Contemporary Issues in Marketing and Consumer Behaviour

Contemporary Issues in Marketing and Consumer Behaviour

Elizabeth Parsons
Senior Lecturer in Marketing, Keele University,
Keele University, Keele, Staffordshire, UK

Pauline Maclaran
Professor of Marketing and Consumer Research,
Royal Holloway, University of London, UK

AMSTERDAM • BOSTON • HEIDELBERG • LONDON • NEW YORK • OXFORD
PARIS • SAN DIEGO • SAN FRANCISCO • SINGAPORE • SYDNEY • TOKYO
Butterworth-Heinemann is an imprint of Elsevier

Butterworth-Heinemann is an imprint of Elsevier
Linacre House, Jordan Hill, Oxford OX2 8DP, UK
30 Corporate Drive, Suite 400, Burlington, MA 01803, USA

First edition 2009

British Library Cataloguing in Publication Data
A catalogue record for this book is available from the British Library

Library of Congress Cataloging-in-Publication Data
A catalog record for this book is available from the Library of Congress

ISBN: 978-0-7506-8739-3

For information on all Butterworth-Heinemann
publications visit our website at www.elsevierdirect.com

Typeset by Macmillan Publishing Solutions
(www.macmillansolutions.com)

Printed and bound in Great Britain
09 10 11 12 13 10 9 8 7 6 5 4 3 2 1

Contents

Preface

The need for marketers to be flexible and adaptable to the changing world around them has never been greater. As competition in markets grows apace, and consumers make ever more demands on the companies from which they choose to purchase, marketers must be increasingly sensitive to a multitude of shifting socio-cultural nuances. This book is intended to draw together a range of key topics that provide an overview into the changing dynamic context within which marketing is taught and practised. Overall, the topics are designed to keep students abreast of current thinking in marketing and consumer research. With an emphasis on socio-cultural perspectives, all of the chapters have been written by experts and often challenge traditional views of marketing.

The principal market for this book is final year marketing undergraduates and students on post-experience and postgraduate marketing programmes. It is designed to be the recommended reading on courses that explore contemporary issues in marketing and consumer research. As such it functions as a complete off-the-shelf package, including class discussion topics and exercises. On other modules, such as marketing theory, consumer behaviour, ethics, macromarketing, marketing and public policy, social marketing and arts marketing, it is appropriate as supplementary reading. The themes addressed in this book will also be of interest to students in media and cultural studies, sociology, anthropology, CAM and consumer studies programmes. So, whilst the main focus of the book is directed at the marketing community, it will also appeal to anyone who wants an accessible overview of the latest thinking and developments in marketing and consumer research. Together the chapters are designed to provoke debate amongst students and encourage them to enquire further into the topics on their own.

Contributors

Nia Hughes is Senior Teaching Fellow at Keele University, and prior to this she was Principal Lecturer at Staffordshire University. She recently gained a PhD from Lancaster University Management School, focusing upon aspects of consumption in the context of collectors and collecting, and employing an interpretivist approach. She is particularly interested in exploring the familial, social and cultural factors that influence consumers in their every-day lives. Her work draws upon ideas from sociology, anthropology and material culture studies, as well as consumer research.

    Krzysztof Kubacki is Lecturer in Marketing at the School of Economic and Management Studies, Keele University. He is a graduate of the School of Music in Legnica, Poland, and before joining academia was working as a musician for the Helena Modrzejewska Theatre in Legnica and the Opera Theatre in Wrocław, Poland. Although his main research interests lie in the relationship between marketing and music, he carries out research projects on a variety of marketing issues in Poland and Central Europe. He has published extensively across a number of marketing areas, including music, culture, the hospitality industry and knowledge management.

    Pauline Maclaran is Professor of Marketing and Consumer Research at Royal Holloway, University of London. Her research interests focus on cultural aspects of contemporary consumption, and she adopts a critical perspective to analyse the ideological assumptions that underpin many marketing activities. In particular, her work has explored socio-spatial aspects of consumption, including the utopian dimensions of fantasy retail environments. She has published in internationally recognized journals such as the *Journal of Consumer Research, Psychology and Marketing, Journal of Advertising,* and *Consumption, Markets & Culture.* She has co-edited several books including *Marketing and Feminism: Current Issues and Research* and *Critical Marketing: Defining the Field,* and is a co-author of *Two Continents, One Culture: The Scotch-Irish in Southern Appalachia.* She is also Co-Editor in Chief of *Marketing Theory,* a journal that promotes alternative and critical perspectives in marketing and consumer behaviour.

    Lydia Martens is Senior Lecturer in Sociology and Director of Post-graduate Training (Social Sciences) at Keele University. Her research interests centre around the intersections between consumption and domestic life. She is working on a research agenda that includes gender and consumption, mundane domestic life, practices and products, and children, families and consumption. Together with Pauline Maclaran, she is currently leading an Economic and Social Research Council seminar series on Motherhoods, Markets and Culture. She is author of *Exclusion and Inclusion: The Gender Composition of British and Dutch Work Forces* (1997), co-author (with Warde) of *Eating Out: Social Differentiation, Consumption and Pleasure* (2000) and co-editor (with Casey) of *Gender and Consumption: Domestic Cultures and the Commercialisation of Everyday Life* (2007). She has also published in various journals, including *Journal of Consumer Culture, Consumption, Markets and Culture, Home Cultures, Sociology* and *British Journal of Sociology of Education*.

Caroline Miller is Lecturer in Marketing at Keele University. She has prior experience as a researcher at Manchester Metropolitan University. She has also practised in the private sector where she spent fourteen years working in the steel industry and has experience of running a family owned small/medium sized business. She gained a PhD in Philosophy studying women and entrepreneurship at Keele University and also has a Masters in Research and a degree in Business Studies and English. Her research interests have a wide focus and include business start-up, gender, social exclusion (difference), sustainable practices in marketing and critical marketing. Her publications are international and interdisciplinary; examples appear in *International Journal of Business and Economics* and *International Journal for Management Theory* and *Practice*.

Daragh O'Reilly is Lecturer in Marketing at the University of Sheffield Management School. Before joining the academic sector, Daragh spent several years working in a range of international sales and marketing roles. His recent research has focused on critical and cross-disciplinary work on the relationship between marketing, consumption and culture. His particular interests are arts marketing, and popular music branding. He was Chair of the Academy of Marketing's Arts & Heritage Marketing SIG from 2004 to 2007, and Principal Organizer of the ESRC seminar series on 'Rethinking Arts Marketing' (2005–2007). He is also a member of a current AHRC grant-aided Research Workshops project led by Elizabeth Carnegie to work with Audiences Yorkshire on qualitative research into the arts consumption experience and its impact. He holds an MA in Modern Languages and Literature (Dublin), an MBA (Bradford) and a PhD in the Marketing and Consumption of Popular Music (Hallam). He is a Member of the Chartered Institute of Marketing, and a holder of its Diploma.

Elizabeth Parsons is Senior Lecturer in Marketing at Keele University. She has prior experience as Lecturer in Marketing at the University of Stirling and gained a PhD in Human Geography from Bristol University. Her research interests bring critical and ethnographic perspectives to two key areas: the cultures of consumption, in particular the marketing and consumption of the non-new, and the construction of gender and identity in organizational life. Her publications are strongly inter-disciplinary, spanning journals in marketing, retailing, consumer research, geography and voluntary sector studies. She has recently co-edited the Sage three volume major work on *Nonprofit Marketing*.

Effi Raftopoulou is currently Lecturer in Marketing at Keele University and gained her PhD in Marketing at the University of Manchester. Her research interests relate to two principal subject areas: the field of marketing communications (in particular, advertising), and the field of discourse analysis. In particular she is concerned with the broader functions and role of marketing communications from an ideological perspective. In addition to this, she is interested in multi-semiotic analysis within discourse analysis and its potential contribution to the study of adverts. One of the areas that she has looked at relates to social/government advertising.

Emma Surman is a Lecturer in the School of Economic and Management Studies at Keele University. After completing her PhD at Keele in 2004, Emma was a Research Fellow at the University of Exeter and subsequently a Lecturer at the University of Warwick before returning to Keele in August 2007. Prior to her career in academia, she held marketing posts in a variety of organizations that encompassed the private, public and charity sectors. Her research interests include: telework, emotion in the workplace, the production and consumption of organizational space, and gender, identity and power relations.

Mark Tadajewski is Lecturer in Critical Marketing at the School of Management, University of Leicester. His research interests are wide-ranging and include the history of marketing theory and thought, the philosophy of science as it relates to marketing, critical theory and consumer research, amongst others. He has co-edited several books, including *Critical Marketing: Issues in Marketing* and Sage three volume major works on: *The History of Marketing Thought*; *Marketing Theory*; *Nonprofit Marketing*; and *Critical Marketing Studies*.

CHAPTER 1

Introduction: Marketing in the Contemporary Organization

Elizabeth Parsons and Pauline Maclaran

This book aims to provide an overview of the latest developments in scholarship and practice in marketing and, importantly, make clear links between the two. We have selected key topics that are currently impacting on the way marketing is researched and practised, and we use these to explore newly emergent marketing ideas and applications. By locating these topics in their wider global, social and economic contexts, we also raise a series of theoretical concerns surrounding the interrelationships between marketing, society and culture. We do this against the backdrop of marketing's relevance in the contemporary organization. During a discussion of current business opportunities with CEOs from five major UK companies Brown noticed that 'The term "marketing" was mentioned only a couple of times in an hour of intense exchange. Yet customers, clients and competitiveness were on the executives' minds throughout the discussion' (2005, p. 3). Marketing's perceived lack of relevance is worrying. Many commentators have blamed this decline on an inadequate conception by both academics and practitioners of what marketing actually is. Thus, before we go on to give an outline of our topic selections, we review some of the current debates about the nature of the marketing role in contemporary organizations. This review provides a background context for the specific topics that follow. First, however, we highlight some of the problems with the definition of marketing.

PROBLEMS WITH THE DEFINITION OF MARKETING?

Marketing as a phenomenon has changed significantly over the last 20 years. New fields of study have emerged such as relationship marketing, services marketing and the network perspective on business-to-business marketing. Alongside this, attempts have been made to redefine both the terminology and the terrain of marketing. Recently, several scholars have aired their concerns about the direction in which marketing conceptualizations are moving (i.e. Wilkie, 2005; Grönroos, 2006). In this respect, the following AMA (American Marketing Association) remodelled 2004 definition of marketing has been subject to particular scrutiny:

> *Marketing is an organizational function and a set of processes for creating, communicating, and delivering value to customers and for managing customer relationships in ways that benefit the organization and its stakeholders.*

A series of issues have been raised with this definition, pertaining to its conception of the role of marketing within the organization, the role of consumers within the marketing relation and the wider societal role of marketing. Grönroos (2006) argues that the definition views marketing as one function amongst others, and that such a conception of marketing is ill-equipped to deal with new forms of relationships with customers.

> *The traditional marketing definitions are based on a view that marketing is one function alongside other functions and, therefore, these are perceived as non-marketing. This view has become a straight jacket for marketing research, where at least mainstream marketing research has not been able to cope with the changes that have taken place in the customer interfaces. The content of customer interfaces has grown far beyond what a one function marketing approach can handle. (Grönroos, 2006, p. 410)*

A particular problem with the AMA definition, however, is the way in which it characterizes the role of *consumers* in the marketing relation. Consumers are defined as having value delivered *to* them. Wilkie sees this as a social problem as 'In the aggregate, all marketers simply propose too much consumption for each consumer' (2005, p. 8). He observes that, in this definition, the marketing system is structured as if finances were no object for the consumer. The delivery of value *to* customers also ignores their role in actively producing value (see Vargo and Lusch, 2004). For example, consumer researchers have long recognized that value emerges both in interactions *between* the consumer and supplier, and also through a series of subsequent consumption practices and rituals where goods are appropriated by consumers in their everyday contexts (see in particular the Consumer Culture Theory approach to understanding consumer value, Arnould and Thompson, 2005). These consumption processes may include an individual, or group characteristic (as in the case of consumer collectives discussed in Chapter 6). Taking the concept of value co-creation one step further, Peñaloza and Venkatesh (2006) argue for the importance of examining markets as social constructions. This has significant implications for our understandings of value in markets: 'our view emphasizes value as constituted by marketers and consumers in their activities and discourses via an enacted process, a social construction that takes place prior to, during and after the actual exchange and use(s) take place' (2006, p. 303).

The dangers in adopting the AMA 2004 definition are that it only captures the role of the marketing manager, and ignores the wider role of marketing within society. Wilkie (2005, p. 1) argues for a 'larger sense of marketing and scholarship' which takes into account the role of both government and other organizational operations, particularly those which may be well beyond the marketing manager's control. Schultz (2007) similarly argues for a definition of marketing that embraces a macro-marketing perspective where marketers engage with the 'big issues' in society (see Chapter 12). This would involve an opening out of marketing, and necessitates 'greater understanding of historical and cultural forces, coupled with far-reaching systemic analysis' (2007, p. 299). Given the debate generated by the earlier 2004 definition of marketing, the AMA produced a second updated version in 2007, as below:

> *Marketing is the activity, conducted by organizations and individuals, that operates through a set of institutions and processes for creating, communicating, delivering and exchanging market offerings that have value for customers, clients, marketers and society at large.*

This definition has yet to be fully applied and debated (although see Sheth and Uslay, 2007), but it certainly seems to represent a step in the right direction.

WHAT IS HAPPENING TO MARKETING'S ROLE IN THE ORGANIZATION?

A series of scholars have charted the decline of marketing within the organization, observing that it has deteriorated in both influence and prominence (McGovern et al., 2004; Welch, 2004; Brown, 2005; Cassidy, 2005; Webster et al., 2005). Several elements of this decline have been observed including: the loss of credibility of marketers and marketing at board level; and the downwards devolvement of marketing responsibility in the organization.

In a survey of 30 large US companies more than 30 per cent indicated that they spend less than 10 per cent of their time discussing marketing or customer related issues at board level (McGovern et al., 2004). It is undeniable that marketing has been in decline within organizations for some time. Following the closure of corporate marketing departments, companies have plugged the gap by creating the position of chief marketing officer (CMO). This has been viewed as a positive move by commentators. According to a recent study by Booz Allen Hamilton (Hyde et al., 2004), 47 per cent of fortune 1000 companies have a designated CMO. However, while marketing is represented once more at board level, concerns have been raised about the high turnover of these positions (Welch, 2004). Kerin (2005, p. 12) observes that this is because 'the position is often ill-defined, there is little formal authority, corporate expectations are frequently unrealistic, and credibility and legitimacy with other company "chieftains" is absent'. Cassidy's (2005) survey of more than 30 European CEOs and CMOs likewise found a 'credibility gap' for marketers in their organizations. She puts this down to the creative approach taken by successful marketers, which is at odds with the more structured and disciplined approach required in other parts of the organization. This often makes for a significant amount of tension between CMOs and other board members.

The problem may be one of a skills gap, according to McGovern et al. (2004, p. 74) who highlight that the marketing field is 'chockablock with creative thinkers, yet it's short on people who hew toward an analytic, left-brain approach to the discipline'. This analytical skills gap is becoming increasingly problematic as developments in information technology are at the forefront of understanding consumer behaviour (see for example the data mining techniques discussed in Chapter 11). In addition, the difficulties in measuring marketing outcomes mean that marketers struggle to demonstrate returns on organizational investments in marketing programmes. As McGovern et al. (2004, p. 75) observe, 'Boards need a thorough understanding of how their companies are meeting customers' needs and how their marketing strategies support those efforts. No company we know of provides its board with a scorecard that allows this.' The combination of tensions between individual skill valuations, and an often hostile organizational context, makes the CMO position a particularly difficult one to perform well in. As Webster observes, 'only rarely has this position been filled by a person with the necessary strategic and analytical skills, the true support of a committed CEO, and a clear mandate to build marketing competence and strategic thinking throughout the organization' (2005, p. 5).

In addition to problems at board level, many key marketing functions have been dispersed throughout the organization. According to Webster et al. (2005), many activities that might ordinarily be the preserve of the marketing department have been redistributed and embedded in functions such as human resource management, sales and product engineering. 'Today, marketing in many large companies is less of a department and more a diaspora of skills and capabilities spread across and even outside the organization' (2005, p. 36). Sheth and Sisodia further highlight how 'many strategically important aspects of marketing … are being taken away by other functions in the organization' (2005, p. 11). This means that there is often little direct responsibility for, and control over, marketing activity in the organization. The seriousness of the situation becomes clear when we consider the issue of brand equity which is a key indicator of a company's health. The decentralization of responsibility for brand equity in many companies is a worrying trend. Brands can be hugely unpredictable, often rising to prominence, or tumbling from pole position, almost overnight, so it is vital to have at least some centralized control over them. For example, in the brand consultancy Interbrand's (2008) Best Global Brands rankings, the internet search engine company 'Google' was ranked 20th in 2007, by 2008 the brand had risen to 10th in the rankings, achieving a 43 per cent increase in brand value in just one year. In the same year, Apple computer hardware saw a 24 per cent increase in brand value, Amazon internet service a 19 per cent increase and ZARA apparel a 15 per cent increase. Equally, brands can crash overnight, in the same period the brand value of Merrill Lynch financial services dropped 21 per cent, Gap apparel dropped 20 per cent and Ford automotive dropped 12 per cent. These examples highlight just how volatile markets can be, and therefore, how important it is to keep a close eye on the brand's performance.

WHAT DO CONSUMERS THINK OF MARKETING?

Given that serving consumers is marketing's central purpose, their sentiments towards marketing activity deserve attention. In a survey by the market research company Yankelovich (cited in Sheth and Sisodia, 2005) 60 per cent of consumers reported that their opinions of advertising and marketing activity had worsened in recent years. However, a long run survey of US consumers' sentiment towards marketing, conducted annually over the past two decades, suggests that, while consumers generally have a negative opinion of marketing, these sentiments have slightly improved over the period (Gaski and Etzel, 2005). Gaski and Etzel (2005) also observe that we are only just beginning to understand the breadth of phenomena that influence these sentiments. Perhaps not surprisingly, they find that of the four marketing functions, product quality carries most importance in influencing consumer sentiments, followed in order of decreasing importance by price, retail service and advertising. In addition, while this study finds that consumers do have a negative view of marketing, in the aggregate and over a long period of time this negative view is only slight and 'not nearly as unfavorable as popular stereotype may have represented' (Gaski, 2008, p. 212).

However, Sheth and Sisodia (2006) report a growing cynicism amongst consumers with few consumers viewing their interactions with companies as fulfilling relationships. From their online survey they found that over 60 per cent of consumers had a negative view of marketing. While positive connotations included creativity, fun, humorous advertising and attractive people, on the negative side frequently used words included: lies, deception, deceitful, annoying, manipulating, gimmicks, exaggeration, invasive, intrusive and brainwashing (see Chapter 8 for a discussion of marketing ethics). In terms of marketing practices telemarketing, online pop-up advertisements and junk mail were viewed most negatively (2006, p. 30).

HOW SHOULD MARKETING BE DONE DIFFERENTLY?

Given the decline of marketing in organizations, and the generally poor view consumers have of marketing activity, how should marketing be done differently? This is not an easy question to answer, but two key suggestions are discussed here: the linking of marketing productivity with strategy; and the development of a collaborative approach to marketing. The latter approach would involve productive practitioner–scholar relations and require organizations to work more closely 'with' the consumer.

As we discussed in previous sections, marketers are being marginalized in the organization. Whenever they do have a role to play, their hands are often tied by a lack of wider organizational commitment to a market-focused perspective. Marketing is often viewed as a variable cost on the balance sheet, rather than a committed cost. Thus, in times of financial hardship, marketing budgets are often the first to be cut. To avoid this situation, from marketing programmes need to be measured more accurately and applied to strategic decision making. For example, a strong brand can result in a whole host of cost savings for the organization, such as the ability to negotiate lower distribution costs. Savings of this nature need to be accounted for as positive outcomes of marketing programmes. This ability to account for marketing expenditure will help in persuading board members of the true value of marketing activity and, hopefully, precipitate a move towards a commitment to marketing within the organization.

There remains a significant scholarship–practitioner gap in marketing. One of the solutions Brown (2005) offers is for scholars to broaden their conception of practitioner audience, to embrace not only marketers, but also strategic management, operations, supply chain, human resources and finance. The 'thought leadership in relation to customer focus and competing through service' offered by marketers is 'too good to be confined to marketing practitioners', he argues (2005, p. 4). Certainly the time is ripe to forge fruitful partnerships between academics and business leaders. Business leaders have little time or encouragement to reflect on the role and nature of marketing in their organizations. They can offer insights, however, into the ways in which marketing is playing out in the business context. This will include a focus on the challenges they face, as well as new ideas surrounding what might and what might not work in their company contexts. The potential for scholars to contribute to marketing thought and practice has never been greater. The need for organizations to develop measurable return on marketing spending, the development of new forms of customer interfaces brought about by new technologies, and the rise of the brand as a central guiding principle in organizations, all cry out for sustained and in-depth reflective analysis that practitioners simply do not have the time or, indeed, the resources to undertake.

A final comment regarding the doing of marketing 'differently' relates to companies working with the consumer. This can be achieved by creating systems which result in mutual value through actively supporting, rather than directing, consumer creation of value. The internet technology available to marketers, while being a potential threat in its empowerment of the consumer through information and connectivity to other consumers, must be seen as an opportunity in enabling a more equal and co-operative relationship between companies, marketers and their consumers. The increasing popularity of the internet is resulting in a form of 'do it yourself' marketing where consumers cut out the marketing middle man in accessing information on pricing and product features and quality. As Sheth and Sisodia observe, consumers can 'self-inform, self-evaluate, self-segment, self-support, self-organize, self-advertise, self-police and self program' (2005, p. 11). The online trading community eBay is perhaps one of the most obvious examples of these elements of consumer marketing in action. Another example is the whole range of online consumer communities where experiences of using products, and opinions about brands are shared (see Chapters 6 and 11). In fact, Sheth and Uslay point out that value co-creation can extend to a whole spectrum of activities:

> coconception (military and defense contracts), codesign (Boeing and United Airlines), coproduction (Ikea), copromotion (word of mouth), copricing (eBay, negotiated pricing), codistribution (magazines), coconsumption (utility), comaintenance (patient–doctor), codisposal (self-serve), and even co-outsourcing (captive business process outsourcing). (2007, p. 305)

The value co-creation view of marketing has significant repercussions for the means marketers should use to try and understand consumers and markets. Chapter 11 documents a range of new techniques in this respect (i.e. videography, netnography, blogs and virtual life worlds) which not only involve the consumer in a dialogical relationship with marketers but benefit from being used in conjunction with more traditional techniques to facilitate the triangulation suggested by Peñaloza and Venkatesh 'Over time then, and with greater triangulation across interpretavist and positivist paradigms in the context of market development, value may be seen to be constituted in exchange and use, simultaneously and sequentially' (2006, p. 303).

There is still a feeling that marketers can do more to work with the consumer. As Lafley, chief executive of Proctor and Gamble Company commented recently, 'we're on a learning journey together' with the consumer 'choosing when to tune in and when to tune out. Consumers are beginning in a very real sense to own our brands and participate in their creation. We need to learn to begin to let go' (cited in Elliott, 2006). When talking about the fact that some Mini owners dress their cars up in costumes for Halloween and some have mounted shark fins on the roof of their Minis – McDowell, managing director at Mini USA, commented 'It's a great thing every day to wake up and see what consumers have done to the brand, even though it's not a culture we necessarily would have come up with on our own' (cited in Elliott, 2006). Putting the customer in charge is often very uncomfortable for organizations with a history of 'consumer management'. Flanagan, executive vice president and chief marketing officer at MasterCard Worldwide, whose recent 'Priceless' campaign was adopted and adapted by consumers, observes 'when you're tapping into that consumer desire to have a piece of it, you have to take the good with the bad' (cited in Elliott, 2006).

So, there are many uncertainties for the marketing role, both inside and outside the organization. The one certainty is that marketers need to become more flexible and adaptable than ever before, ready to respond to a volatile and fast-changing marketplace that increasingly demands they act responsibly and play an active role in good citizenship. Our selection of topics is intended to give students a greater understanding of the changing dynamics in which marketing is researched and practised.

OUTLINE OF THE BOOK

Our first two topic areas in this book consider aspects of the theoretical and practical context in which we undertake marketing activities. In an overview of 'A History of Marketing Thought' (Chapter 2), Mark Tadajewski provides an important foundational, historical background against which to understand the development of the contemporary issues that follow, enabling us to locate them in relation to the overall development of marketing thought. He tracks marketing's emergence and growth as a discipline, together with the influences that have impacted this evolution. Importantly, he reveals the impact of particular sets of power relations during key periods of development in marketing thinking. To this end, he looks at the close ties between the genealogy of marketing thought and practice, and the changes in the US political and economic climate.

Likewise, the next chapter on 'Postmodern Marketing and Beyond' (Chapter 3) provides a base from which to appreciate our other topics. In it we explore the defining characteristics of the postmodern turn, and the many ways postmodernism has represented a critique of, and challenge to, the underpinnings of conventional marketing wisdom. We also chart recent developments of the postmodern concept within marketing and explore its links with cultural branding and interpretive consumer research. Despite its own critique of traditional assumptions, postmodernism is itself open to critique, and we consider the various limitations of using a postmodern lens. Significantly, certain current trends indicate that we may now be moving beyond postmodernism and we consider the potential impact of this for marketers.

Following these two contextualizing chapters, we shift our focus to consider more specific socio-cultural contexts in which marketing practice takes place. Our postmodern analysis reveals how art and life are now inextricably intertwined and the next chapter pursues this theme from a marketing management perspective. 'Arts Marketing' (Chapter 4) is a relatively new subdiscipline of marketing. In this chapter, Krzysztof Kubacki and Daragh O'Reilly locate arts marketing within the larger framework of cultural production and consumption, before exploring the complexities of the relationship between art and the market. They highlight a range of special considerations for arts marketers, considerations that mean conventional product marketing approaches do not work in this context. In so doing, their analysis reveals two main approaches to arts marketing that offer very different conceptualizations of it. In the preceding chapter, we see how, from a postmodern perspective, brands are infused with art, whereas this chapter shows how art is infused with brands.

Brands are everywhere in contemporary society. In 'Building Brand Cultures' (Chapter 5) we look at how meaning systems are established around brands, and how these can take on a life of their own as the brand intersects with other cultural phenomena such as, for example, the art world just discussed. Adopting an 'inside out' approach, we explore important synergies between organizational and brand cultures, illustrating the important role of employees in building brand culture. Shifting our focus outside the organization, we consider how brand cultures are also co-created with consumers and other external stakeholders. The evolution of brand culture is concerned with story telling, but not, as we might expect, just on the part of marketers. Employees, customers and the media are continually relating experiences about brands and, as they do so, certain meanings evolve, meanings that may not have been intended by marketers. Highly successful brands achieve iconic status through responding insightfully to the wider cultural environment and being aware of the stories circulating about them. Other brands are less watchful, however, and become tainted through negative perceptions that arise and over which marketers sometimes have little control. Whether we like them or not, brands play an increasingly significant role in contemporary lifestyles. They are also increasingly coming under attack from the anti-branding movement, which heavily critiques the role of brands and the impact of brand culture on our lives.

Many critiques can be levelled at the marketing system, not least that it contributes to a fragmentation of society through the increasing proliferation of smaller and smaller market segments. Conversely however, in Chapter 6, 'Consumer Collectives', Nia Hughes illustrates the communal bonds that can be forged through marketing phenomena. Contemporary consumer culture is often implicated in the breaking down of traditional bonds between people such as class, caste, family or village. Yet, as this chapter shows, consumers find new ways to establish collective identities through selecting specific products, services and activities that define themselves and create a social identity that they communicate to others. A range of marketing collectives have been identified: lifestyle groupings, subcultures, subcultures of consumption, brand communities, consumer micro-cultures and tribes. All of these concepts share the same underlying principle, that choices of goods and services make a statement about who we are and, importantly, with whom we wish to identify (or with whom we do not). In reflecting a group identity, consumption activities can be highly symbolic and often the meanings that consumers create collectively can be beyond the control of marketers. This chapter explores the similarities and differences between these different concepts of consumer collectives.

In Chapter 7, Lydia Martens uses a sociological perspective to understand the topic of 'Gender and Consumer Behaviour', a topic that has been largely overlooked in marketing. Once again, as in Chapter 2, we are reminded of the importance of understanding historical perspectives to better appreciate the subtleties of contemporary issues. Lydia highlights the significance of feminist thought in shaping social and cultural agendas and applies this to our understanding of how gender impacts consumer behaviour. She explores various theories of consumption and gender that try to explain how gender shapes particular patterns of consumer behaviour and meanings, and vice versa, how consumption patterns and meanings shape gender culture.

The next three topic choices move us away from specific socio-cultural contexts to focus more on the ethical and political context of marketing theory and practice. In 'Ethical Debates in Marketing' (Chapter 8), we review debates surrounding the moral principles that guide the conduct of marketers. Here we include discussion of marketing as a profession and also as a wider societal force. The growing diversity of the socio-cultural environment in which marketers operate means that they will need to be capable of assessing the ethical implications of their actions across an increasingly broad range of contexts. Marketers have to take into account three key viewpoints – the company, the industry and society – and it is when these groups have conflicting needs and wants that ethical problems arise (e.g. the tobacco industry).

In 'Sustainable Marketing and the Green Consumer' (Chapter 9), Caroline Miller highlights the paradoxical nature of the term sustainable marketing. She discusses how marketing activities can be heavily critiqued for their encouragement of wastage and for their contribution to the destruction of the environment. One of the major challenges for marketing lies in how it can help to encourage organizations and industry sectors along a more environmentally sustainable path. This chapter explores the birth and evolution of sustainable marketing and looks at the significant steps and setbacks in its development. It also discusses key aspects of green marketing and the green consumer, and looks at how the balancing of consumption and conservation is a challenge, not only for individuals but also for organizations. Emphasizing the need for a more holistic view to be taken by marketers, leading scholars in the field of sustainable marketing are now calling for a significant rethinking of the nature/culture divide.

Faced with mounting pressure from consumers and companies, marketers are becoming increasingly aware of their citizenship role in society. This emerging topic is the focus of the next chapter by Effi Raftopoulou. 'Social Marketing and Consumer Citizenship' (Chapter 10) explores the emergence of social marketing as a subdiscipline which can be associated with broader shifts in the boundaries of marketing in the late 1960s. Social marketing as a concept has gained ascendancy in a range of professional circles and is used in a range of spheres including: societal (i.e. re-educating against racism), political (i.e. promoting the EU), environmental (i.e. saving energy, re-cycling) and health (i.e. safer sex, healthy eating, smoking cessation). However social marketing is not confined to marketing communications and can make a unique contribution to both behaviour change and critical marketing.

Many fast-changing technological innovations have recently impacted on the marketing role and our two concluding chapters explore this new technological environment. In 'New Technologies of Marketing Research' (Chapter 11) we explore recent developments in marketing research and relate them to broader technological and cultural changes in society. Technological developments have had a huge impact on the practices of marketing research, offering marketers vast amounts of data on the consumer. Indeed some commentators have observed the birth of 'data driven' marketing. However an important second shift has seen moves towards more interpretive understandings of consumers. This shift might be located more broadly in the postmodern turn within marketing, a turn which has resulted in a more eclectic approach to marketing research, making new uses of the available technologies, for example netnographies, videographies blogs and virtual life worlds. These new techniques can be seen as emancipatory when they involve the consumer more fully in a dialogical relationship with marketers. Trends also reflect a willingness to look outside traditional marketing to other disciplines for inspiration. Evidence of this can be seen in the proliferation of marketing research agencies staffed by anthropologists, sociologists and cultural theorists.

Technological advances have also driven an increasing globalization of products and services. Through technology, we are increasingly linked to people and activities throughout the rest of the world. Our final chapter by Emma Surman, 'The Global Consumer' (Chapter 12), explores the intertwining of the technological, cultural, political and economic environments. It provides an overview of the process of globalization and discusses many of the resulting debates. Emma encourages us to question the power and influence of multinational companies and to think about how local cultures are affected by global production and consumption.

Written as an introductory overview, each of the above chapters includes a range of current examples of research and practice and concludes with a more detailed case study. There are recommended discussion and group exercises which, together with key readings and internet resources, are designed to stimulate debate and further exploration. Enjoy!

REFERENCES

Arnould, E.J. and Thompson, C.J. (2005), 'Consumer culture theory (CCT): Twenty years of research', *Journal of Consumer Research*, 31 (4), 868–882.

Brown, S.W. (2005), 'When executives speak, we should listen and act differently', *Journal of Marketing*, 69 (October), 1–4.

Cassidy, F. (2005), 'A credibility gap for marketers', *McKinsey Quarterly*, 2, 9–10.

Elliott, S. (2006), 'Letting consumers control marketing: Priceless', *The New York Times*, October 9.

Gaski, J.F. (2008), 'The index of consumer sentiment toward marketing: Validation, updated results, and demographic analysis', *Journal of Consumer Policy*, 31, 195–216.

Gaski, J.F. and Etzel, M.J. (2005), 'National aggregate consumer sentiment toward marketing: A thirty-year retrospective and analysis', *Journal of Consumer Research*, 31 (March), 859–867.

Grönroos, C. (2006), 'On defining marketing: Finding a new roadmap for marketing', *Marketing Theory*, 6, 395–417.

Hyde, P., Landry, E. and Tipping, A. (2004), 'Making the perfect marketer', *Strategy and Business*, (winter), 37–43.

Interbrand (2008), *Best Global Brands 2008*. http://www.interbrand.com/best_global_brands

Kerin, R.A. (2005), 'Strategic marketing and the CMO', *Journal of Marketing*, 69 (October), 12–14.

McGovern, G.J., Court, D., Quelch, J.A. and Crawford, B. (2004), 'Bringing customers into the boardroom', *Harvard Business Review*, 82 (November), 70–80.

Peñaloza, L. and Venkatesh, A. (2006), 'Further evolving the new dominant logic of marketing: From services to the social construction of markets', *Marketing Theory*, 6 (3), 299–316.

Schultz, II., C.J. (2007), 'Marketing as constructive engagement', *Journal of Public Policy and Marketing*, 26 (2), 293–301.

Sheth, J.N. and Sisodia, R.S. (2005), 'Does marketing need reform?', *Journal of Marketing*, 69 (October), 10–12.

Sheth, J.N. and Sisodia, R.S. (eds) (2006), *Does Marketing Need Reform: Fresh Perspectives on the Future*. New York: M.E. Sharpe.

Sheth, J.N. and Uslay, C. (2007), 'Implications of the revised definition of marketing: from exchange to value creation', *Journal of Public Policy and Marketing*, 26 (2), 302–307.

Vargo, S.L. and Lusch, R.F. (2004), 'Evolving to a new dominant logic for marketing', *Journal of Marketing*, 68 (January), 1–17.

Webster, Jr., F.E. (2005), 'Back to the future: Integrating marketing as tactics, strategy and organizational culture', *Journal of Marketing* (October), 4–6.

Webster, Jr., F.E. Malter, A.J. and Ganesan, S. (2005), 'The decline and dispersion of marketing competence', *MIT Sloan Management Review*, 46 (4), 35–43.

Welch, G. (2004), *CMO Tenure: Slowing the Revolving Door*. New York: Spencer Stuart.

Wilkie, W.L. (2005), 'Needed: a larger sense of marketing and scholarship', *Journal of Marketing*, 69 (October), 8–10.

CHAPTER 2

A History of Marketing Thought

Mark Tadajewski

INTRODUCTION

Whenever we begin to study a new discipline, we must begin somewhere. That much is obvious. A good starting point is by reviewing the history of the field, from its earliest inception as an academic discipline, tracing the influences that have impacted on the way the subject appears in the present day. This is the purpose of the present chapter: an historical overview of the key developments in the history of marketing.

Most students will probably ask themselves: Why should I study the history of marketing thought? The immediate response is that before you can even begin to critique a discipline, you must first understand it. Secondly, there is a famous saying, often written in a variety of ways, but generally attributed to George Santayana, a famous philosopher, that those who do not know their history are likely to make similar mistakes to those of their intellectual predecessors. In this case, reinventing concepts, making errors of attribution and so on (see Hollander, 1995, pp. 98–99).

Another famous scholar, this time of 'the history of systems of thought', has said that all systems of knowledge are ineluctably tied up, often in very complex ways, with systems of power (Foucault, 1977/1991). As Foucault famously wrote, 'power produces knowledge ... power and knowledge directly imply one another ... there is no power relation without the correlative constitution of a field of knowledge, nor any knowledge that does not presuppose and constitute at the same time power relations' (Foucault, 1977/1991, p. 27). In conceptualizing his views on power, Foucault does not propose that the powerful dominate the powerless – a Hobbesian view – rather that power flows through society, as a spider might move along a web. When reading this chapter, you may well want to think about the power relations between groups as relatively fluid; certain groups might be more powerful than others at any given point – even for a long historical period – but this invariably means that at some point, those groups subject to power – whether consumers, academics or whoever – will resist. And the way we understand appropriate forms of marketing practice or marketing theory, will change accordingly.

So, this chapter reviews the origins of marketing thought, examining when the term 'marketing' was first used, and its subsequent development. The chapter will also provide an overview of the development of marketing thought and practice. Since the genealogy of marketing is closely tied up with changes in the US industrial landscape, discussion of major theoretical debates is woven in with important, indeed seismic, political and economic changes in the US.

THE EARLY DEVELOPMENT OF MARKETING THOUGHT: A COMPLEX BEGINNING

When we turn to Robert Bartels' (1988) influential history of marketing, we are told relatively quickly that the term 'marketing' was first used 'as a noun', that is, as a label for a particular practice, sometime 'between 1906 and 1911' (Bartels, 1988, p. 3). Nonetheless, Bartels' historical account has recently been challenged in a variety of papers. According to Bussière (2000), Bartels' account of the emergence of the use of the term marketing is incorrect; there were in fact scholars writing and commenting on the subject before 1906. In appraising the contents of the *American Economic Review* (AER), Bussière found that the term marketing was actually used far earlier than Bartels suggested, in 1897 (cf. Weld, 1941, p. 381).

Taking us slightly away from the academic context with which Bartels (1988) and Bussière (2000) were concerned, Shaw (1995) has challenged Bartels' account on two fronts that we should note. Firstly, Shaw draws attention to the statement from Bartels referred to above, but then points out that there was a section of an 1880 cookery book called 'Miss Parloa's New Cookbook and Marketing Guide' that discussed marketing (Shaw, 1995, p. 16). In this cookery book, Shaw tells us, the term 'marketing' related to 'buying and selling activities' (see Dixon, 2002). But he does not stop here in his critique of Bartels, as he says that if we examine dictionaries prior to the Bartels' statement, that the intellectual genealogy of marketing becomes decidedly more complicated. He writes,

> ... the definition of marketing rooted in buying and selling activities
> is noted in early dictionaries of the English language, even before
> marketing emerged as an academic discipline in the twentieth-
> century United States. The American Encyclopedic Dictionary
> (1896) for example, defines marketing as "the act or process of
> transacting business in markets" as well as "goods offered for sale

[and] purchased in a market". A century later, Webster's Collegiate Dictionary (1994) continues to define marketing as "the act or process of selling or purchasing in a market" (p. 172), and it notes that the earliest recorded English language use of the term as a noun was in 1561. (Shaw, 1995, p. 16)

There have been further objections to Bartels' history of marketing that we should acknowledge. Jones and Monieson (1990) have claimed that the first courses in marketing did not actually appear in American universities at all, as we might otherwise have supposed. Jones and Monieson propose that, in contrast to Bartels who claimed that the first marketing courses did appear in the US, that the first courses were actually found in Germany, 'around' the cusp of the twentieth century (Jones and Monieson, 1990, p. 111 n. 2). The history of marketing is obviously subject to quite a degree of intellectual contestation.

THE FIRST COURSES ON MARKETING IN THE EARLY TWENTIETH CENTURY

But we do, as a matter of fact, have a great deal of information about those courses that were offered in the early twentieth century US, as well as about those scholars who have been called the pioneers of marketing (see Hagerty, 1936; Weld, 1941; Bartels, 1951; Jones, 1994, 2004, 2007; Cochoy, 1998). We know that the earliest courses were delivered in 1902 at the Universities of Michigan, California and Illinois. These were not called 'marketing' per se, but labelled with a variety of other names such as 'Distributive and Regulative Industries', 'trade' or 'commerce', among others (Bartels, 1988). H.H. Maynard, in an early historical account, makes reference to what he considers the 'first course' in marketing 'offered at the University of Michigan by Dr. E.D. Jones in 1902' (Maynard, 1941, p. 142; see also Weld, 1941, p. 380; Bartels, 1988, p. 21). The 1902 course covered 'the various methods of marketing goods' (Bartels, 1988, p. 22) and studied a range of institutions that were useful in aiding the performance of marketing activities, such as trade associations who were influential drivers of industrial and business-to-business marketing research (Tadajewski, 2009b). Other courses touched upon issues that we also associate with the study of marketing today, including 'Advertising, its psychological laws, its economic importance and the changes it has introduced into selling goods' (Bartels, 1988, p. 23).

In summarizing his understanding of the field of marketing, as it was then emerging, Ralph Butler Starr said:

In considering the whole field of selling, I developed the idea that personal salesmanship and advertising had to do simply with the final expression of the selling idea. My experience with the Proctor & Gamble Company had convinced me that a manufacturer seeking to market a product had to consider and solve a large number of problems

> *before he ever gave expression to the selling idea by sending a salesman on the road or inserting an advertisement in a publication ... In brief, the subject matter that I intended to treat was to include a study of everything that the promoter of a product has to do prior to his actual use of salesmen and of advertising. (Bartels, 1988, p. 24)*

On a more theoretical level, there is some agreement in the historical literature that marketing developed as a form of 'applied economics' (cf. Cassels, 1936; Jones and Monieson, 1990). Scholars say 'applied economics' because early and later marketing thought often contested the assumptions of classical and neoclassical economics. In particular contesting the view of the self-interested utility-maximizing consumer, who made their consumption decisions on the basis of full, accurate information in a rationalistic manner, much like a computer processing information (Belk, 1987). Marketing can also be considered 'applied economics' in view of the fact that marketing knowledge was intended to improve marketing practice (eventually).

Certain marketing researchers – notably L.D.H. Weld – were critical of the way that theoretical reflections on the marketplace were not actually used to inform business practice (see Kemmerer et al., 1917, p. 267). Others lamented the lack of engagement by economic theorists with consumption (see Mason, 1998). At the most basic level, we can say that the early pioneer marketing academics/practitioners[1] 'were more interested in developing practice than theory' (Bartels, 1988, p. 29). 'Contributions' to the academic study of marketing

> *'were made for the purpose of describing, explaining, and justifying prevailing marketing practices and institutions, particularly newer ones. They were offered to clarify misconceptions held among the public, such as the belief that the wholesaler was parasitic and would disappear from the distributive system, fear of the annihilation of small stores by chain organizations, and dismay at the plight of consumers before the ruthless practices of vendors'* (Bartels, 1988, p. 29)

To effectively understand the rapidly expanding industrial economy of the US, these practically minded researchers refused to cogitate 'in a cupboard' – to paraphrase Weld slightly – but actively studied the practice of marketing, sometimes extremely literally, as we shall see.

STUDYING THE MARKETPLACE

Because the first scholars required material for their own teaching, they needed to study marketing related topics in real life. This meant literally

---

[1] Many were actively involved in public policy debates relating to the marketplace or associated with industry as 'marketing counsellors'.

following products from their point of production and manufacture, all the way through to their distribution to the ultimate consumer. Weld, for instance, describes a number of his own research projects where he 'personally followed shipments of butter and eggs and other commodities from the country shipper in Minnesota through the wholesalers, jobbers, and retailers to New York, Chicago, and other cities. I analyzed each item of expense involved in this passage through the channels of trade' (Weld, 1941, p. 381).

This concern for the processes involved in moving a product from its point of origin – where it was harvested, for example – to the final consumer, was a result of scholarly and public concern over marketplace efficiency and what was called 'the marketing problem' (Jones and Monieson, 2008). This related to the exorbitant mark-up that many considered middlemen to be adding to the price of goods. With this sentiment circulating in public discourse, it is hardly unexpected that research projects undertaken at the time (1910–1920), asked questions about whether there were any elements in the supply chain that could be eliminated to save costs. In other words, were certain intermediaries (middlemen) actually adding any value to a product, such as getting it to the right place, at the right time, in a satisfactory condition, or did they simply only add further cost to the product (see Benton, 1987)? This cost factor was notably important to people living in the late 1920s and 1930s US, as the Great Depression left many people unemployed, lacking the financial wherewithal and ability to search for the highest quality, cheapest products; so any efficiency savings that could be made in terms of the distribution of products was considered a very important subject.

In one of the first marketing publications, Arch Shaw (1912) examined the functions of middlemen in considerable detail, especially regarding whether their services did add value to a product offering. This is in part a response to the criticism relating to 'the marketing problem' already gestured toward above (see Jones, 1994). Jones and Monieson (2008) have revealed that there was quite serious concern that middlemen were taking advantage of their knowledge of marketplace conditions, charging higher prices wherever possible (see also Jones, 2007). In response to such criticism, Shaw reasoned that middlemen did provide highly valuable services (they stored goods, assumed an element of risk in doing so, if the market conditions changed, etc). Consequently, middlemen deserved to be compensated properly for their activities.

Moving away from the academic marketing literature, as the American marketplace expanded exponentially in size, with ever larger firms, serving ever more distant customers, it was no longer possible for many firms to actually know their customers on a one-to-one basis, much as the old small shop owner had known the requirements of their patrons. Neither was managerial intuition regarding the products or services the consumer might deign to buy, a sufficient basis upon which to plan and manage business activities. As a case in point, Arch Shaw (1912, p. 755) had long been critical of business people who failed to engage in systematic market research, even when they invested 'tens, even hundreds, of thousands of dollars in a selling campaign'. Systematic understanding of buyer behaviour was vital and management needed to understand what products the marketplace demanded, if they were to scientifically manage their levels of production in line with likely consumption (White, 1927). So we can assert that marketing scholars and practitioners did appreciate that by producing the kinds of products that consumers said they desired, that such a production strategy was likely to be consistent with consumer demand (Coutant, 1936), as well as 'long-run ... consumer satisfaction' (Tosdal, 1939, p. 511).

Further encouraging the business community to register that the marketplace was no longer a sellers' market, if indeed it ever was (Rassuli and Hollander, 1987), business faced an important situation that it had not confronted on a large scale previously: demand was less than supply. Simply producing a particular line of goods did not mean that the market would automatically clear: consumers would not buy products just because they were available. One means of competing in this environment that firms turned to was 'pricing'. The problem with this, is that each manufacturer then pushes their price slightly lower than the competition; their competitors respond likewise, resulting in what Arthur Jerome Eddy (1912/1915) called 'destructive competition'. Without access to appropriate marketplace information about supply, demand, current prices, etc., manufacturers could inadvertently promise to supply goods at a price that left them unable to recoup their costs (see Coutant, 1937, p. 96).

Nor were consumers generally convinced that low cost equalled good quality. Not just for the reason that there is something obviously jarring about such an equation, but because manufacturers were reducing the quality of the products that they offered to consumers, as the price declined (see also Tadajewski, 2008). Consumer trust in manufacturers consequently fell for good reason. As Paul Nystrom (1932, p. 872) highlights:

> ... cuts in quality are being made in practically every line of goods. Almost unbelievable junk goes into the inside construction of both men's and women's shoes. Furs are stretched to twice their original and natural dimensions. Scraps that would formerly have been thrown away are patched together to make fur trimmings for coats and suits to be sold to unsuspecting customers.

A more feasible option for the firm interested in actively competing for the consumers' discretionary income, given the above issues, was for firms to pursue 'nonprice' forms of competition. Zaltman and Burger (1975, p. 4) list various forms of this type of competition, including: 'competing for consumer awareness through mass media promotion, and the use of special incentives such as coupons, samples, and premium offers'. Such methods of approaching the customer have been criticized by prominent marketing commentators as still being a 'short-term and tactical' approach to marketing strategy (Webster, 1988, p. 31). This is because a firm pursuing these policies is still essentially trying to encourage the customer to buy those products that the firm is already offering, rather than tailoring products and services to the customer's requirements (Webster, 1988, p. 31). At the same time, however, there *were* calls for increased attention to customer needs, wants and desires. Let us pause briefly to consider the appearance of the marketing concept in marketing thought.

THE MARKETING CONCEPT

This attentiveness of industry, marketing academics and consultants alike to consumers, and their desires and product requirements, generally passes unacknowledged, even in very influential studies that deal with the history of marketing in some respect (e.g. Webster, 1988; Vargo and Lusch, 2004). Notwithstanding this, ideas associated with the marketing concept were surprisingly widespread from the seventeenth century onwards, and probably before (e.g. Fullerton, 1988; Hollander, 1986; Jones and Richardson, 2007; Tadajewski, 2008, 2009a). The reason why this historical fact is not usually appreciated, is due to an important paper by Robert J. Keith (1960) that is routinely cited in introductory textbooks and discussed throughout business schools worldwide, usually in a week one introduction to marketing lecture.

Keith's paper was based on changes in business and customer relations that characterized the history of the company where he worked: The Pillsbury Company. In a compelling fashion, Keith maintained that his firm, and others, were currently revolutionizing the way they thought about marketing and sales. Marketers were no longer producing whatever products they could manufacture, just because they possessed the manufacturing capacity and skill to do so: 'In today's economy the consumer, the man or woman who buys the product, is at the absolute dead center of the business universe. Companies revolve around the customer, not the other way around' (Keith, 1960, p. 35).

It was hardly surprising then, with statements such as these, which were written in a very accessible fashion (and in a short paper), that academics leapt on to Keith's argument with nary a moment of critical reflection (see Jones and Richardson, 2007). Thus Webster (1988, p. 31), claimed that 'Until the mid-1950s, the business world equated "marketing" with "selling." Under this traditional view of marketing, the key to profitability was greater sales volume, and marketing's responsibility was to sell what the factory could produce'. In a slightly later paper, Webster (1992) develops this point further, when he opines that the 1950s mark the point when the marketing concept was first articulated. According to Webster, the core thesis associated with the marketing concept is 'that marketing was *the* principle function of the firm (along with innovation), because the main purpose of any business was to create a satisfied customer' (Webster, 1992, p. 2; emphasis in original).

Obviously, high pressure selling was still used in some industries, and not all marketers were equally attentive to customer requirements. The same is true nowadays (e.g. Boru, 2006; Brown, 2007). As Brown (2001a) has detailed, up to the 1950s there were a range of industries known to utilize very high pressure sales tactics. Patient medicine producers, and the travelling quack medicine acts, were also willing to bamboozle and hoodwink customers wherever possible (Brown, 2001b). There were, all the same, some very consumer centric, progressive marketing scholars writing, publishing and consulting during the 1920s, 30s, 40s, and 50s, who recognized the value of customer satisfaction and its importance in fostering long-term relations between a customer and a firm, to the benefit of all. It *is* odd that scholars should have failed to notice this, given that two well known papers by Borch (1958) and McKitterick (1957) expressed this point extremely clearly.

In his paper, McKitterick was careful to underscore that many of the theoretical debates surrounding various business philosophies were not new. They were further developments of arguments already found in the historical record, rebranded and repackaged with new names and labels. Borch (1958) also appreciated this:

> *I have gotten the feeling that what we hear about marketing and customer orientation these days is being regarded as something really new. I do not think that it is. Years ago, when our economy was much younger, customer-orientation was a built-in feature of a business enterprise. Before the days of mass communication, national markets, and mass production, the business pioneers were cognizant of their customers and their markets. They knew their customers individually, and these customers formed their collective market. These predecessors of ours built their relationships through personal contact and got very rapid feedbacks [sic] of customer needs and wants. (1958, p. 19)*

Or, in McKitterick's words:

> *Anyone who gets a new idea bearing on business philosophy and who then takes the trouble to scan corresponding utterances of preceding generations will return to this thought with increasing awareness of its apparent lack of originality. In an attempt to locate the historic significance of this marketing concept that we are going to discuss today, I started reading the 1930 and 1940 issues of the* Journal of Marketing *and the* Harvard Business Review. *To my surprise, I found that many of the viewpoints expressed and the stances advocated on business philosophy bear striking resemblance to current writings. (1957, p. 71; emphases in original)*

Key figures who talked about issues relating to 'the marketing concept' before the 1950s included Harry Tosdal, Percival White, Paul Ivey, Arthur Farquhar, Lee Bristol, Simon Litman and Oswald Knauth. These figures all, in slightly differing ways, advocated that firms should begin all organizational activities (Coolsen, 1960/2008; Jones, 2004; Tadajewski and Jones, 2008), whether this was new product development, enhancing existing offerings, and so on, from the perspective of the target consumer[2] (see Tadajewski, 2009a; Tadajewski and Saren, 2009). Firms were told, quite simply, to produce those products that the consumer desired provided, that is, such ventures were likely to be profitable in the short or longer term, or otherwise contributed to the satisfaction of organizational objectives (e.g. increasing market share or, preventing a competitor from entering a market).

Note, that firms were not expected just to listen to *all* customers and produce *any* product that was demanded: a company had to have the technical skill or the means of rapidly developing such skills, cheaply and effectively. There also had to be sufficient levels of present or anticipated future demand. Consistent with this emphasis, marketing writers from the 1920s onwards were quick to spell out the benefits of accurate, scientific market research in ensuring a better fit between those products an organization manufactured, and actual customer requirements (see White and Hayward, 1924; Engel, 1938; Cherington, 1938).

As Zaltman and Burger register, marketing research was a further tool in the armoury of manufacturers who did not want to follow the price competition route: 'Marketing research was ... used to provide a competitive edge in the form of knowledge about customers which the company could use in developing marketing plans' (Zaltman and Burger, 1975, p. 3). In an excellent illustrative case, Cherington (1938) discussed the 'insulation between producer and consumer which has developed from the enlargement of the scale of business operations' (1938, p. 178). In this paper, Cherington is actually talking about market research and its value in connecting supply and demand. But he seems to claim that there are various factors stopping effective consumer demand for goods being communicated to the firm, and offers advice regarding the use of market research to remedy such problems. He states:

> On the theory that the human wants which underlie the business are the eventually controlling factors, some survey of the types of consumer, or final user, usually takes its place early in the work. In this the chief essential is to get back of the surface indications and find out how the case in hand really lies in the customer's mind and in his actually living habits. (1938, p. 179)

---

[2]This is a very sweeping generalization. I also translate the arguments of these scholars and practitioners into contemporary language. Percival White's (1927) position comes closest to those stated here.

Whilst there was still concern among prominent marketing scholars and practitioners that firms were not engaging in sufficient research (cf. White, 1940, p. 185; Tosdal, 1942, p. 72), there was also little doubt that an increasingly competitive marketplace would mean, in the future, that 'consumers will have more to say' about those products being produced (Nash, 1937, p. 255). It was thought that if some marketers failed to respond to consumer requirements, others would be perfectly happy to service the customer. Practitioners, therefore, were frequently called upon to pay due attention to the benefits associated with 'good marketing research' (Coutant, 1936, p. 28), which was able to detect the 'incipient wants' consumers possessed. Marketers were then able to stimulate these, so that they grew 'to profitable proportions' (Coutant, 1938, p. 28).

DEMAND STIMULATION AND THE 'DUAL CORE' MARKETING CONCEPT

In the above reading of the history of marketing theory and practice, marketing is concerned – to some extent – with demand stimulation. 'Marketing students', Converse (1951, p. 3) proposed, 'are interested in increasing or stimulating human wants, in general and for the good of individual sellers. This leads them to the study of advertising, salesmanship, and merchandizing, marketing research and packaging.' Marketing has not, clearly, simply been an academic subject, or practical business endeavour, that has *only* been concerned with responding to those product or service requirements that people already have; it is involved with demand creation, that is, with actively selling and marketing those products that companies do produce, which customers may not have even realized they required originally (Borch, 1958). This is what Borch (1958) called the 'dual core' aspect of the marketing concept: sometimes consumers did not know what they required, or what products were technologically feasible. Therefore marketers had to engage in selling and promotion; activities that were otherwise criticized as part of the much derided 'sales' era (see Jones and Richardson, 2007, p. 18).

Since marketers were seriously interested in selling to consumers, business organizations *slowly* began to grow steadily more interested in marketing research, so that it assumed a much more prominent role in organizational decision-making. Zaltman and Burger (1975, p. 6) go so far as to identify a shift in the way 'market research' was translated into 'marketing research'. This change appears to have been noted previously by Engel, who discussed the need to:

> ... *distinguish between* marketing research *and* market research *on the basis that the latter applies only to fact-finding, with perhaps some analysis of a* single-market *or marketing area, whereas*

*the broader term includes not only the collection of facts about
particular markets, but about marketing organizations, marketing
methods and policies, the analysis of the facts, and the deduction
of appropriate conclusions there-from. (1938, p. 280; emphases in
original)*

What Zaltman and Burger do confirm is that during the 1940s 'Marketing research became a significant management activity. Management
decision-making became the central *raison d'etre* of marketing research'
(Zaltman and Burger, 1975, p. 6).

Historically speaking, there are always a large number of factors that
influence the receptivity of business managers to marketing innovations or
that encourage marketing scholars to study particular marketplace phenomena; but one key event that had a dramatic impact on marketing during the
1940s, and well in to the 1950s, was World War II.

WORLD WAR II

The reason why marketing practice was increasingly viewed in far more
favourable terms in the boardrooms of large companies in the 1950s, is
perhaps attributable to World War II. During a dramatic world-wide con-
frontation, such as the two World Wars, industry is not usually permitted
to continue producing those products and services which it, or even the
consumer, deems appropriate. To be sure, there is a level of give and take
here, but generally the government is the largest buyer in a market, and can
consequently dictate those products that are produced. This occurred during World War II to such an extent that industry again massively expanded
on the back of the requirements of the Army, Navy and other military bodies. Tosdal reviews the seismic changes to the industrial infrastructure, as
follows:

*It seems now that the end of the war will find the United States with
the greatest productive capacity that it has ever had. In the United
States, new plants have been constructed and old plants converted to
augment enormously the flow of commodities. New processes have
been developed and have been introduced; ideas that once seemed
visionary have been made realities and have increased production in
an unheard of degree. (1942, p. 75)*

Predictably, Tosdal (1941, p. 216) talked about the significance of 'consumer attitudes as an important factor in the making of decisions as to
products and prices'. According to Tadajewski (2006b), it was the fear that
they were losing contact with their consumers that really motivated firms
to begin to hire the available marketing research agencies, or to conduct

research seriously themselves. The latter option was quite costly, which meant that small firms were still restricted with respect to the types of research that they could commission. In addition, the late 1940s and, early 1950s witnessed the increased use of psychological and psychoanalytical theory and techniques in marketing research. Consultants such as Ernest Dichter, who were well versed in such methods, claimed to be able to tap into consumer motivations beyond those available to questionnaire studies, drawing out subconscious motives that were influential forces in structuring consumer behaviour. This type of 'motivation research' was interested in understanding 'why' consumers bought specific products and tried to understand consumer buying motives and behaviour through a range of qualitative research approaches, including in-depth interviews and ethnography (Tadajewski, 2006b). These motivation studies avoided posing direct questions to the consumer, as it was thought that they would rationalize their buying motives (e.g. I needed a new car, because it had better fuel efficiency), rather than admit to subjective influences (e.g. the next door neighbour bought one, so I picked one up).

And Dichter, the foremost practitioner of motivation research, frequently presented himself as able to probe consumer motivations, while at the same time, affirming the financial benefits of motivation research to the interested firm: 'We are consumers' representatives. We pass on this information to the advertiser and the industrialist, showing him how he can make more money by giving people what they truly want' (Dichter, 1960, p. 259). Motivation research was, in short, very successful. Even so, it ultimately declined in prominence during the 1960s and 1970s for a range of reasons. Among the most important were Dichter's increasingly flamboyant claims about what he, and motivation research, could accomplish (Tadajewski, 2006b). Nor was it ever an especially popular subject in academia. On a related matter, the further development of the qualitative methods associated with motivation research was effectively rendered moot on the basis of a shift in the nature of research in the business school. This shift resulted from the influence of two reports into business education issued by the Ford and Carnegie Foundations respectively.

THE BEHAVIOURAL REVOLUTION IN MARKETING THEORY AND PRACTICE

In his review of the history of consumer behaviour, Kassarjian maintains that 'by the end of World War II, business schools in general and marketing departments in particular were in a very weak position ... Academic research was impressionistic ... Good research might consist of a case study or perhaps detailed interviewing with a couple of middlemen' (Kassarjian, 1989,

p. 123). By the end of the 1950s, however, two important reports criticized the state of business education, lamenting the lack of engagement by business academics with mathematically oriented, behavioural science research.

Both the Ford and Carnegie reports were influential in stimulating a whole range of changes in business education: management educators were pushed to earn PhD degrees and to 'upgrade' (Bartels, 1988) their research skills, mainly in terms of improving their ability to manipulate complex mathematics. It was the funding provided by the Ford Foundation that 'served to usher in a new age for marketing' (Tadajewski, 2006a, p. 179). This Foundation financially supported a whole range of textbooks, seminars and, training programmes that diffused their scientific vision for business research. Research had to be objective, scientific and rigorous (see Kernan, 1995a, 1995b). Academic journals soon reflected this emphasis, notably the newly founded *Journal of Marketing Research*. Ideally, says Kernan (1995a), a published research paper had to contain some element of mathematical symbolism or involve 'laboratory research, experimental design, computer simulation, operations research, mathematical models, and high powered statistics' (Kassarjian, 1989, p. 124).

Many of the leading marketing thinkers to the present day were either directly involved in the Ford Foundation mathematical seminars, or have been taught by scholars that were. Neither was this simply an academic preoccupation, of little relevance to practicing marketing managers. Practitioners were interested in these new methodological tools in anticipation that they could enhance managerial decision-making (Silk, 1993; Tadajewski, 2006b). Still, disaffection with highly quantitative, behavioural scientific research was not far away.

Regardless of the positive comments made by Stewart (1991, p. 28), when he referred to the growth in 'graduate-level courses in marketing research [which] include treatment of multivariate statistics', and the extensive proliferation of 'courses on mathematical modelling of marketing phenomena', not all were convinced that the mathematization of marketing research and education was useful. Tadajewski (2006a, p. 183) documents the comments made by a range of marketing scholars who criticize the use of quantitative methods, and the wholesale theory borrowing from the behavioural sciences, that was encouraged by the research environment (cf. Silk, 1993).

Approaching this period from a slightly different angle, Shimp argued that irrespective of the analytical sophistication made possible by this 'upgrading' (Bartels, 1988) of marketing education and research, it actually rendered marketing research less relevant to its traditional constituency: the business person. As he put it, 'Influenced by these reports … We in marketing and consumer behavior turned away from business practitioners and toward fellow scholars around campus for theoretical ideas, analytical tools, and perhaps even our source of approbation' (Shimp, 1994, p. 2). And yet, business research could not try to uncouple itself from the needs of industry, without expecting a response from taxpayers and related critics, as Shimp (1994, p. 2) revealed:

> ... the situation began changing in the mid-to-late 1980s. The economy deteriorated, American corporations became less globally competitive, and jobs were lost. The conditions were ripe for attack and attacked we were. The B-School became the whipping boy of critics in the mass media. Detractors caricatured B-school research as trivial and largely irrelevant.

For industry, the behavioural revolution did not provide the much hoped for insights into market and consumer behaviour. The 'numbers' had indeed been 'seductive' (Hodock, 1991). Numbers, and large reams of electronic data processing, did not make up for human frailty and failures to ask the right questions prior to computerized data analysis. 'Technical sophistication does not necessarily guarantee success. Our academic institutions must share some of the blame for our [industry] obsession with sophisticated techniques. Too many textbooks are long on technique and short on reality' (Hodock, 1991, p. 18). Hodock continues: 'Too many researchers are tied up with their numbers, statistics and rating scales – all of which have their place – but they lose sight of the reason for it all, which is insight into the consumer' (Hodock, 1991, p. 19).

THE 'IRRELEVANCE' OF MARKETING SCIENCE: MARKETING AND THE MILITARY–INDUSTRIAL COMPLEX

Other critics rallied against the growing irrelevance of 'marketing science', which was perceived to be ignoring the impact of marketing on society, focusing instead exclusively on issues related to managerial and firm competitiveness. Many interested observers called for marketing intellectuals to devote attention to research issues that were central to contemporary policy debates; or to study the impact of marketing on society, and vice versa – that is, the study of macromarketing (see Dawson, 1971; Wilkie and Moore, 2003, 2006; Shapiro, 2006). For Kassarjian (1994/2008, p. 307) the movement away from a preoccupation with managerial, technical issues, was instigated by younger marketing academics rebelling against the alignment of marketing with the 'military–industrial complex' (i.e. big business).

The principal way in which they tried to ensure the legitimacy of marketing in this climate, was to broaden the domain of marketing, to include not just business exchanges (i.e. the selling of soap and toothpaste), but to stress that most, if not all, organizations in society engaged in marketing (Kotler and Levy, 1969; Levy, 2002, 2003). For these writers, marketing tools and techniques could be used to market the value of church attendance, increase donations to charity organizations and more generally expand the boundaries of marketing beyond a myopic concern for for-profit groups. Non-profit and other interested parties were further possible beneficiaries of marketing know-how (see Parsons et al., 2008). Social marketing – the promotion of particular forms of socially responsible behavioural change – also appeared on the intellectual agenda of marketing, during the time frame Kassarjian is discussing (late 1960s, early 1970s) (see Andreasen, 1994, 2003).

Importantly, these politically motivated changes were institutionally supported by the formation of a group who considered themselves far removed from issues of managerial relevance, namely the Association for Consumer Research. This association:

> … was not to be an arm of the business establishment and it was not intended to be an offspring of marketing. It was intended to function as a legitimate interdisciplinary field during difficult social times. Consumer research could be used for the good or evils of trade. We wanted to believe that it could be applied to the protection of consumers as well as to their exploitation … From the local court house to the nation's capital, marketing and consumer researchers were plying their trade … Articles on deceptive advertising, on counter and corrective advertising, on research on labelling, on nutritional information, and on information overload abounded. The outcasts were those who worked for or defended the military–industrial complex and those who asked, What are the managerial implications. (Kassarjian, 1994/2008, p. 307)

ENGAGING WITH SOCIETY

More recently, criticism surrounding the lack of engagement by marketing scholars and practitioners with the impact of marketing on society has had a major influence on the American Marketing Association's recent redefinition of marketing. Marketing academics publically condemned the 2004 definition of marketing for its explicitly managerial slant, and concomitant elision of the impact of marketing activities on a whole range of stakeholders (i.e. non-consumers, society, etc.), other than the marketing firm itself (see Mick, 2007; Shultz, 2007; Tadajewski and Brownlie, 2008). In view of the vociferous criticism that took place in the pages of the *Journal of Public Policy and Marketing* and elsewhere, marketing has been redefined in such a way that its impact on society is taken into account. The latest definition of marketing calls 'marketing' 'the activity, set of institutions for creating, communicating, delivering, and exchanging offerings that have value for customers, clients, partners, and society at large' (Lib, 2007).

In line with this broadening of the scholarly and definitional focus of marketing, many researchers have, since the mid to late 1980s, engaged in research that studies 'people', not customers or consumers necessarily. They have also focused on the actual processes involved in all manner of consumption activities, ranging from purchase through to divestment behaviours. In terms of the methods used to study people as they went about their everyday consumption behaviours, marketing and consumer researchers have, in effect, returned to roots of consumer behaviour as a distinct discipline (Levy, 2003), using interpretive methods such as ethnography, photo-elicitation and phenomenological interviewing (Tadajewski, 2006b). Naturally, such approaches retain an element of managerial relevance in that interpretive consumer research does have utility when it comes to studying consumption phenomena that marketing managers may find interesting (e.g. Elliott and Jankel-Elliott, 2003). But far from just investigating consumer buying behaviour, researchers now analyse all the many facets of consumption phenomena, including 'neglected experiential, social, and cultural dimensions of consumption in context' (Arnould and Thompson, 2005, p. 869). And they do this by drawing on the theoretical resources of multiple paradigmatic perspectives, including among others critical theory (Murray and Ozanne, 1991; Tadajewski and Brownlie, 2008), feminism (Maclaran and Stevens, 2008), postmodernism (Firat and Dholakia, 2006) and postcolonialism (Jack, 2008).

It would seem, therefore, that as long as there are marketing historians studying the development of the discipline, we can expect this history to be fleshed out in further detail, adding nuance where there was little previously, challenging the dates for the so-called 'marketing revolution' (Jones and Richardson, 2007) and rethinking the development of interpretive research (Tadajewski, 2006b) or the marketing concept (e.g. Fullerton, 1994; Tadajewski, 2009a). In recognition of the complexity of the history of marketing and the extent to which this chapter skates over important debates, some references are provided below that offer more detailed readings on specific aspects of the subject.

SUMMARY

Over the course of this chapter, it has been demonstrated that the history of marketing thought is complex. The date of the emergence of the subject has been debated and rethought on numerous occasions. And the development of both thought and practice have been shaped by external environmental changes in the US industrial landscape, as well as by the interests of the scholars and practitioners intimately involved with the subject itself.

Case study: Rethinking the influence of the *Hidden Persuaders* on marketing thought

In the main part of this chapter, the motivation researcher, Ernest Dichter was mentioned. As was remarked upon, Dichter was a very colourful individual. He made a great deal of money promoting his own motivation research consultancy group, which was housed in a castle in Croton-on-Hudson, in New York City. Again, as I said above, motivation research disappeared from research agendas. According to Professor John Bargh (2002, p. 282), academic researchers 'seemed to shy away from the study of motivational influences over the past 40 years' for a variety of reasons, but the main one he provides was the influence of Vance Packard's (1960) *The Hidden Persuaders* book. Packard's book was nothing if not sensational. He detailed the growth in marketing research that was psychologically and psychoanalytically informed, based on information provided by a number of sources. His primary source, however, was Ernest Dichter, whose information was used to paint a picture of American consumers' being manipulated by marketing and advertising communications to a far greater extent than they had hitherto appreciated (see Brown, 2001a, pp. 32–35) and whose subconscious thoughts could be accessed by the probing techniques of psychologically adept researchers.

According to Packard, 'Americans have become the most manipulated people outside of the Iron Curtain' (Packard, 1960, Preface); 'and he argues that all of this probing and manipulation has its constructive and its amusing aspects; but also, I think it is fair to say, it has seriously anti-humanistic implications. Much of it seems to represent regress rather than progress for man in his long struggle to become a rational and self-guiding being' (Packard, 1960, p. 13).

In reference to the interviewing techniques used by the shadowy 'depth-men', Packard said: 'These interviews are conducted very much as the psychiatrist conducts his interviews, except there is no couch since a couch might make the consumer-guinea pig wary' (Packard, 1960, p. 38). It is no surprise that these comments caused an uproar. Legal challenges were made to ban subliminal advertising (Schwarzkopf, 2005); motivation research had little academic respectability, but did this bother Dichter? Not really, as the following quote reveals:

> Whenever somebody tries to make other people aware of my "fame" or the controversial nature of what I am doing, they sooner or later use as

a memory trigger Vance Packard's The Hidden Persuaders. It was in 1956 and we were lost in our castle with our staff of six. He spent a few days in our offices, studied a number of our reports, and a few months later showed me a rough manuscript. Despite my supposed knowledge of public relations, I must admit that nothing in the manuscript led me to expect the spectacular, literally world-wide attention which was created through this book. Since I am quoted on almost every page, I became known as the chief villain – the Chief Hidden Persuader. Some of my clients who read the book told me facetiously, "We wish you were half as good as Packard makes you out to be." Others seriously suspected me of having paid Packard to write the book. My reminding them that it was an attack against me did not seem to impress them. Indeed, very soon after the appearance of the book, I received invitations to go to India, Australia, and to some of the remotest regions of the world. I could not possibly imagine that these people would be interested in motivational research. My business started booming. I appeared on many television and radio programs, in discussions with Mr. Packard and, since I modestly think that I am a better speaker than he is, I felt that I was up to the challenge. The argument was centred, for the most part, around the morality and immorality of what I was doing: manipulating and persuading people with mysterious means to do things that they never intended to do; to get them to vote, to buy, to act in almost an hypnotic state. What was my answer? I tried to explain in a previous chapter what I am really doing: cultural anthropology. I concern myself with the customs and habits of the people living in this world, regardless of whether their habitat happens to be in Paris, Frankfurt, Chicago, New York or Samoa. I try to take a fresh approach, and not be misled by stereotypes. In other words, to first set up creative hypotheses, as any good researcher will do, and then to use the techniques discussed previously to prove or disprove my hypotheses as to what makes these people behave in a special way. (Dichter, 1979, pp. 82–83)

INTERNET RESOURCES

Bartels, R. (1976), 'The History of Marketing Thought,' 2nd edn, pp. 1–33, 123–243, Chapters 1, 2, 3, 4, 9, 10, 11, 12, 13, 14. http://www.faculty. missouristate.edu/c/ChuckHermans/Bartels.htm

CHARM (Conference on Historical Analysis & Research in Marketing). http:// faculty.quinnipiac.edu/charm/

John W. Hartman Center for Sales, Advertising and Marketing History. http:// library.duke.edu/specialcollections/hartman/

KEY READINGS

Jones, D.G.B. and Shaw, E.H. (2005), 'A history of marketing thought', in B. Weitz and R. Wensley (eds), *Handbook of Marketing*. London: Sage, pp. 39–65.

Shaw, E.H. and Jones, D.G.B. (2005), 'A history of schools of thought in marketing', *Marketing Theory*, 5 (3), 239–281.

Sheth, J.N., Gardner, D.M. and Garrett, D.E. (1988), *Marketing Theory: Evolution and Evaluation*. Chichester: John Wiley and Sons.

Tadajewski, M. and Jones, D.G.B. (eds) (2008), *The History of Marketing Thought* Volumes I, II and III. London: Sage.

Wilkie, W.L. and Moore, E.S. (2003), 'Scholarly research in marketing: exploring the "4 eras" of thought development', *Journal of Public Policy and Marketing*, 22 (2), 116–146.

Wilkie, W.L. and Moore, E.S. (2006), 'Macromarketing as a pillar of marketing thought', *Journal of Macromarketing*, 26, 224–232.

SEMINAR EXERCISES

Discussion Topics

1. What are the main reasons why we should study the history of marketing? Try to think of other ways in which you think history can be useful, apart from those included in the chapter.

2. Search the Internet and find some information on the Great Depression. How do you think this will have influenced the development of marketing?

3. Given the debate that took place in the *Journal of Public Policy and Marketing*, why do think marketing scholars believed the 2004 definition of marketing to be too restrictive? Do you agree that it was too limiting? You may want to search the American Marketing Association website for further information (http://www. marketingpower.com/Pages/default.aspx).

4. Is marketing simply a managerial discipline that is only interested in responding to consumer desires?

Group Exercises

1. Having read the chapter, case study and Baragh (2002) and Tadajewski (2006a, 2006b), prepare a 10 minute seminar presentation that discusses the following:

   (i) What methods did the motivation researchers use to study consumer behaviour?

   (ii) With which paradigm would you associate them? Positivist, Interpretive or Critical Theory? (You may want to search the papers available on the CHARM (Conference on Historical Analysis & Research in Marketing) website to help you here: http://faculty.quinnipiac.edu/charm/)

   (iii) Was the use of motivation research ethically problematic?

   (iv) Should we be worried about being influenced by subliminal messages? Are marketers really as powerful as cultural critics like Vance Packard, Theodor Adorno and Erich Fromm claim?

2. Select a paper from the CHARM website to discuss and analyse:

   (i) What new insights into marketing history does this paper give us?

   (ii) How is this relevant to contemporary marketing?

REFERENCES

Andreasen, A.R. (1994), 'Social marketing: its definition and domain', *Journal of Public Policy and Marketing*, 13 (1), 108–114.

Andreasen, A.R. (2003), 'The life trajectory of social marketing: some implications', *Marketing Theory*, 3 (3), 293–303.

Arnould, E.J. and Thompson, C.J. (2005), 'Consumer culture theory (CCT): twenty years of research', *Journal of Consumer Research*, 31 (4), 868–882.

Bargh, J.A. (2002), 'Losing consciousness: automatic influences on consumer judgment, behavior, and motivation', *Journal of Consumer Research*, 29 (2), 280–285.

Bartels, R. (1951), 'Influences on the development of marketing thought, 1900–1923', *Journal of Marketing*, 16 (1), 1–17.

Bartels, R. (1988), *The History of Marketing Thought*, 3rd edn. Ohio: Publishing Horizons.

Belk, R.W. (1987), 'A modest proposal for creating verisimilitude in consumer information processing models and some suggestions for establishing a discipline to study consumer behavior', in A.F. Firat, N. Dholakia and R.P. Bagozzi (eds), *Philosophical and Radical Thought in Marketing*. Lexington: Lexington Press, pp. 361–372.

Benton, R. (1987), 'The practical domain of marketing: the notion of a 'free' enterprise economy as a guise for institutionalized marketing power', *American Journal of Economics and Sociology*, 46 (4), 415–430.

Borch, F.J. (1958), 'The marketing philosophy as a way of business life', in E.J. Kelley and W. Lazer (eds), *Managerial Marketing: Perspectives and Viewpoints A Source Book*. Homewood: Richard D. Irwin, pp. 18–24.

Boru, B. (2006), 'Ryanair: the cu chulainn of civil aviation', *Journal of Strategic Marketing*, 14 (1), 45–55.

Brown, S. (2001a), *Marketing: The Retro Revolution*. London: Sage.

Brown, S. (2001b), 'Torment your customers (they'll love it)', *Harvard Business Review*, 79 (9), 82–88.

Brown, S. (2007), 'The failgood factor: playing hopscotch in the marketing minefield', *The Marketing Review*, 7 (2), 125–138.

Brussière, D. (2000), 'Evidence of a marketing periodical literature within the american economic association, 1895–1936', *Journal of Macromarketing*, 20 (2), 137–143.

Cassels, J.M. (1936), 'The significance of early economic thought on marketing', *Journal of Marketing*, 1 (2), 129–134.

Cherington, P.T. (1938), 'Market studies in theory and practice', *Journal of Marketing*, 2 (3), 177–180.

Cochoy, F. (1998), 'Another discipline for the market economy: marketing as a performative knowledge and know-how for capitalism', in M. Callon (ed.), *The Laws of the Markets*. Oxford: Blackwell, pp. 194–221.

Converse, P.D. (1951), 'Development of marketing theory: fifty years of progress', in H.G. Wales (ed.), *Changing Perspectives in Marketing*. Urbana: University of Illinois Press, pp. 1–31.

Coolsen, F.G. (1960/2008), 'Appraisal of contributions to marketing thought by late nineteenth century liberal economists', in M. Tadajewski and D.G.B. Jones (eds), *The History of Marketing Thought*, Volume I. London: Sage, pp. 65–105.

Coutant, F.R. (1936), 'Where are we bound in marketing research?', *Journal of Marketing*, 1 (1), 28–34.

Coutant, F.R. (1937), 'Orderly marketing for greater profits', *Journal of Marketing*, 2 (2), 95–97.

Dawson, L.M. (1971), 'Marketing science in the age of aquarius', *Journal of Marketing*, 35 (July), 66–72.

Dichter, E. (1960), *The Strategy of Desire*. New York: Double Day.

Dichter, E. (1979), Getting Motivated by Ernest Dichter: *The Secret Behind Individual Motivation by the Man Who Was Not Afraid to Ask "Why?"*. New York: Pergamon Press.

Dixon, D.F. (2002), 'Emerging macromarketing concepts: from Socrates to Alfred Marshall', *Journal of Business Research*, 55, 737–745.

Eddy, A.J. (1912/1915), *The New Competition*. Chicago: A.C. McClurg and Co.

Elliott, R. and Jankel-Elliott, N. (2003), 'Using ethnography in strategic consumer research', *Qualitative Market Research: An International Journal*, 6 (4), 215–223.

Engel, N.H. (1938), 'A program for marketing research', *Journal of Marketing*, 1 (3), 280–282.

Firat, A.F. and Dholakia, N. (2006), 'Theoretical and philosophical implications of postmodern debates: some challenges to modern marketing', *Marketing Theory*, 6 (2), 123–162.

Foucault, M. (1977/1991), *Discipline and Punish: The Birth of the Prison*. Tr. A. Sheridan. London: Penguin.

Fullerton, R.A. (1988), 'How modern is modern marketing? marketing's evolution and the myth of the "production era"', *Journal of Marketing*, 52 (January), 108–125.

Fullerton, R.A. (1994), '"And how does it look in america?": H.F.J. Kropff's historic report on US marketing', *Journal of Macromarketing*, Spring, 54–61.

Hagerty, J.E. (1936), 'Experiences of an early marketing teacher', *Journal of Marketing*, 1 (1), 20–28.

Hodock, C.L. (1991), 'The decline and fall of marketing research in corporate America', *Marketing Research*, June, 12–22.

Hollander, S.C. (1986), 'The marketing concept: a déjà vu', in G. Fisk (ed.), *Marketing Management as a Social Process*. New York: Praeger, pp. 3–29.

Hollander, S.C. (1995), 'My life on Mt. Olympus', *Journal of Macromarketing*, 15 (1), 86–106.

Jack, G. (2008), 'Postcolonialism and marketing', in M. Tadajewski and D. Brownlie (eds), *Critical Marketing: Issues in Contemporary Marketing*. Chichester: John Wiley, pp. 363–383.

Jones, D.G.B. (1994), 'Biography and the history of marketing thought: Henry Charles Taylor and Edward David Jones', in R.A. Fullerton (ed.), *Explorations in the History of Marketing*. Greenwich: JAI Press, pp. 67–85.

Jones, D.G.B. (2004), 'Simon Litman (1873–1965): pioneer marketing scholar', *Marketing Theory*, 4 (4), 343–361.

Jones, D.G.B. (2007), 'Theodore N. Beckman (1895–1973): external manifestations of the man', *European Business Review*, 19 (2), 129–141.

Jones, D.G.B. and Monieson, D.D. (1990), 'Early development of the philosophy of marketing thought', *Journal of Marketing*, 54 (January), 102–113.

Jones, D.G.B. and Monieson, D.D. (2008), 'Origins of the institutional approach in marketing', in M. Tadajewski and D.G.B. Jones (eds), *The History of Marketing Thought*, Volume III. London: Sage, pp. 125–144.

Jones, D.G.B. and Richardson, A.J. (2007), 'The myth of the marketing revolution', *Journal of Macromarketing*, 27 (1), 15–24.

Jones, D.G.B. and Shaw, E.H. (2005), 'A history of marketing thought', in B. Weitz and R. Wensley (eds), *Handbook of Marketing*. London: Sage, pp. 39–65.

Kassarjian, H.H. (1989), 'Review of philosophical and radical thought in marketing', *Journal of Marketing*, 53 (1), 123–126.

Kassarjian, H.H. (1994/2008), 'Scholarly traditions and European roots of American consumer research', in M. Tadajewski and D.G.B. Jones (eds), *The History of Marketing Thought*, Volume III. London: Sage, pp. 301–312.

Keith, R.J. (1960), 'The marketing revolution', *Journal of Marketing*, 24 (3), 35–38.

Kemmerer, E.W., MacGibbon, D.A., Bilgram, H., Weld, L.D.H., Anderson, B.M. and Fisher, I. (1917), 'Money and prices – discussion', *The American Economic Review*, 8 (1), 259–270.

Kernan, J.B. (1995a), 'Declaring a discipline: reflections on ACR's silver anniversary', *Advances in Consumer Research*, 22 (1), 553–560.

Kernan, J.B. (1995b), 'Framing a rainbow, focusing the light: JCR's first twenty years', *Advances in Consumer Research*, 22 (1), 488–496.

Kotler, P. and Levy, S. (1969), 'Broadening the concept of marketing', *Journal of Marketing*, 33 (January), 10–15.

Levy, S.J. (2002), 'Revisiting the marketing domain', *European Journal of Marketing*, 36 (3), 299–304.

Levy, S.J. (2003), 'Roots of marketing and consumer research at the University of Chicago', *Consumption, Markets and Culture*, 6 (2), 99–110.

Lib, A. (2007), 'Definition of marketing', *ELMAR: Electronic Marketing*, December 24.

Maclaran, P. and Stevens, L. (2008), 'Thinking through theory: materializing the oppositional imagination', in M. Tadajewski and D. Brownlie (eds), *Critical Marketing: Contemporary Issues in Marketing*. Chichester: Wiley, pp. 345–361.

Mason, R.S. (1998), 'Breakfast in Detroit: economics, marketing, and consumer theory, 1930 to 1950', *Journal of Macromarketing*, 18 (2), 145–152.

Maynard, H.H. (1941), 'Early teachers of marketing', *Journal of Marketing*, 7 (2), 158–159.

McKitterick, J.B. (1957), 'What is the marketing management concept?', in F.M. Bass (ed.), *The Frontiers of Marketing Thought and Science*. Chicago: American Marketing Association, pp. 71–81.

Mick, D.G. (2007), 'The end(s) of marketing and the neglect of moral responsibility by the American Marketing Association', *Journal of Public Policy and Marketing*, 26 (2), 289–292.

Murray, J.B. and Ozanne, J.L. (1991), 'The critical imagination: emancipatory interests in consumer research', *Journal of Consumer Research*, 18 (2), 129–144.

Nash, B. (1937), 'Product development', *Journal of Marketing*, 1 (3), 254–262.

Nystrom, P.H. (1932), 'A restatement of the principles of consumption to meet present conditions', *Journal of Home Economics*, 24 (10), 869–874.

Packard, V. (1960), *The Hidden Persuaders*. Harmondsworth: Penguin.

Parsons, E., Maclaran, P. and Tadajewski, M. (2008), 'Editors' introduction: nonprofit marketing', in E. Parsons, P. Maclaran and M. Tadajewski (eds), *Nonprofit Marketing*, Vol. I. London: Sage, pp. xvii–xxxvi.

Rassuli, K.M. and Hollander, S. (1987), 'Comparative history as a research tool in consumer behavior', *Advances in Consumer Research*, 14 (1), 442–446.

Schwarzkopf, S. (2005), 'They do it with mirrors: advertising and British Cold War politics', *Contemporary British History*, 19 (2), 133–150.

Sheth, J.N., Gardner, D.M. and Garrett, D.E. (1988), *Marketing Theory: Evolution and Evaluation*. Chichester: John Wiley and Sons.

Shapiro, S.J. (2006), 'Macromarketing: origins, development, current status and possible future direction', *European Business Review*, 18 (4), 307–321.

Shaw, A.W. (1912), 'Some problems in market distribution', *Quarterly Journal of Economics*, 26 (4), 703–724.

Shaw, E.H. (1995), 'The first dialogue on macromarketing', *Journal of Macromarketing*, 15 (1), 7–20.

Shaw, E.H. and Jones, D.G.B. (2005), 'A history of schools of thought in marketing', *Marketing Theory*, 5 (3), 239–281.

Shimp, T.A. (1994), 'Presidential address: academic appalachia and the discipline of consumer research', *Advances in Consumer Research*, 21, 1–7.

Shoup, E.C. (1942), 'Post-war marketing responsibilities need changed marketing executives', *Journal of Marketing*, 7 (2), 125–128.

Shultz, C.J. (2007), 'Marketing as constructive engagement', *Journal of Public Policy and Marketing*, 26 (2), 293–301.

Silk, A.J. (1993), 'Marketing science in a changing environment', *Journal of Marketing Research*, 30 (November), 401–404.

Stewart, D.W. (1991), 'From methods and projects to systems and process: the evolution of marketing research techniques', *Marketing Research*, September, 25–36.

Tadajewski, M. (2006a), 'The ordering of marketing theory: the influence of McCarthyism and the cold war', *Marketing Theory*, 6 (2), 163–200.

Tadajewski, M. (2006b), 'Remembering motivation research: toward an alternative genealogy of interpretive consumer research', *Marketing Theory*, 6 (4), 429–466.

Tadajewski, M. (2008), 'Relationship marketing at Wanamaker's in the 19th and early 20th centuries', *Journal of Macromarketing*, 28 (2), 169–182.

Tadajewski, M. (2009a), 'Eventalizing the marketing concept', *Journal of Marketing Management* (forthcoming).

Tadajewski, M. (2009b), 'Competition, cooperation and open price associations: relationship marketing and Arthur Jerome Eddy (1859–1920)', *Journal of Historical Research in Marketing*, 1, 1.

Tadajewski, M. and Brownlie, D. (2008), 'Critical marketing: a limit attitude', in M. Tadajewski and D. Brownlie (eds), *Critical Marketing: Contemporary Issues in Marketing*. Chichester: Wiley, pp. 1–28.

Tadajewski, M. and Jones, D.G.B. (eds) (2008), *The History of Marketing Thought* Volumes I, II and III. London: Sage.

Tadajewski, M. and Jones, D.G.B. (2008), 'The history of marketing thought: introduction and overview', in M. Tadajewski and D.G.B. Jones (eds), *The History of Marketing Thought*, Volume I. London: Sage, pp. xix–xlii.

Tadajewski, M. and Saren, M. (2009), 'Rethinking the emergence of relationship marketing', *Journal of Macromarketing* (forthcoming).

Tosdal, H.H. (1939), 'The consumer and consumption in recent literature', *Harvard Business Review*, 17 (4), 508–514.

Tosdal, H.R. (1941), 'Significant trends in sales management', *Journal of Marketing*, 5 (3), 215–218.

Tosdal, H.R. (1942), 'Sales management: retrospect and prospect', *Harvard Business Review*, 21 (1), 71–82.

Vargo, S.L. and Lusch, R.F. (2004), 'Evolving to a new dominant logic for marketing', *Journal of Marketing*, 68 (1), 1–17.

Webster, F.E. (1988), 'The rediscovery of the marketing concept', *Business Horizons*, 31 (3), 29–39.

Webster, F.E. (1992), 'The changing role of marketing in the corporation', *Journal of Marketing*, 56 (4), 1–17.

Weld, L.D.H. (1941), 'Early experience in teaching courses in marketing', *Journal of Marketing*, 5 (4), 380–381.

White, P. (1927), *Scientific Marketing Management: Its Principals and Methods*. New York: Harper.

White, P. and Hayward, W.S. (1924), *Marketing Practice*. New York: Doubleday, Page & Company.

White, W.L. (1940), 'Marketing research', *The Annals of the American Academy of Political and Social Science*, 209, 183–192.

Wilkie, W.L. and Moore, E.S. (2003), 'Scholarly research in marketing: exploring the "4 eras" of thought development', *Journal of Public Policy and Marketing*, 22 (2), 116–146.

Wilkie, W.L. and Moore, E.S. (2006), 'Macromarketing as a pillar of marketing thought', *Journal of Macromarketing*, 26 (2), 224–232.

Zaltman, G. and Burger, P.C. (1975), *Marketing Research: Fundamentals and Dynamics*. Hinsdale: The Dryden Press.

CHAPTER 3

Postmodern Marketing and Beyond

Pauline Maclaran

INTRODUCTION

Postmodernism can be a difficult concept to comprehend because of its richness and complexity. An elaborate lexicon surrounds it, full of 'ologies', 'ities' and 'isms', that often obscures and confuses its would-be audiences. Our ambition in this chapter is to take away some of the term's mystique, by clarifying and, we hope, simplifying some of its key principles.

The postmodern era signalled a major change in Western thinking and philosophizing. Leading commentators consider that it commenced around the end of the 1950s when the term 'postmodern' was first applied to describe changing characteristics in art and culture (Lyotard, 1984). For example, it was used in architecture to describe the distinct break that occurred during the 1960s with the type of rational thinking that had given rise to modern functionalism (a perspective dictating that the design of an object or building should be determined by its function). In contrast to functionalism, postmodernism focused more on style, and, indeed, a mixture of styles that also often playfully harked back to the past. As a cultural movement, postmodernism is characteristically sceptical about many of the key assumptions that have underpinned Western thinking for several centuries. Accordingly, the postmodern critique questions authority, sources of knowledge and many other cultural, social, economic and political taken-for-granted assumptions in society.

Over the last three decades, postmodernism has spread to affect all disciplines and branches of knowledge, including marketing, where it has made its biggest impact in relation to the understanding of consumers. This has given rise to many new theories around the hedonic and experiential nature of consumption.

In this chapter we consider the implications of postmodernism for marketing and consumer behaviour. First, in order to set it in its historical context, we give a brief overview of postmodernism in relation to modernity. Next we discuss how the characteristics of what Lyotard (1984) termed 'the postmodern condition' are manifested in marketing phenomena. We then explore the influence of postmodern critique in overturning some of marketing's basic assumptions. Finally, we consider some of the criticisms that have been levelled at postmodernism and discuss how we may be moving beyond postmodernism.

MODERNITY VERSUS POSTMODERNITY

As the name suggests, postmodernity marks the end of modernity – variously referred to as *The Age of Reason* or *The Enlightenment* – a period in Western history running from the mid-eighteenth to the mid-twentieth century. Widepread industrialization marked the first phase of modernity, together with the rise of capitalism and the increasing role of science and technology. Its second phase, in the twentieth century, was marked by the huge proliferation of mass media. In general terms, modernity was characterized by a belief in the intrinsic power of humankind to be master of its own destiny, principally through the control of nature.

Postmodernism recognizes that the modernist notion of improving human existence by controlling nature through scientific technologies is an illusion (Firat, 1991). This has been forcefully spelt out in recent decades by major scares such as Mad Cow Disease, AIDS, the thinning of the ozone layer, and the many other implications of humankind's environmental pollutants. In addition, rationalist thinking has witnessed the many extremes of ethnic cleansing during the twentieth century. In the face of these many disasters and tragedies there has been a loss of faith in the notion of 'progress', together with an accompanying scepticism concerning the many hopes for science and technology.

This sceptical questioning is characteristic of the postmodern era, an era that marks the disintegration of what Lyotard (1984) refers to as grand 'metanarratives'. These are systems or ideologies, for example, Christianity and the rationalist thinking of the Enlightenment (see Adorno and Horkheimer, 1997) that set standards to measure dualistic/binary values such as good and bad, high and low, true and false. Hence, a postmodernist perspective challenges traditional value systems with such dichotomous modes of thinking and merges categories in a relativistic way, thereby producing complex mixtures of those binaries. Categories of true and false, genuine and fake, high and low are blurred and mutually dependent. For example, clear demarcations between high and low art no longer exist. An advertisement is just as likely to be labelled an artwork as a Van Gogh painting. In the multicultural world of the twenty-first century, there is no one perspective that is privileged, or one source that provides any absolute 'truth'.

We now go on to consider all these issues in greater depth. In order to do so we have found it useful to distinguish between the **characteristics** of postmodernism and the postmodern **critique**. This follows on from Zymunt Bauman's (1988) distinction between 'a sociology of postmodernism' and 'a postmodern sociology'. Whereas the former looks at postmodernism through a lens that uses traditional sociological tools, the latter introduces new tools to analyse social phenomena. Accordingly, first we look at the characteristics of postmodernism as they are manifested by changing trends in marketing and, second, we look at how the tools of postmodern critique have influenced our understanding of marketing phenomena.

MARKETING AND THE CHARACTERISTICS OF POSTMODERNISM

Marketing and consumption have been pinpointed as key phenomena of the postmodern era (Baudrillard, 1988; Brown, 1995, 1998; Firat et al., 1995), to the extent that marketing, as the main purveyor of signs, symbols and images, has been identified as more or less synonymous with postmodernism (Firat and Venkatesh, 1993). Increasingly, the emphasis is on product intangibles such as brand name and overall image, the fantasy aspects that surround a product as opposed to any intrinsic, tangible value in the product itself. Thus the image becomes the marketable entity and the product strives to represent its image rather than vice versa. Firat et al. (1995) describe this as the quintessential post-modern approach. Of the various authors who have identified and discussed postmodernism's key features in relation to marketing (Firat, 1991, 1992; Firat and Venkatesh, 1993, 1995; Firat et al., 1995), Brown's (1995, p. 106) list of seven characteristics is the most comprehensive for our present analysis:

1. *Fragmentation* – a sense that all things are disconnected pervades our everyday experiences, particularly through the disjointed images of mass advertising and the media. This is heightened by other factors such as the demise of political stability, social organization and mass market economy, the nature and grounds of knowledge. With the collapse of mass marketing approaches, we are witnessing the fragmentation of markets into smaller and smaller market segments. This is encouraged by the huge growth in database marketing, the increasing prevalence of one-to-one marketing and the concept of mass customization.

2. *De-differentiation* – this involves the blurring of established hierarchies such as high/low culture, local/global marketplaces,

education/training, politics/showbusiness and so forth. Formerly clearcut boundaries have become opaque, with one category merging into the other. On the pages of *Hello* magazine we are likely to see footballers and their wives (e.g. David and Victoria Beckham), alongside Royalty (e.g. Prince William and his girlfriend, Kate Middleton). Here we are witnessing the collapse of traditional social class distinctions into an overriding category of celebrity culture. Similarly, high and low art blur, with displays of advertising 'art' occurring regularly in the Tate Gallery in London. These have included exhibits of Bovril labels and shopping bags. During 2002 and 2003 the Tate Liverpool held an exhibition entitled *Shopping – A Century of Art and Consumer Culture* which was the first exhibition to carry out an in-depth examination of the interrelationships between contemporary art and the display, distribution and consumption of goods. This included Barbara Kruger's famous photographic screenprint depicting a large hand carrying a sign that reads 'I shop therefore I am'.

Andy Warhol famously predicted that 'All department stores will become museums and all museums will become department stores' (Gawker.com). We can see this prediction coming to pass with the increasing trend for large companies, such as Nike, Guinness and Coca-Cola, to develop museums devoted to their history and the development of their brand. In the following report, posted on a travel website, we can see how consumers enthusiastically communicate with each other and how their cultural sightseeing now includes such museums:

Coca-Cola Museum – Las Vegas (consumer report)

Couldn't help not miss this place as it totally stood out of its place. A semi-glass building in the shape of a Coca-Cola bottle … wow. Small entrance fee I forgot how much … 2 or 3 dollars to go in. They have a lovely Coke gift shop as you enter. If you're a Coke lover, then this is Paradise! Inside there's the complete history of Coca-Cola plus a room where one can view the best Coke-Cola commercials of all time. Plus you get to try some of the different cokes from around the world. They have around 6–8 coke dispensers where you grab a little plastic coke cup and help yourself. Careful not to drink yourself silly. I honestly enjoyed myself there as I am an avid Coke bottle collector.

3. *Hyperreality* – is the becoming real of what was originally a simulation. This is exacerbated by the dream worlds created by advertising and promotion. Nowadays alternative meanings may even be attached to many mundane products like toothpaste, soap

and deodorant (i.e. sex, money, power and so forth). The many trends towards consumer fantasy, for example, themed environments (pubs, shopping centres, restaurants and hotels), virtual reality and computer games, exemplify this characteristic. The Irishness conveyed in Irish theme pubs becomes what we think of as 'Irish'. In Las Vegas, the casino, New York, New York, is very similar to its 'real' counterpart's neon-lit Times Square (Firat and Dholakia, 2006).

The West Edmonton Mall in Canada, one of the world's largest shopping malls, recreates a Parisian Boulevard, Bourbon Street, New Orleans and Chinatown, among many other fantasy-evoking simulations. One of Europe's biggest shopping and leisure centres, the MetroCentre, in Gateshead, England, has themed shopping in the Roman Forum, Antiques Village, Garden Court and Mediterranean Village.

Alongside this continual simulation there is an accompanying sense of loss of authenticity, and confusion over what is real and what is not. This leads to a quest on the part of consumers to experience what is really 'real'. Farmers' markets are making a comeback to city centres as people tire of the sameness of out-of-town shopping malls. The market is burgeoning for guides (books and people) that cater for travellers who shun the managed tourism of package holidays and seek 'authentic' experiences in the countries they visit (see Caruana et al., 2008). Chapter 5 discusses in detail the importance of perceived authenticity in the development of brand culture.

4. *Chronology* – instead of looking towards a future that it mistrusts, postmodernism adopts a retrospective perspective (see Brown, 2001 for a very detailed discussion of this). It has a nostalgic concern for the past and its representations, rather than the progressive orientation of modernism. This links very much to the desire for authenticity and the 'real' just discussed. Another manifestation of this is the trend for retro products as illustrated, for example, by the launch of the new Mini (see the case study in Chapter 5); Volkswagen Beetle cars which hark back to the 1960s/70s; and Citroen C3s modelled on the original 2CVs of the 1950s.

Nostalgic consumption is particularly associated with the ageing baby boom generation (those born between 1948 and 1964). However, Goulding (2002) has highlighted an increasing trend for what she terms 'vicarious nostalgia', a preference for objects associated with 10–15 years before one's actual birth date. Evidenced by the growing numbers of 'retro' clubs and shops, this type of nostalgia focuses on the aesthetic consumption of a particular period. Her research documents many consumers who live the lifestyle as closely as they can of a decade outside their living memory. This passion pervades all their consumption experiences. For example, one young woman, Caroline, who drives a Vespa scooter and a 1960s Mini, lives in an apartment full of 60s memorabilia and only likes music from that era as well. For an evening's entertainment she goes to a 60s club where she and her friends follow the dress codes of the 60s, and dance the night away to the music of the Stones, Beetles, Sandy Shaw, Lulu and the many other 'pop singers' of that decade. The website, retrowow.co.uk, caters for just such lovers of retro style (check it out!). Apart from including details of a vast range of retro collectibles, it also gives advice on retro lifestyles that intermingles with snippets of social history of the particular period being discussed.

5. *Pastiche* – this concerns postmodernism's tendency to mix styles, past and present, often achieving the effect of a collage. As we already saw, in the example of the West Edmonton Mall, quite incongruous styles are juxtaposed (i.e. Chinatown and New Orleans). Pastiche is done in a playful and often ironic or self-referential way with a blending of existing codes, be they architectural, musical, literary and so forth. Often these result in parody advertisements or even advertisements about advertising. A good illustration of this is the Energizer Bunny advertising series that commenced in 1989 and ran through the 1990s. The first advertisement featured the now iconic pink toy rabbit, wearing dark glasses and beating a drum. It escapes from the studio where the advertisement is being made and rampages through other commercials that are being made in adjacent studios (wikipedia. org). The concept of the Energizer Bunny was itself a parody of Energizer's arch rival, Duracell, whose advertisements at that time showed a series of toy animals playing instruments and slowly coming to a halt with only the one powered by Duracell continuing to play.

    Pastiche also includes intertextuality which means that one text draws on its audiences' understanding of another text to give it meaning. Advertisements frequently draw on elements from other popular cultures sources such as TV programmes or music. The recent Magners Irish Cider advertising campaign features the husky tones of Steve Earle singing 'Galway Girl' (a song well known to its target audience for being featured in the romantic film, *PS I Love You*, which was released just prior to the advertisement's release). Such intertextuality serves to enhance a brand's mystique.

6. *Anti-foundationalism* – this is postmodernism's tendency to eschew mainstream, traditional approaches and beliefs and is typified by

anti-fashion fashion movements such as Grunge. It is inherently deconstructive of anything that is orthodox and representative of the establishment. In the Magners' campaign referred to above, Steve Earle is a perfect example of the 'rebel' archetype in mass culture (Holt and Thompson, 2004). In his youth, the singer was a hard drinking man who refused to conform to society's norms and was revered for his anti-establishment attitude. This 'rebel sell' is discussed in more detail in Chapter 5. Developing counter-cultural brand images and advertising messages has become big business. Think of French Connection United Kingdom's infamous acronym, FCUK, which helped turn a £5 million loss (in 1992) into a £39 million profit (Spencer, 2004). There are now many subversive advertising campaigns, such as the infamous 'You know when you've been Tango'd'.

The green movement can also be identified with postmodern anti-foundationalism. This critiques the basic structures of Western social organization and, in particular, excessive lifestyles that are encouraged by increasing consumerism. Green marketing and sustainable marketing are becoming very important areas for marketers to understand and are discussed in more depth in Chapter 9.

7. *Pluralism* – the effect of the previous six characteristics leads to an acceptance of incongruous phenomena typified by the 'anything goes' syndrome. It welcomes and embraces diversity in all areas. Postmodern pluralism is associated with relativism, a perspective that eschews any belief in absolute truth. Instead, relativism embraces the idea that knowledge is dependent on an individual's perspective which will be highly influenced by his/her socio-cultural background. Reality is thus socially constructed and there can be no objective knowledge or absolute representation of reality. Multiculturalism is a manifestation of this, respecting as it does all cultural positions and religious backgrounds. In his book, *Shopping for God* (2007), James Twitchell highlights how religious pluralism is leading to a market-based approach to spiritual practice in America, where consumer choice and church competition are the order of the day (Scott and Maclaran, 2009). Twitchell uses the term 'vernacular religion' to describe how consumers either produce their own ritual objects, use traditional religious props in unintended ways, or incorporate elements from other religious traditions—to use for their creative, and highly personalized, spiritual practices. (Twitchell, 2007)

Overall, then, our above analysis of postmodernism's seven key characteristics shows the large extent to which postmodernism and marketing phenomena are intertwined. Indeed, consumer society is at the heart of postmodernism. In the next section we go on to look at how the postmodern critique has introduced new ways for us to understand our changing, increasingly marketing-driven, consumerist world.

MARKETING AND THE POSTMODERN CRITIQUE

The postmodern critique is usually associated with French poststructuralist thinkers such as Jacques Derrida, Michel Foucault and Jean-François Lyotard, among others, although postmodernism and poststructuralism are by no means synonymous. We are not going to attempt to give a detailed overview of this highly complex and abstract body of thinking. We will, however, discuss some of the areas in marketing and consumer behaviour that this theorizing has influenced.

Poststructuralism shows how meanings are constructed through discourse (systems of expression with in-built power relations and ideological implications), and that meanings are constantly shifting and evolving. It exposes how conceptual opposites, referred to as 'binary oppositions' (e.g. male/female, reason/emotion, speech/writing, etc.), depend on each other for their meaning, meaning which is also hierarchical in that one term is usually seen as superior to the other (i.e. reason is usually privileged over emotion). Poststructuralism tries to deconstruct these paired relationships of meaning, showing how the more privileged term depends on its relationship to the other, less privileged term. For example, to be male depends on not being female and being rational depends on not being emotional. Through the act of deconstruction, poststructuralism exposes the assumptions and knowledge systems that underpin such binary, hierarchical oppositions and unsettles the idea that there are any essential meanings that stay fixed over time. Instead it shows how meaning shifts with historical and cultural contexts. What it means to be male or female in one culture, or one period in history, varies considerably.

Within consumer research, interpretivist research has frequently been conflated with postmodernism (Sherry, 1991), although not all interpretivist research takes a postmodern perspective. Certainly this body of scholarship (now also referred to as Consumer Culture Theory, see Arnould and Thompson, 2005 for a detailed overview) has contributed many new theoretical insights that have been influenced by the postmodern critique and, in particular, by poststructuralism through its analysis of discourse. Fundamental to these insights has been the recognition of the changing relationship between the production/consumption binary. During modernism, production and the political economy were privileged over consumption and the domestic sphere. Postmodernism shifts the emphasis from production to consumption, however, privileging culture instead, and meaning creation through consumption. The consumer becomes a producer of meanings through his/her consumption acts and, hence, the binary division between production/consumption becomes blurred, with production no longer assuming the privileged position. Rather the consumer becomes the creative hero, playfully seeking out an identity, or identities, in the marketplace. This is very much the position taken by two leading interpretivist researchers, Firat and Venkatesh (1995), who celebrate the overturning of modernist conceptions of the consumer in their seminal article on 'liberatory postmodernism'. In this highly influential article, they argue that postmodernist developments in our knowledge of consumption processes offer emancipatory potential because they release us from traditional roles and constraints (e.g. gender, class, race), and allow a multiplicity of consumption forms and identity positions. It is in this respect particularly, that Firat and Venkatesh recognize the potential of individuals to 'register rebellion' (op. cit., p. 260) in the marketplace, through creating identity positions that could be subversive to the meanings intended by marketers. Other interpretivist studies have shown the emancipatory potential of, and within, the marketplace, in relation to: subcultures of consumption (Schouten and McAlexander, 1995); ethnicity (Peñaloza, 1994); fashion discourses (Thompson and Haytko, 1997); and the gay community (Kates, 2000).

Experiential consumption

We have already discussed how, from a postmodern perspective, contemporary consumption is not so much to do with use value or even exchange value, but rather more to do with symbolic value. As the symbolic meanings around products and services become increasingly important to consumers, so too do the experiences that are associated with those products and services. Experiential consumption is one of the dominant theoretical themes to emerge in interpretivist research (Belk, 1995), and it has its origins in the postmodern notion of consumers as manipulating signs and symbols in the marketplace in order to communicate with those around them. An experiential consumption perspective conceptualizes consumers as socially connected beings rather than merely as potential purchasers of a product or service. There is a realization that choosing depends on using, that customer choice depends on their experiences, and that buying depends on consuming (Holbrook, 1995). This overturns traditional marketing assumptions of a rational, information-processing consumer. Instead it emphasizes the primacy of emotions over rationality, experience over cognition, and the subconscious over the conscious. Usage experiences become a basis for 'hedonic' consumption and the role of 'fantasies, feeling and fun' in the lives of consumers (Hirschman and Holbrook, 1982).

As consumers seek more meaningful associations from products and services, they are moving away from wanting value for money to wanting value for time. As part of this shift, they expect more experiences from the brands they buy, experiences that also link them to other like-minded consumers. Thus, rather than being interested in the use value of goods and services, postmodern consumers seek a 'linking value' (Cova, 1996, p. 21). For example, Liberty, the upmarket London department store hosts 'stitch 'n' bitch' sessions in its café to help create a community around its brand. T-mobile invites customers to 'Street Gigs' where they can try out the newest technology. Innocent Smoothies runs an event called 'Fruitstock' as a way to encourage consumers to engage with the brand. Because consumers are increasingly sceptical about brand claims made through advertising (part of the postmodern scepticism referred to above), they want to experience brands for themselves, and discuss what other consumers feel about them, before making up their minds. The influence of brand communities is discussed in detail in Chapter 6.

Many major brands are now investing in permanent brand experiences. At Cadbury World we can learn about the history of chocolate before buying it in a vast emporium dedicated to lavish displays of enticingly packaged chocolates. We can also explore the set where the television soap opera, *Coronation Street*, sponsored by Cadbury's, was filmed. Similarly, Volkswagen's headquarters in Germany features a complete mini town, Autostadt, with streets, train stations, marketplaces, parks, rivers and bridges. There are also plenty of other entertainments and restaurants. Here consumers can study the technology behind Volkswagen cars and see Volkswagen's vision for the future, as well as browse around a museum of vintage VWs. There is even a special centre for children where they can drive miniature Beetles.

The key to experiences such as these is that they are interactive, both consumer-to-marketer and consumer-to-consumer. These interactive experiential strategies are designed to co-create meanings with consumers (discussed further in Chapter 5). Again, this is a further illustration of the breaking down of the production/consumption binary that has been influenced by the postmodern critique. Marketers may create certain meanings around their brands, but unless these resonate with consumers they will not be accepted, or be seen as authentic, by them. Experiential marketing encourages consumers to weave their own personal and social meanings alongside those created by marketers. Of course, we need to maintain a healthy (postmodern) scepticism as to marketers' motives in empowering consumers in this way. Arvidsson (2006), for example, accuses marketers of building on the immaterial labour of consumers, namely the values, commitments and forms of community around many products and services that are sustained by consumers. In other words, in a postmodern marketplace, consumers do a lot of the work and actually pay the company to be able to do so! We now go on in our final section to consider other limitations of a postmodernist approach.

BEYOND POSTMODERNISM

From a critical perspective, this emphasis on a playful, imaginative consumer, as he or she creatively appropriates marketplace signs and symbols, also reinforces the achievement of personal freedom through economic means. It must be remembered that there are many marginalized groups who cannot afford the luxury of such marketplace play. Unlike their more prosperous counterparts, consumers in poverty and those who are homeless do not have the luxury of constructing and reconstructing consumer identities at will (Hamilton, 2007; Hill and Stamey, 1990). For such destitute groups of consumers, it is survival strategies, rather than identity strategies that count.

Moreover, a postmodernism lens is only relevant to advanced consumer societies and cannot be applied to the large majority of the world's subsistence and developing economies. This is the theme of a key article by Rohit Varman and Ram Manohar Vikas (2007) who focus on subaltern consumers in India. They demonstrate how consumer freedom remains, as yet, only for the elite. Highly critical of a postmodern lens whereby consumption increasingly defines human freedom, they make an important contribution to the debate by calling for a re-emphasis on production which, they argue, has become separated from consumption. Their research with subaltern consumers shows how these consumers are disempowered in the workplace and, consequently, lead wretched lives which are barely at subsistence levels. Varman and Vikas conclude that powerlessness in relation to production, ensures powerlessness in the sphere of consumption.

Another criticism of postmodernism has been that, while many interpretivist studies have given us greater insights into consumer culture theory and individual agency through the marketplace, this has sometimes been to the detriment of the wider social landscape and its structures. Catterall et al. (2005) argue that because rebellion takes place on an individual basis in the marketplace or within market-based subcultures (see Chapter 6), this has stifled much collective critique of wider social, economic and political structures. This is in part encouraged by the relativist stance that postmodernism adopts and its reluctance to privilege any one perspective which also weakens its political potency.

Bearing these significant limitations in mind, (see Tadajewski and Brownlie, 2008 for further discussion of these) there is some evidence that we are now beginning to move beyond the postmodern condition. Throughout this chapter we have highlighted the consumer quest for authentic goods and services as part of the characteristics of a postmodern era. According to Holt (2002), what he refers to as 'the postmodern branding paradigm' relies on the fact that, when perceived as authentic, brands are viewed by consumers as key resources for identity construction (for a more detailed discussion of these issues, see Chapter 5). However, Holt warns that this paradigm is now threatened because of the core paradoxes it

Case study: Experiencing a postmodern marketplace

Developed out of a beautiful eighteenth century building, the Powerscourt Townhouse Centre opened as a festival marketplace in 1981, a short walk away from one of Dublin's busiest shopping areas, Grafton Street. The centre comprised three levels of retail outlets grouped around an enclosed courtyard. The majority of shops sold specialist merchandise, with jewellery, ladies fashion, antiques and eating places predominating. Like its American and European counterparts (e.g. Harborplace, Baltimore and Covent Garden, London), Powerscourt offered an allegedly unique shopping environment, the 'Powerscourt Experience', as it was described on promotional material. Festival malls provide an alternative to the uniformity of shopping malls which offer mass-produced goods via high street chains such as Next, Miss Selfridge, New Look and Zara. They typically occupy a refurbished building of acknowledged architectural merit, retail an eclectic mix of speciality goods and services, are tenanted by independent retailers rather than national chain stores, encourage recreational as opposed to utilitarian shopping activities, and adopt an essentially aesthetic ethos involving artworks, craft activities and designer goods.

On the ground floor in Powerscourt there was a central café where shoppers could pass the time chatting or people-watching. Surrounding this were small market stalls, selling an eclectic mix of products, from ice cream to bonsai trees. Rising up from the courtyard was a stage for cultural events, with a grand piano to provide special recitals and enhance the centre's ambience. More exclusive shops, on the higher levels, proffered a range of designer jewellery, clothing, antiques and paintings. Its quirky mix of shops and entertainment gave Powerscourt a special ambience that consumers loved. Its combination of arts and crafts and the sense that there was something for everyone, made it very different from other high street shopping. Many people came just to sit with friends over coffee or food in the many restaurants that were interspersed throughout the centre. Visually, a plethora of colourful signs, restaurant canopies and plant greenery greeted shoppers as they entered the courtyard. Powerscourt's somewhat haphazard layout encouraged exploration, and gave shoppers a sense of discovery. It was not unusual for some to actually lose their way as they wandered around the different floors.

During the 1980s and 1990s, Powerscourt typified the nature of postmodern retailing (although it has subsequently been refurbished), as we go on to show using the previously discussed seven characteristics of postmodernism identified by Brown (1995).

Fragmentation

In its espousal of unique retail as opposed to the mass market, Powerscourt offered many richly contrasting opportunities for (re)creation of the self. The centre provided much scope for imaginings that centred around changing one's image or identity and engaging in the creative exploration of many celebratory identities. The setting's many associations with arts, crafts and aesthetics encouraged consumers to seek this self-expression in many different ways and to consider the many possible variations of Belk et al. (2003) 'myself-that-could-be'. For example, the Design Centre with its exclusive Irish designer labels together with other designer goods shops, proffered many possibilities for self-transformation, as did many other smaller stores: the Colour Me Beautiful stall, Buttercups (the beauty salon), Pzazz (the hair salon), Townbride and Wigwam (the wig boutique).

De-differentiation

The design and setting of Powerscourt challenged many traditional marketing notions around segmentation and targeting. Whereas the higher levels were devoted to designer labels, craft shops, goldsmiths, antiques and art galleries, the ground floor was characterized by an abundance of bric-à-brac shops and cheap jewellery stalls. Many consumers commented that there was something for everyone. The extremes of bric-à-brac and expensive designer outfits catered for very different budgets. Thus the boundaries between high and low culture became indistinct in an environment where you could obtain anything ranging from high-quality antiques to the downright 'kitsch'.

Furthermore, for consumers, Powerscourt represented a very local marketplace that took its identity from the character of its immediate surroundings. This was in sharp contrast to the perceived uniformity of the global marketplace. Hence the special significance to consumers of the localized and contextualized nature of the symbolic meanings that were created. In turn, this meaning creation blurred boundaries between production and consumption, art and life, in a characteristically postmodern way, with consumers becoming the producers of their own meanings and dream artists of their own imaginings (Campbell, 1987).

Hyperreality

The abundance of spectacle and dreamlike images in Powerscourt encouraged a sense of being in a world apart, and this effect contributed greatly to it being a hyperreal environment. Powerscourt looked like a Georgian residence or a traditional market, depending on which entrance one looked at. In either case, once inside it was not as it had seemed from the outside. Its airy vistas opened up to a profusion of colourful and enticing shopping spectacles around the tiered courtyard. The serendipitous nature of this discovery frequently surprised and entranced consumers, provoking many expressions of amazement and lending a hyperreal quality to consumers' shopping experience.

The centre stage that housed the grand piano epitomized this hyperreal ambience and the notion of postmodern consumption as a symbolic activity and as a consumption of meaning. Even when unplayed, it created an air of expectancy and anticipation. Its associations with performance reminded consumers of the theatre, the concert hall and the opera house, thereby simulating a more cultured environment, an environment normally very much removed from the more mundane task of shopping.

Chronology

In its eclectic blending of the old with the new, a blending that did not attempt to make chronological sense, Powerscourt typified the postmodern tendency to adopt a retrospective perspective. With its historic setting, its sweeping mahogany staircases, the grand piano, its antiques and arts galleries, and other fixtures and fittings such as mock-Victorian gas street lamps, wrought iron balustrades and creaking wooden floorboards, Powerscourt evoked a strong sense of the living past in the present.

This, then, is a good illustration of our earlier point about how the very ubiquity of hyperreality stimulates a countervailing desire for authenticity. Powerscourt was considered authentic on several levels: its 'sympathetically restored' historic building with many original features preserved intact; its many hand-made products that testified to the craftsmanship that had made them unique; and the overall impression conveyed to consumers of a dedication to more subtle aesthetic values rather than blatant commercial interests. In respect of the latter, the piano in Powerscourt was a further symbolic reinforcement of the centre's longstanding traditions and cultural superiority, signifying what was lacking in other shopping environments and experiences.

Pastiche

Styles were unashamedly mixed in Powerscourt to achieve the effect of a giant collage that greeted consumers as they entered the main courtyard. With no uniformity to shopfront design or layout, an array of different codes and references intermingled both vertically and horizontally within the centre. On the ground floor more contemporary shops mixed with others trying to convey a more historical ambience. For example, Wigwam displayed its brightly coloured blue and red wigs in close proximity to Joseph Appleby Diamond Jewellers, with its mock-Georgian wooden façade that framed the opulent jewellery displays within.

The hotch-potch of small market stalls and kiosks, informally placed around the ground floor, belied the more formal Georgian lines of the courtyard in which they were housed. Its two entrances symbolized these inherent contradictions. The original front entrance with its marbled black and white floor, its empty fireplace and its high ceiling, was somewhat cold and forbidding, reminiscent of the distant aristocracy that had previously inhabited its surrounds. In sharp contrast, the original back entrance (used more frequently as the front) was a profusion of flowers and fruit that spilled out onto the street. Its welcoming earthen flagstones and cosy ambience invited consumers to enter and go beyond, to investigate and explore. Contradictions in these two entrances abounded: urban/rural, high culture/low culture, aristocracy/peasantry, coldness/warmth, temperance/indulgence.

Anti-foundationalism

In eschewing mainstream forms of shopping, the ethos of Powerscourt, as a festival marketplace, was inherently anti-foundational. Everything about the centre was read by consumers as standing in opposition to the mass market with its over-commercialization and its loss of more traditional and aesthetic values. In addition, it symbolized a localized resistance to fears of an anonymous globalization, a uniqueness retained despite the encroaching efficiency of mass production lines. This perceived anti-foundationalism played an important role, allowing consumers 'to live their own myths or stories (narratives) instead of otherwise enforced or imposed ones' (Venkatesh et al., 1993, p. 216).

Pluralism

This last characteristic can be seen reflected in all the others. The eclectic and paradoxical mix that made up the shopping experience in Powerscourt contributed to a rich diversity on which the consumer imagination could feed. There was something for everyone, and anything seemed to go. Consumers found it difficult to categorize Powerscourt in relation to other forms of shopping. With its subversive mixing of class-based ambiences under one roof – designer chic alongside tourist 'tack' – it conveyed a social ambivalence that evaded categorization.

contains whereby marketers are taking riskier strategies to appear authentic and original. As consumers become more and more sceptical of marketing activities, they are not easily taken in by such techniques and quickly see through inauthentic, money-making gambits. Holt envisages that in the future marketers will not be able to conceal their profit-making bias and they will have to acknowledge their commercial interests more readily. In turn, consumers will view the products and services marketers provide as cultural materials for identity projects that are no different from other cultural resources such as music, theatre, film and television. Marketers will then be judged, not by the perceived authenticity of the goods they offer, but by the creativity of those goods in helping consumers express themselves.

SUMMARY

In this chapter we have looked at the impact of postmodernism on our knowledge of marketing and consumer behaviour. In particular, we have looked at how a postmodern perspective conceptualizes the consumer as a communicative subject who reinforces his or her identity through the marketplace. Postmodernism emphasizes interpretivist, qualitative ways of knowing, rather than survey-based, or experimental quantitative research. Interpretivist perspectives have given us many new ways to understand the relationship between consumers and marketing phenomena, and how marketplace cultures develop through these ongoing interactions. We have also considered some of the drawbacks of postmodernism perspectives, not least that they are relevant only to a relatively wealthy minority of the world's population.

INTERNET RESOURCES

For lovers of retro style. www.retrowow.co.uk
Professor Stephen Brown's website (author of *Postmodern Marketing*): http://www.sfxbrown.com/

The classic Energizer Bunny 1989 advertisement. http://www.youtube.com/watch?v=fILdYrxnrf8&feature=related

The Metrocentre, UK. http://www.metrocentre-gateshead.co.uk/

The West Edmonton Mall, Canada. http://www.westedmall.com/

KEY READINGS

Brown, S. (1995), *Postmodern Marketing*. London: Routledge.

Catterall, M., Maclaran, P. and Stevens, L. (2005), 'Postmodern paralysis: the critical impasse in feminist perspectives on consumers', *Journal of Marketing Management*, 21 (5–6), 489–504.

Firat, A.F. and Venkatesh, A. (1995), 'Liberatory postmodernism and the reenchantment of consumption', *Journal of Consumer Research*, 22 (3), 239–266.

SEMINAR EXERCISES

Discussion Topics

1. Using the library and internet, discover further sources of information on modernity. What other characteristics can you identify that are not discussed in this chapter?

2. Search various media sources (magazines, TV ads, the Internet) and identify a retro product. Discuss what market you think this is targeting and why?

3. Choose an advertisement that you think best illustrates an experiential approach and analyse its various experiential elements.

4. What are the key criticisms of postmodernism? Can you think of other examples besides those already discussed?

Group Exercises

1. Look for an advertisement that you think could be described as postmodern.

   (i) How many of the seven postmodern characteristics can you relate to this?

   (ii) Are there different ways the advertisement can be interpreted (i.e. depending on your sex/age/cultural background)?

2. Choose a themed consumptionscape that all your group can visit at least once (preferably alone or in pairs but not the whole group together). Then each member should write an individual account (minimum 400 words) of their experience there and the feelings and emotions that were evoked. Try not to think too rationally and be as creative as you want. You can use photographs also or anything else that you feel is appropriate (brochures, advertisements, etc.).

(i) Compare and contrast the differing viewpoints that group members expressed about their visit.

(ii) Are there key themes that run through these accounts and, if so, what are they?

(iii) What are the key emotions and feelings that you all had?

(iv) Have you found the seven characteristics useful in understanding and interpreting your experiences?

(v) Make a 10 minute presentation in your seminar to give an overview of your group's experiences and reactions to the consumptionscape.

REFERENCES

Adorno, T. and Horkheimer, M. (1997), *Dialectic of Enlightenment*. trans. J. Cumming. London: Verso.

Arnould, E.J. and Thompson, C.J. (2005), 'Consumer Culture Theory (CCT): twenty years of research', *Journal of Consumer Research*, 31 (4), 868–882.

Arvidsson, A. (2006), *Brands: Meaning and Value in Media Culture*. London & New York: Routledge.

Baudrillard, J. (1988), M. Poster, (ed.), *Jean Baudrillard: Selected Writings*. Oxford: Blackwell.

Bauman, Z. (1988), 'Sociology and postmodernity', *The Sociological Review*, 6 (4).

Belk, R.W. (1995), 'Studies in the new consumer behaviour', in D. Miller (ed.), *Acknowledging Consumption*. London: Routledge, pp. 58–95.

Belk, R.W., Ger, G. and Askegaard, S. (2003), 'The fire of desire: a multisited inquiry into consumer passion', *Journal of Consumer Research*, 30 (3), 326–351.

Brown, S. (1995), *Postmodern Marketing*. London: Routledge.

Brown, S. (1998), *Postmodern Marketing 2: Telling Tales*. London: ITP.

Brown, S. (2001), *Marketing: The Retro Revolution*. London: Sage.

Campbell, C. (1987), *The Romantic Ethic and the Spirit of Modern Consumerism*. Oxford: Basil Blackwell.

Caruana, R., Crane, A. and Fitchett, J. (2008), 'The paradox of the independent traveller', *Marketing Theory*, 8 (3) pp. 253–272.

Catterall, M., Maclaran, P. and Stevens, L. (2005), 'Postmodern paralysis: the critical impasse in feminist perspectives on consumers', *Journal of Marketing Management*, 21 (5–6), 489–504.

Cova, B. (1996), 'The postmodern explained to managers: implications for marketing', *Business Horizons*, Nov/Dec, 15–23.

Firat, A.F. (1991), 'The consumer in postmodernity', *Advances in Consumer Research*, 18, 70–76.

Firat, A.F. (1992), 'Fragmentation in the postmodern', *Advances in Consumer Research*, 19, 70–76.

Firat, A.F. and Dholakia, N. (2006), 'Theoretical and philosophical implications of postmodern debates: some challenges to modern marketing', *Marketing Theory*, 6 (2), 123–162.

Firat, A.F., Dholakia, N. and Venkatesh, A. (1995), 'Marketing in a postmodern world', *European Journal of Marketing*, 29 (1), 40–56.

Firat, A.F. and Venkatesh, A. (1993), 'Postmodernity: the age of marketing', *International Journal of Research in Marketing*, 10 (3), 227–249.

Firat, A.F. and Venkatesh, A. (1995), 'Liberatory postmodernism and the reenchantment of consumption', *Journal of Consumer Research*, 22 (3), 239–266.

Gawker.com. http://gawker.com/386202/the-department-stores-have-all-become-museums

Goulding, C. (2002), 'An exploratory study of age related vicarious nostalgia and aesthetic consumption', *Advances in Consumer Research*, 29, 542–546.

Hamilton, K. (2007), 'Making sense of consumer disadvantage', in M. Saren, P. Maclaran, C. Goulding, R. Elliott, A. Shankar and M. Catterall (eds), *Critical Marketing: Defining the Field*. Oxford, UK: Butterworth-Heinemann, pp. 178–192.

Hill, R.P. and Stamey, M. (1990), 'The homeless in America: an examination of possessions and consumption behaviors', *Journal of Consumer Research*, 17 (3), 303–320.

Hirschman, E.C. and Holbrook, M.B. (1982), 'Hedonic consumption: emerging concepts, methods and propositions', *Journal of Marketing*, 46 (Summer), 92–101.

Holbrook, M.B. (1995), *Consumer Research*. New York: Sage.

Holt, D.B. (2002), 'Why do brands cause trouble? a dialectical theory of consumer culture and branding', *Journal of Consumer Research*, 29 (1), 70–90.

Holt, D.B. and Thompson, C.J. (2004), 'Man-of-Action heroes: the pursuit of heroic masculinity in everyday consumption', *Journal of Consumer Research*, 31 (2), 425–440.

Kates, S.M. (2000), 'Out of the closet and out on the street: gay men and their brand relationships', *Psychology and Marketing*, 17 (6), 493–513.

Lyotard, J-F. (1984), *The Postmodern Condition: A Report on Knowledge*. Minneapolis, MN: University of Minnesota Press.

Peñaloza, L. (1994), 'Crossing Boundaries/Crossing Lines: a Look at the Nature of Gender Boundaries and their Impact on Marketing Research', *International Journal of Research in Marketing*, 11 (4), 359–379.

Schouten, J.W. and McAlexander, J.H. (1995), 'Subcultures of consumption: an ethnography of the new bikers', *Journal of Consumer Research*, 22 (1), 43–61.

Scott, L. and Maclaran, P. (2009), '"Roll Your Own" religion: consumer culture and the spiritual vernacular', *Advances in Consumer Research* (forthcoming).

Sherry, J.F. (1991), 'Postmodern alternatives: the interpretive turn in consumer research', in T.C. Robertson and H.H. Kassarjian (eds), *Handbook of Consumer Research*. Englewood Cliffs: Prentice-Hall, pp. 548–591.

Spencer, N. (2004), "Connecting with culture: profit and loss", August 27. http://www.licc.org.uk/culture/profit-and-loss

Tadajewski, M. and Brownlie, D. (2008), *Critical Marketing: Issues in Contemporary Marketing*. Chichester, UK: John Wiley & Sons.

Thompson, C.J. and Haytko, D.L. (1997), 'Speaking of fashion: consumers' uses of fashion discourses and the appropriation of countervailing cultural meanings', *Journal of Consumer Research*, 24 (June), 15–42.

Twitchell, J. (2007), *Shopping for God*. New York: Simon and Schuster.

Varman, R. and Vikas, R.M. (2007), 'Freedom and consumption: toward conceptualizing systemic constraints for subaltern consumers in a capitalist society', *Consumption Markets & Culture*, 10 (2), 117–131.

Venkatesh, A., Sherry, J.F. and Firat, A.F. (1993), 'Postmodernism and the marketing imaginery', *International Journal of Research in Marketing*, 10 (3), 215–223.

CHAPTER 4

Arts Marketing

Krzysztof Kubacki and Daragh O'Reilly

INTRODUCTION

This chapter explores the latest developments in the relatively new discipline of arts marketing. It is located within the larger framework of cultural production and consumption; however, its main focus is on marketing in the context of art. The relationship between art and the market is a complex one, which means that arts marketers need to pay attention to a range of issues which may not arise in the same way, or to the same degree, in conventional product marketing. Within Western culture, these issues are longstanding and have to do with notions of *art* and the *artist*. Most readers should be already familiar with various definitions of marketing, though, there are very few concepts as controversial and vague as *art*. It has provoked numerous and heated discussions among philosophers, from Socrates' view of 'art as mirror held up to nature' (Danto, 1964, p. 571), through famous Andy Warhol's poster 'art is what you can get away with', to Morris Weitz's argument that art cannot be defined as it is an open concept. Throughout over two thousand years, many have attempted to answer the question: *what is art?* In consequence, definitions of art have been conditioned by their authors' aesthetic preferences, culture, current debates and the development of art itself. Thus countless of these definitions have failed the test of time. This chapter therefore starts with an attempt to clarify what is meant by *art* and *artist* by exploring how understanding of both concepts has changed throughout history. We then outline two main approaches to arts marketing, offering very different conceptualizations of it. It is followed by an overview of some of the most important aspects of arts marketing, discussing issues such as the characteristics of the artworld as an industry and the production and consumption of art in our society. The chapter concludes with some observations on the relationship between art and brands, and the role of arts marketer.

DEFINITIONS OF ART AND THE ARTIST

Early conceptualizations of *art*, stretching from Aristotle to late nineteenth century Post-Impressionists, were concerned mostly with distinctive features of artworks. They can be broadly divided into two main streams: representational and expressive definitions. One example of the former, depicting visual appearance of objects, is Kant's (1790) philosophy, which describes art as 'a mode of representation which is intrinsically final, and which, although devoid of an end, has the effect of advancing the culture of the mental powers in the interests of social communication'. One of the more popular examples of the latter is, on the other hand, Tolstoy's definition of art as 'infectious communication of emotions' (Knox, 1930, p. 65). Music, in that sense, has been inseparable from people throughout the ages, and for hundreds of years has been used to warn about danger, wars, herald animal hunting or to make rain; it has also been an intrinsic element on social occasions such as coronations, weddings, funerals and banquets.

Nonetheless, the development of art in the twentieth century was followed by the dominant view amongst theorists that it became impossible to define art, as it progressed into a concept devoid of any common functions or essential and unique characteristics. Wolff (1983), for example, rejecting earlier essentialist definitions of art, argued that social history of art proved some artefacts or activities became art accidentally; hence, we cannot identify any features or characteristics which differentiate them from other, similar works. Therefore, over the past few decades we can observe the growing popularity of non-essentialist definitions of art, moving away from formalistic discussion about physical characteristics of artworks. One of them, so called the *institutional definition of art*, put forward by Georg Dickie in 1969 and based on Arthur Danto's original concept of *artworld* (1964), has significantly influenced our contemporary thinking about art. Criticized by many philosophers for its vagueness, it was later revised in 1984 (Torres and Kamhi, 2000): 'a work of art is an artefact of a kind created to be presented to an artworld public' (p. 96).

Several later attempts to define *art* also circled around Dickie's approach and added very little to his definition. Recently, Danto's definition of art was stretched to its limits by Carey (2005), who provocatively argued that 'a work of art is anything that anyone has ever considered a work of art, though it may be a work of art only for that one person' (p. 29). And while in the *institutional theory of art* recognition by a member of the artworld is what gives the work of art aesthetic value, Binkley (1992) argued that that member should be the artist him-/herself, deciding and specifying what the artwork is. A social constructionist view of art which seeks to accommodate these lines of thinking might assert that art is a construct which is contextually and strategically mobilized by individuals and social institutions to discuss a human signifying practice, whereby a historically situated artist, working from his/her lived inner and outer experiences, and from his/her creative imagination, selects and configures material and symbolic resources – including ideas, images, sounds, smells, tastes, actions and gestures – in accordance with certain art-generic ideas, and arranges them in an expressive text which refers to different dimensions of human experience. The meanings of a work of art are construed within the broad constraints of the cultural codes which apply contextually, of the signifiers encoded in the work of art, and of the socio-economico-political positions of its interpreters.

However, as much as defining art causes a lot of problems, identifying *artists* is equally difficult. Within the Romantic tradition in particular (Wu, 2006), the *artist* was seen as a person of exceptional ability, a genius, who was inspired to produce wonderfully original works of the creative imagination, suffering poverty, neglect, obscurity and a tragic, early death in the process. This notion of the individual genius sometimes drew attention away from the social processes and cultural context within which art was produced, and from the mechanisms by which art reached its market. Indeed, artists have a reputation, not always deserved, for being focused on their inner processes and their products, and therefore being out of touch with the marketplace. The tensions between art and commerce are well known and often cited, for example in indie music. This tension, too, has a long past, and can be seen in the *art for art's sake* movement of the nineteenth century (Fillis, 2004). More recently Karttunen pointed out that 'anybody at all is free to follow the trade and call himself an artist without any formal degree or any officially recognized demonstration of competence' (1998, p. 3), which takes us back to earlier Weitz's argument, highlighting the open character of concepts such as *art* and *artist*. We may therefore argue that an *artist* is anyone who produces *art*.

DEFINITIONS OF ARTS MARKETING

While *art* and *artist* appear to be very complex and controversial concepts, one may not be surprised that up until very recently there was no agreement as to what arts marketing is either (Rentschler, 1998). Rentschler and Wood (2001) reviewed 128 articles in the arts marketing literature and suggested three periods in the development of the field. At the very beginning, the focus of research activities was predominantly on education of audiences, organizational awareness and economy of the arts (*Foundation Period* 1975–1984). It was then followed by the dominance of studies into applicability of marketing concept to non-profit arts organizations (*Professionalization Period*

1985–1994), and finally by studies into methodologies of the behavioural and social sciences, with emphasis on discoveries of new economic realities and new view of audiences (*Discovery Period* 1995–2001). A significant amount of those studies has focused on museums and different venues within performing arts (e.g. music and theatre), and to a lesser extent on still relatively under-researched film marketing (see for example Kerrigan et al., 2004).

Currently we may broadly distinguish two approaches to arts marketing. First one, more concerned with arts marketing as a managerial tool, locates it within the domain of cultural intermediaries (Venkatesh and Meamber, 2006), and positions marketing mix as a method used by artists and arts organization to promote cultural goods on a very competitive arts market. Hill et al. (2003, p. 1); for example, define arts marketing as 'an integrated management process which sees mutually satisfying exchange relationships with customers as the route to achieving organizational and artistic objectives'. This approach to arts marketing has as many supporters as opponents, and has been for many years popular in arts marketing education, research as well as in practice. The majority of work in this stream has focused on the application of various elements of the marketing mix in the arts, building loyalty through subscriptions and other loyalty programmes, and quantitative marketing research tools and techniques (e.g. surveys) (see for example Kotler and Scheff, 1997).

In the second approach, followed in this chapter, marketing is an integral element of artistic production; it postulates 'a broad understanding of the arts as a context for marketing' (Butler, 2000, p. 345). Butler, for example, identified fifteen distinctive characteristics of arts marketing (Table 4.1), all of which should be considered by arts marketers. However, his list should not be treated as an end in itself, and more importantly it is beyond the scope of this chapter to discuss all of them. Thus in the remaining part

Table 4.1 The characteristics of arts marketing

Structural characteristics	Process characteristics
The Product	**Value definition**
Cultural domain	Source of value definition
Human performance	Discovery of new art
Location as identity	
The Organization	**Value development**
Role of the artist	Education and development of artists
Clash of commerce and culture	Education and development of audiences
Arts networks	
The Market	**Value delivery**
Resource base	Access
Diversity of audience	Pricing
Influence of critics	

Source: Butler (2000, p. 346)

of the chapter we are going to introduce, in our view, some of the most important aspects of arts marketing, namely arts industry, consumption and production of arts, and art brands.

ART WORLDS OR CULTURAL INDUSTRIES?

Butler (2000) maintains that structural issues are amongst the most distinctive characteristics of arts marketing. Therefore, we need to start our journey through arts marketing by drawing its boundaries. Dickie's understanding of one of the basic concepts in arts marketing – *artworld* – as 'the totality of all artworld systems' remains vague enough to add even more to the earlier perplexity with the definitions of art and artist (Torres and Kamhi, 2000, p. 96). Becker offers us a much more precise account of what in his view *art worlds* are (1982, p. 34):

> *all the people whose activities are necessary to the production of the characteristic works which that world, and perhaps others as well, define as art.*

Although his definition does not clarify who those people are, Venkatesh and Meamber (2006) in their discussion of cultural production and aesthetic consumption within the marketing context identify those 'cultural actors' as producers (artists), consumers (public) and intermediaries (individuals and organizations involved in communication and distribution of art).

Regardless of whether we like it or not, the arts are nowadays widely perceived as an industry, with all its economic, cultural and political consequences. Arts marketing is usually linked to the creative and cultural industries (CCIs). Governments are spreading this new terminology as part of their projects of inner city or wider economic redevelopment. *Creative* places the emphasis on the production side, on processes of the imagination, of origination, of creative production. *Cultural* places the emphasis on the offering, the idea that the output of the industry has some cultural value for somebody. The word *industries* suggests mass production along factory lines, and there is a sign here of the tension between art and industry. Howkins (2002) defines the creative industries as including those that create copyright, including advertising, computer software, design, photography, film, video, performing arts, music . . . publishing, radio and TV, and video games, design industries and those dealing in patents and trademark. Caves (2003, p. 10) argues that the 'social processes and organizational structures surrounding high and low forms of culture do not fundamentally differ'. This is an argument for not differentiating heavily between high and low culture. Hesmondhalgh (2007, p. 14) suggest that the core cultural industries are those 'based on the industrial production and circulation of texts and centrally reliant on the work of symbol creators'. The term CCIs is perhaps best understood as referring to those parts of the arts business which bear a resemblance to conventional industrial sectors, for example, record labels, book publishers, video game development companies or mainstream film studios. The globalization of CCIs has opened the way for the rapid and widespread international circulation of cultural products.

Different organizations use CCIs to tap into the artistic talent and products to which the latter have bought the rights. Celebrities are used to endorse products (and presidential candidates). Art texts, such as films, carry references to commercial brands in a practice known as product placement. Major cultural products, such as Star Trek, the James Bond movies and the Harry Potter books, become platforms for the realization of product rights in a wide range of formats, from paperbacks to board-games and T-shirts. Commercial brands sponsor arts organizations in order to add personality to their own brands. Each of these mechanisms may bring needed cash to arts organizations, but this may come at a price.

One of the key characteristics of CCIs is what Negus (1992) identified in the popular music context as 'a conflict between commerce and creativity or art and capitalism'. Other authors take the argument further arguing that mcdonaldization of culture already led to the situation where 'the development of literature, theatre, music and art has been subjected more to the law of supply and demand of the expanding cultural market' (Smart, 1999, p. 136). However, some writers suggest that commerce can offer many advantages to artists. Frequently, Le Cocq (2002) argues, commercial considerations in the production of art may give artists more freedom of expression than employer-patronage or public subsidy; there is a place on the arts market for all artists, even if it may be a very small niche. Commerce also makes art more communicative and accessible to audiences and therefore establishes a bridge between artists and their public. The requirements of the market may be also interpreted as the boundaries of artistic creativity, which, we may argue, are necessary for artists.

The same dilemma is faced by non-profit arts organizations, whose role is to re-distribute any public funding they may receive. They are often charged with preserving valuable works of art and encouraging the most talented artists, while at the same time governments and donors expect them to broaden the demographics of their audiences, and to address an aesthetic imperative in society. In order to accomplish these objectives, arts organizations often have to modify the products to make them more accessible to wider audiences; that in turn can negatively affect artistic integrity.

THE ART PROJECT

Because an arts *offering* may be from a single artist, a local government organization or a large commercial business, it is not always easy to model what is going on. The looseness and fluidity of arts networks and the social nature of art production and consumption suggest moving away from the notion of an arts organization towards the idea of an art project. In any art project, there may be a wide range of roles, including producer, director, artist, consumer, critic, investor, regulator, cultural intermediary, business intermediary, policy intermediary, owner, administrator, trustee, beneficiary, archivist, and . . . marketer. The question is what roles can be defined as marketing roles. In a narrow sense, promotion/publicity, and selling products are marketing roles. In a wider sense, marketing would like to claim that every role contributes something to marketing, e.g. a singer performing at a concert is marketing himself. This kind of talk may make sense to marketing people, but would not always carry conviction with artists themselves. It is also important to note that although market transactions take place between people inside the project and outside it, not every exchange is a buy/sell one. In addition to sales as conventionally understood, e.g. the purchase of a DVD, art transactions also include auctions (whether at Sotheby's or on eBay), loans (e.g. of paintings), endowments, bequest, inheritances, gifts and trusts.

PRODUCTION OF ART

Although the arts are an industry, we need to bear in mind that often 'art is sold like a commodity but produced like a religious calling, as an object of intense personal expression' (Plattner, 1996, p. 23). This intense relationship between artists and their work lies in the heart of the art world, and therefore must be the centre of attention for arts marketers. The art market as a phenomenon is also very different from more traditional markets. Its pyramid-like shape is due to its relatively low barriers to entry (as we already mentioned anyone can call themselves an artist), and rich and diversified supply of artists-to-be and their potential works of art. However, only very few of them manage to climb up the ladder and have their work published, released by a record label or exhibited in a gallery, achieving critics' acclaim, fame and wealth. In the music industry, for example, no more than 5 per cent of musicians signed by leading record labels break even (Seifert and Hadida, 2006).

One of the defining characteristics of arts communities since the nineteenth century has been the previously mentioned 'art versus commerce' dilemma. With the decline of arts patronage at the end of eighteenth century, artists found themselves forced to rely on other members of the art world, for example dealers and publishers, for their art to reach consumers. This situation pushed them to fall under the law of profit. And despite increasing commercialization of culture, particularly since the second half of the twentieth century, romantic and bohemian ideals, epitomized by artists in an image of anti-social creative mavericks struggling to make a living from their arts, have remained strong among many artists. And even if many of today's artists do not subscribe to the *art for art's sake* philosophy, research shows us they still find it difficult to effectively engage with marketing (Kubacki and Croft, 2004; O'Reilly, 2005).

A different view on artists is presented by authors such as Fillis (2002), Guillet de Monthoux (2004) and Schroeder (2005). Fillis (2002), indeed, identified many positive examples of entrepreneurial practice amongst artists. Schroeder (2005, p. 1295), on the other hand, in his research into successful and famous visual artists (e.g. Thomas Kinkade, Andy Warhol), portrayed them as brand managers oriented on selling their art, 'actively engaged in developing, nurturing and promoting themselves as recognizable "products" in the business of art'. In his opinion, marketers can actually learn from artists how to 'use consumer culture themes and images', 'create[. . .] distinctive products, segment[. . .] the market', extend brands or 'control[. . .] distribution and foster[. . .] exclusivity' (ibid.).

CONSUMPTION OF ART

> . . . all forms of cultural and leisure activities are positive
> manifestations of the quality of community life. (Blau, 1988, p. 884)

Everybody seems to agree on the importance of the arts for a society, particularly their role in creating and defining our culture; but maybe due to the controversial character of the arts, fewer people follow the belief up with closer investigations of many of the ways the arts are consumed in everyday life. Blau's opinion may lead to the conclusion that communities with better quality of life produce more works of art. Therefore, the argument runs, governments should remember not only 'the need to ensure a "healthy" variety of artistic experience available to the public, but also the need to further the "civilized values" of the community' when considering financial support for the arts (Gainer, 1989, p. 144). This way, it becomes the arts marketer's task to understand the ways in which the meaning of art is created and transferred to consumers through consumption, in increasingly blurred boundaries between art and everyday life (Featherstone, 1991; Szmigin, 2006). And it may be a daunting job – the seminal work of Kreitler and Kreitler (1972) on the psychology of the arts tells us that people respond to the same work of art in many, often very different and subjective ways, reflecting their individual preferences and familiarity with cultural codes.

One possible explanation of consumer behaviour in the arts lies in environmental psychology and the theory of forms of behaviour (Mehrabian and Russell, 1974), which emphasizes the role of emotions and describes two general attitudes – approach and avoidance – determined by the three so-called PAD dimensions:

- pleasure (positive versus negative character of a feeling),

- arousal (strength of a feeling), and

- dominance (lever of freedom associated with a feeling).

These emotional responses, leading to approach-avoidance behaviour, may be direct results of a person's characteristics, but often they arise from physical or social stimuli coming from the surrounding environment. For example, loud music may be perceived by many as a negative condition, therefore some people unconsciously tend to avoid rock concerts or shorten their time in this kind of environment.

Although there might be countless reasons to consume the arts, within the framework indicated by Mehrabian and Russell several aspects of consumers' motivation can be identified. For example, Pine and Gilmore (1999) talk about four 'realms' of experiential consumption, ranging from purely passive entertainment (e.g. listening to a jazz gig in a bar while having a conversation at the same time), through centred on aesthetic pleasure 'passive immersion' (e.g. watching a theatre play) and escapist active participation (e.g. singing with music at a rock concert), to educational participation (e.g. attending music workshops and learning how to play an instrument). Botti (2000) on the other hand draws our attentions to factors influencing motivation to attend. He identified four main needs:

- cultural (e.g. knowledge),

- symbolic (e.g. using the arts as a source of meaning for communicating personality),

- social (e.g. building social relationships through consumption of the arts), and

- emotional.

We can observe that some of the dimension suggested by those authors overlap. For example, Botti's cultural needs can be satisfied through educational participation in the artistic experience, passive entertainment can be a form of building social relationships, and emotional needs may correspond to escapist character of an artistic experience. The last aspect of arts consumption, focusing on consumption for pleasure and unifying experiences with emotions, links back to earlier work of Hirschman and Holbrook (1982). Their notion of hedonic consumption is concerned with issues such as consumer fantasies, feeling and fun. For detailed analysis of the consumption of various types of the arts see for example Urrutiaguer (2002) for theatre and Shankar (2000) for music.

As much as it is important to know why we consume the arts, recent activities aiming to increase participation in the arts show that often it is much more relevant to know why we do not do it. It cannot come as a surprise that frequently we do not go to a theatre or a jazz gig for exactly the same reasons why others do. Colbert (2003) pointed out that there are several risks involved in arts consumption, such as feeling uncomfortable in a place where others seem to know each other and be knowledgeable about the arts, not wanting to be seen by others in a wrong place, or simply worrying about wasting time and money on something that we may not enjoy. Nowadays, the arts consumer comes in many different guises. S/he may be a metalhead, a goth, an avid film-goer, a ligger, a Trekkie, or a balletomane (see Chapter 6). The discourse of fandom is increasingly used to talk about arts consumers. Art *fans* cluster around the objects of their affections and form knowledge and distance hierarchies as they vie for cultural capital. They use their consumption of art to symbolize something about themselves, both to themselves as well as to others. They will sacrifice significant amounts of leisure time and money to consume the object of their fandom. They are in search of profound and transformative experiences, sensory pleasures, and moments of intimacy with the artist. They form passionate attachments and loyalties to artists. They are active, agentic, and use their fantasies and feelings in the consumption of art products. Art is a symbolic resource for the construction of identities, images, experiences and relationships. Arts consumers do their consumption both online and offline. Their passionate identification, frequency of attendance or purchase, and the size of their groups works to the benefit of the artist's income. However, tensions between fans and artists can lead to accusations of artists selling out, moving too far ahead of the fans and leaving them behind, or getting above themselves.

ART BRANDS

From a culturalist point of view, brands may be read as signs which are exchanged or meanings which are constructed through the dialogue between and amongst producers, consumers and other stakeholders (see also Chapter 5). Art and brands have in common their symbolic dimension. However, when talking about *art brands*, it is important to be clear whether one is using the word *brand* in a strictly commercial sense, or in a wider sense which is synonymous with *sign* or *symbol*. Using the word *brand* in relation to art buys the user access to a repertoire of terms used by businesspeople to discuss the symbolic aspects of doing business. Many of these words however already come from the domain of culture. This means, for example, that when we talk about *brand identity*, the word *brand* is arguably redundant.

Lash and Lury (2007, pp. 5–7) argue that 'global culture industry works through brands'. In a general symbolic sense, an artist may be considered a brand, e.g. Madonna, and the celebrity literature can be used to inform this discussion. For example, issues of identity/image attractiveness, credibility, authenticity and legitimacy are often salient in assessments of artists' effectiveness, not only amongst ordinary fans, but particularly amongst their peers and specialist critics, and these are topical issues in branding and the arts. An art brand in terms of a tangible art product can be assessed for its consumer benefits, and also for its symbolic positioning.

In some art projects, the different dimensions of branding can be complex. For example, in film, the producer, director, screenwriter and stars may be regarded as brands in their own right. The film may include product or service brands whose presence in the film has been sponsored by commercial brands such as Fedex, Nike or Starbucks. The musical score may include songs or tunes which are marketed separately, or which index a particular composer who him/herself is a distinctive brand in the world of music. Finally, the film itself may be regarded as a product brand in a studio's project management portfolio or back catalogue. The media play a major role in the creation and dissemination of art brands, for example through televised talent search shows which simultaneously act as launch-pads for artists.

Heritage plays an important role in the development of commercial brand identity, for example in the case of alcohol, jeans and cars. Within the arts sector, however, are organizations whose role is to preserve and interpret cultural heritage in a wider sense. These *heritage brands* include places such as the Guggenheim in Bilbao, stately homes, World Heritage Sites as well as traditional museums. There are other ways, too, in which art forms can construct a kind of *heritage*, for example the Rock'n'Roll Hall of Fame, or the Hollywood Walk of Fame.

ARTS MARKETERS

The conventional notion of marketing strategy imagines the marketer segmenting an audience, targeting some or all of those segments and positioning the offering in relation to them in a way which gives him/her an advantage over competition. An arts marketer, however, needs to be a *situationist*, in the sense that s/he takes account of this wide range of factors when formulating arts marketing strategy. These include the role of the organization or artist in the relevant value chain; the artistic conventions and ideologies which historically apply there; the rate, nature and degree of artistic innovation; the sources of funding which are available and the requirements and priorities which they bring with them; the location of the marketer in the art project structure and his/her power or lack thereof; the receptivity of the consumers, fans and critics; the kind of business model which is viable in the relevant arts sector; the tensions between art and commerce; and the influence of government policy, technological developments, the media and the economy, and so on.

An arts marketer should understand his/her *product*, and any attempt to understand an artistic product must engage with its symbolic content, its cultural meaning. The art *product* has a powerful symbolic component, whether it be the Mona Lisa, a Don DeLillo novel, a jazz performance, a dance, a DVD cover or a festival. The nature of the art experience varies considerably and is difficult to theorize. Working out what is going on in the heart, soul and mind of the art consumer raises complex research challenges, yet is very necessary if one is to succeed in marketing an art product. Performing arts products in particular are subject to intense competitive pressures. Not only are, for example, shows in the West End of London competing against each other but also against all other kinds of leisure offering, including staying at home and watching television. Some art is complex and is an acquired taste, such as classical music, and not all consumers have the time and desire to become classical buffs. Art's symbolic nature makes it a carrier of ideology(ies) which may or may not be in political flavour at any one time. Art is reflective and productive of cultural, social and political change. This may tend to force the artist into the category of rebel or establishment figure. Nowadays, successful artists are tied up with celebrity and the media, and made the subject of intensive media attention and speculation. The relationship between the artist and his/her audience now involves a potentially very wide range of fan responses, from extreme adulation to darker behaviour such as stalking.

The arts marketer's work is indeed complex. Not only is s/he dealing with economic, competitive and customer dynamics, but also potentially a wide range of artistic, social and cultural issues which are more salient in the arts sector than in the mainstream.

CONCLUSION

We have sought in this chapter to outline some of the ways of thinking about *art*, *artists* and *arts marketing* which are in circulation within the academy and practice. The arts offer rich experiences not just for artists and consumers but also for arts marketers and researchers. The field of arts marketing remains very diversified and is still trying to define its identity and role within the discipline of marketing as much as within broadly understood cultural production and consumption. In the world where it is not only impossible to define art, but also to identify boundaries between artistic production, consumption and everyday life, the relationship between art and marketing is becoming more intimate, but by no means easier and less controversial than ever before.

Case study: It's not about the money (by Robin Croft, University of Glamorgan)

The Brecon Jazz Festival is one of the enduring events of the musical calendar. For more than 25 years it has attracted some of the biggest names in the jazz world, including Sonny Rollins, Lee Konitz, Van Morrison and Courtney Pine. It has also presented more contemporary artists including Amy Winehouse, Jools Holland and Cerys Matthews. It is all about the music.

The Brecon Festival is also unique in the way its location – it is set in an area of outstanding natural beauty in the Black Mountains of Wales – helps to build a carnival atmosphere, captivating a small market town for a weekend every August. The economic value of the event has been estimated at around a million pounds a year, underpinning jobs in tourism, retail and other services. Much of the appeal for the musicians is the setting: small, informal venues such as the Guildhall and the Market Hall in place of the professional arenas of London, New York and Copenhagen. Jazz musicians focus on performance, rarely promoting themselves or their albums.

At the heart of the event is the music: Brecon has used its international reputation to attract big names, which in turn have pulled in the audiences. But there is more than this: as the Jazz Festival Director Jim Smith puts it, 'We have always got to maintain musical integrity of Brecon Jazz'. It is this cultural capital that sustains its appeal to a range of stakeholders, including the media, arts funding bodies as well as local residents and government.

It would be very easy to over-use the tools of marketing and so fatally undermine the Brecon 'brand': even this word sits uncomfortably with an artistic phenomenon such as this. Promotion has to be low key, relying strongly on sustaining long-term relationships with music lovers, on word-of-mouth, on telling the story rather than selling it. This puts the emphasis very much on the calibre of the acts that Jim Smith is able to sign. Historically, world-class performers such as Gerry Mulligan, Stephane Grapelli, Lionel Hampton and Wynton Marsalis have put Brecon on the map.

But this type of line-up comes at a price, and as other artistic venues have found to their cost, you cannot put artistic integrity in the bank. The Festival is run by a non-profit company, the Brecon International Festival of Jazz Ltd, an organization which has to temper the cultural aspirations of its members with harsh economic realities. The intimate venues may be popular with artists and audiences, but they make the business of breaking even more difficult. Entering the twentieth-first century, alongside artistic integrity, the festival has to demonstrate financial probity and corporate and social responsibility in its dealings.

To continue for another 25 years the Festival has to continue to find ways to engage with all of its stakeholder groups, not just audiences. For Brecon Jazz the answer is emphatically not mass marketing.

FIGURE 4.1   *Tom Cawley's Curios performing at the Captain's Walk venue, Brecon Jazz Festival, 2008*

INTERNET RESOURCES

Arts Council England. http://www.artscouncil.org.uk/

Arts, Heritage, NonProfit and Social Marketing SIG (AHNPSM SIG) at the Academy of Marketing, UK. http://www.academyofmarketing.info/artssig/artssig1.cfm

Arts Management Network. http://www.artsmanagement.net/

Arts Marketing Association, UK. http://www.a-m-a.org.uk/

ArtsMarketing.org. http://www.artsmarketing.org/

Arts Professional Magazine. http://www.artsprofessional.co.uk/

Intute: arts&humanities. http://www.intute.ac.uk/artsandhumanities/

KEY READINGS

Butler, P. (2000), 'By popular demand: marketing the arts', *Journal of Marketing Management*, 16, 343–364.

Guillet de Monthoux, P. (2004), *The Art Firm: Aesthetic Management and Metaphysical Marketing from Wagner to Wilson*. Stanford: Stanford University Press.

Kerrigan, F., Fraser, P. and Özbilgin, M. (2004), *Arts Marketing*. Oxford: Elsevier.

Schroeder, J. (2005), 'The artist and the brand', *European Journal of Marketing*, 39 (11/12), 1291–1305.

Venkatesh, A. and Meamber, L.A. (2006), 'Arts and aesthetics: marketing and cultural production', *Marketing Theory*, 6 (1), 11–39.

SEMINAR EXERCISES

Discussion Topics

1. Outline the various definitions of art, artist and arts marketing. Which of those best reflect your perception and understanding of these concepts?

2. Discuss the reasons for which people may want to consume art, identifying those particularly important to you.

3. What are the main challenges faced by arts marketers?

4. Every artistic product has its symbolic component. Choose your favourite artist and discuss his/her cultural meaning.

5. How can arts marketers make use of knowledge of an artist's identity to promote his/her work?

Group Exercises

1. Check several music festivals websites, including the Brecon Jazz Festival, and discuss as a group:

   (i) What do you believe are the positioning strategies of each festival?

   (ii) What do you think is the target audience of each festival?

   (iii) How do you think the Brecon Jazz could make its website more appealing to its stakeholders?

   (iv) How could Brecon Jazz continue to attract music lovers and achieve its financial stability, maintaining at the same time its artistic integrity?

2. Think of your last experience of art, whether it was a music concert or a visit to a gallery. Choose as a group the most interesting experience and answer the following questions:

   (i) How did you become aware of your need? Were you influenced by marketing activities at any point?

   (ii) Why would anyone prefer this artistic experience rather than staying at home and watching television?

   (iii) How would you convince others it was worthwhile?

   (iv) How did you know whether or not your needs were satisfied?

3. Assume the group is an arts marketing firm employed by a new and unknown artist. Prepare a communication plan for the artists including at least the following:

   (i) Artistic identity.

   (ii) Target audience.

   (iii) Main competitors.

   (iv) Communication tools.

REFERENCES

Becker, H. (1982), *Art Worlds*. Berkeley: California University Press.

Binkley, T. (1992), 'Deciding about art', in S. Sim (ed.), *Art: Context and Value*. Reading 19, Milton Keynes: Open University, pp. 257–277.

Blau, J.R. (1988), 'Music as social circumstance', *Social Forces*, 66 (4), 883–902.

Botti, S. (2000), 'What role for marketing in the arts? An analysis of arts consumption and artistic value', *International Journal of Arts Management*, 2 (3), 14–27.

Butler, P. (2000), 'By popular demand: marketing the arts', *Journal of Marketing Management*, 16, 343–364.

Carey, J. (2005), *What Good are the Arts?*. London: Faber and Faber.

Caves, R. (2003), *Creative Industries: Contracts Between Art and Commerce*. Cambridge, MA: Harvard University Press.

Colbert, F. (2003), 'Entrepreneurship and leadership in marketing the arts', *International Journal of Arts Management*, 6 (1), 30–39.

Danto, A. (1964), 'The artworld', *Journal of Philosophy*, 61 (19), 571–584.

Featherstone, M. (1991), *Consumer Culture and Post Modernism*. London: Sage.

Fillis, I. (2002), 'Creative marketing and the arts organization: what can the artist offer?', *International Journal of Nonprofit and Voluntary Sector Marketing*, 7 (2), 131–145.

Fillis, I. (2004), 'The theory and practice of visual arts marketing', in F. Kerrigan, P. Fraser and M. Özbilgin (eds), *Arts Marketing*. Oxford: Elsevier, pp. 119–138.

Gainer, B. (1989), 'The business of high culture: marketing the performing arts in Canada', *The Service Industries Journal*, 9 (4), 143–161.

Guillet de Monthoux, P. (2004), '*The Art Firm: Aesthetic Management and Metaphysical Marketing from Wagner to Wilson*'. Stanford: Stanford University Press.

Hesmondhalgh, D. (2007), *The Cultural Industries*. London: Sage.

Hill, L., O'Sullivan, C. and O'Sullivan, T. (2003), *Creative Arts Marketing*, 2nd edition. Oxford: Butterworth-Heinemann.

Hirschman, E.C. and Holbrook, M.B. (1982), 'Hedonic consumption: emerging concepts, methods and propositions', *Journal of Marketing*, 47 (3), 92–101.

Howkins, J. (2002), *The Creative Economy: How People Make Money From Ideas*. London: Penguin.

Kant, I. (1790), *Critique of Judgment*. Meredith translation, section 44.

Karttunen, S. (1998), 'How to identify artists? Defining the population for "status-of the artist" studies', *Poetics*, 26, 1–19.

Kerrigan, F., Fraser, P. and Özbilgin, M. (2004), *Arts Marketing*. Oxford: Elsevier.

Knox, I. (1930), 'Tolstoy's esthetic definition of art', *The Journal of Philosophy*, 27 (3), 65–70.

Kotler, P. and Scheff, J. (1997), *Standing Room Only: Strategies for Marketing and Performing Arts*. Boston: Harvard Business School Press.

Kreitler, H. and Kreitler, S. (1972), *Psychology of the Arts*. Durham NC: Duke University Press.

Kubacki, K. and Croft, R. (2004), 'Mass marketing, music and morality', *Journal of Marketing Management*, 20 (5–6), 577–590.

Lash, S. and Lury, C. (2007), *Global Culture Industry: The Mediation of Things*. Cambridge: Polity Press.

Le Cocq, J. (2002), 'Commercial Art Music', *Economic Affairs*, 22 (2), 8–13.

Mehrabian, A. and Russell, J.A. (1974), *An Approach to Environmental Psychology*. Cambridge: Massachusetts Institute of Technology.

Negus, K. (1992), *Producing Pop: Culture and Conflict in the Popular Music Industry*. London: Edward Arnold.

O'Reilly, D. (2005), 'The marketing/creativity interface: a case study of a visual artist', *International Journal of Nonprofit and Voluntary Sector Marketing*, 10 (4), 263–274.

Pine, B.J. and Gilmore, J.H. (1999), *The Experience Economy*. Boston: Harvard Business School Press.

Plattner, S. (1996), *High Art Down Home: An Economic Ethnography of a Local Art Market*. Chicago: University of Chicago Press.

Rentschler, R. (1998), 'Museum and performing arts marketing: a climate of change', *Journal of Arts, Management, Law and Society*, 28 (2), 83–96.

Rentschler, R. and Wood, G. (2001), 'Cause related marketing: can the arts afford not to participate?', *Services Marketing Quarterly*, 22 (1), 57–69.

Schroeder, J. (2005), 'The artist and the brand', *European Journal of Marketing*, 39 (11/12), 1291–1305.

Seifert, M. and Hadida, A.L. (2006), 'Facilitating talent selection decisions in the music industry', *Management Decision*, 44 (6), 790–808.

Shankar, A. (2000), 'Lost in music? Subjective personal introspection and popular music consumption', *Qualitative Market Research*, 3 (1), 27–37.

Smart, B. (ed.) (1999), *Resisting McDonaldization*. London: Sage Publications.

Szmigin, I. (2006), 'The aestheticization of consumption: an exploration of "brand. new" and "Shopping"', *Marketing Theory*, 6 (1), 107–118.

Torres, L. and Kamhi, M.M. (2000), *What Art Is: The Esthetic Theory of Ayn Rand*. Chicago and La Salle: Open Court.

Urrutiaguer, D. (2002), 'Quality judgments and demand for French public theatre', *Journal of Cultural Economics*, 26 (3), 185–202.

Venkatesh, A. and Meamber, L.A. (2006), 'Arts and aesthetics: marketing and cultural production', *Marketing Theory*, 6 (1), 11–39.

Wolff, J. (1983), 'Aesthetics and the sociology of art', in T.B. Bottomore and M.J. Mulkay (eds), *Controversies in Sociology: 14*. London: George Allen and Unwin.

Wu, D. (ed.) (2006), *Romanticism: An Anthology*, 3rd edition. Oxford: Blackwell Publishing.

CHAPTER 5

Building Brand Cultures

Pauline Maclaran

INTRODUCTION

Culture refers to the system of symbols and meanings that give human activities significance. Throughout our lives we are part of many different, often intersecting, cultures, such as national culture, music and literature cultures, lifestyle culture and so forth. These cultures can have a profound influence on the attitudes, beliefs and values that underpin our behaviours. Increasingly, it is recognized that brands too can have a powerful influence on us because of the meanings they incorporate, and the 'culture' that evolves around them. According to Jonathan Schroeder, one of the leading experts on the topic, brand culture concerns all the aspects and connotations of brands that have made them an important part of our everyday lives and experiences (Schroeder, 2007).

Brands are deeply embedded in the meaning systems that we use to make sense of our contemporary world. Take, for example, the golden arches of McDonald's or the Nike swoosh that we encounter on a daily basis. These symbols and their meanings are instantly recognizable around the globe, signifying respectively fast food Americana style, and empowerment through sports. Yet, not only do brands create their own unique culture, but they also draw on other cultural phenomena such as history, myths, rituals, artworks, the film industry, theatre and television, to convey meanings that resonate in powerful ways with consumer's lifestyles (Schroeder and Salzer-Morling, 2006). This ongoing iteration, between contributing to culture and drawing from it, makes brand culture a complex and multi-faceted phenomena. It is much more than just a clever name or logo, and also more than the implementation of a successful marketing strategy. Importantly, brand culture is a living entity that evolves and responds to the dynamics of the marketplace. Brand culture is continuously (re)created as the various parties that have an interest in the brand – companies, employees, culture industries, intermediaries, customers – relate stories around their experiences of the brand (Holt, 2004). The strength of a brand's culture lies in the collective perception about it, rather than the psychological aspects of an individual's response to the brand. To begin to understand brand culture we need to break down the traditional barriers that exist between internal and external aspects of organizations, and between separate organizational functions such as human resource and marketing management. To appreciate the underpinning complexities of brand culture we need a cross-disciplinary lens that enables a synthesis, rather than a division, of perspectives.

This chapter examines the building blocks of brand culture by looking at how meanings that circulate around a particular brand evolve as the brand intersects with other cultural phenomena. First, we discuss the important synergies between organizational and brand cultures together with the important role of employees in building brand culture, before looking at how brand cultures are also co-created with consumers and other stakeholders external to an organization. We highlight the importance of competing in 'myth markets' (Holt, 2004) and illustrate how many highly successful brands achieve iconic status through responding insightfully to the wider cultural environment. Finally, we explore some of the ways that a brand's culture can become tainted through negative perceptions that consumers hold about it and discuss the impact of the anti-branding movement.

BUILDING BRAND CULTURE FROM THE INSIDE

Well-known entrepreneurs such as Phil Knight (Nike), Richard Branson (Virgin), Anita Roddick (Bodyshop) and Steve Jobs (Apple) have built strong corporate brand cultures through personal dedication and passion for their enterprises. Their strong, charismatic personalities and missionary zeal have the ability to enthuse employees with a sense of their vision for the organization, often making employees as passionate about the enterprise as the entrepreneurs are themselves. Such entrepreneurial vision intuitively connects corporate identity to organizational mission, a key factor in building a sustainable corporate brand culture.

Following the lead of such inspirational entrepreneurs, many companies are now moving towards corporate branding, as opposed to product branding, in a move to instil a clearer sense of corporate identity and brand culture into their employees, suppliers, customers and other stakeholders. Balmer (2006, p. 34) refers to the growth of the 'corporate brandscape', arguing that brand cultures, and the communities that they engender, are much stronger for corporate brands than those created by product brands. Whether we feel an affinity with them or not, powerful corporate brands, such as Microsoft, IBM, BMW, HSBC and Coca-Cola, convey a rich set of associations in our minds as to what they stand for and who they are. Corporate brand culture is three dimensional, reaching not only inside and outside the organization, but also *across* organizations (Balmer, 2006). Consider the rebellious nature of the Virgin brand and how this is conveyed across many different industries that range from mobile phones to air travel. Embodied in the figure of its flamboyant founder, Richard Branson, the Virgin brand culture is based on the idea of doing things differently, of radical rethinking and of siding with the consumer in the face of bureaucracy and monopoly.

Co-Creation of Meaning with Employees

The role of employees in enacting the corporate vision is one of the core building blocks for brand culture, together with the idea that they should 'live the brand' and be empowered to be 'brand champions' (Ind, 2007). From this perspective, the marketing role diffuses throughout the organization, no longer resting with a specific marketing function or brand manager. Whereas in the past, marketers have been accustomed to thinking of specific externally focused marketing activities, particularly marketing communications, to convey the brand ethos and values, a corporate brand approach emphasizes the customers' brand experience that comes from their dealings with an organization's employees. From chief executive to delivery driver, all employees' actions can be seen as reinforcing the brand values. These actions are responsible for translating the corporate vision into a reality and embedding the brand culture in all employee/customer interactions, as well as throughout the organization. In this way the organization and all its employees provide the basis for the brand's position in the marketplace vis-à-vis its competitors (Elliott and Wattanasuwan, 1998).

Of course, all this is easier said than done. A corporate branding culture cannot simply be dreamt up in a day or be imposed on an organization regardless of the existing organizational culture. It requires a subtle touch and a lot of patience to understand and reconcile the different meaning systems that may already exist in an organization (for example, managerial versus shopfloor cultures). Schultz and Hatch (2006) emphasize that for corporate branding to be successful the strategic vision, organizational culture and stakeholder image must be aligned. Strategic vision is normally dictated by top management, embodying their aspirations for where the company is going in the future. By contrast, organizational culture is 'the internal values, beliefs and basic assumptions that embody the heritage of the company and manifests in the ways *employees* [emphasis in original] feel about the company they are working for' (p. 16). Organizational culture is much more organic than strategic vision, emanating from employee's sense of what the organization is and their sense of identification with their employer. The culture of an organization is often taken-for-granted, going unquestioned and expressed in the familiar phrase of 'just the way we do things around here'. If employees' and managements' visions of the organization are at odds, it will be much more difficult to develop a consistent image with the organization's customers and other stakeholders. Consistency of image is what internal marketing often seeks to address through communications and training to develop a unified sense of purpose within an organization. When employee, management and customer meanings of the corporate brand coalesce, extreme loyalty may be generated for the communities involved with the brand, whether employee or customer centered. This loyalty can be quasi religious in its intensity (Balmer, 2006), as we will see in Chapter 6 when we discuss brand communities.

Successful brands go to great lengths to establish the right culture within their organization, and to ensure that employees believe in the brand. Starbucks, for example, has established its strong brand culture by committing to always treat its employees with dignity and respect, referring to them as 'partners' rather than employees and offering many incentives and benefits (i.e. healthcare packages) not offered by competitors (Simmons, 2005). The company runs intensive training programmes that build knowledge of the brand values and encourage its 'partners' to help create customers' experience of the brand, whilst at the same time allowing them to use their initiative and express their individuality in their interactions with customers. The Starbucks brand has turned coffee-serving into an art. Its employees are more than restaurant servers, they are professional 'baristas', a term that gives them pride in their work and at the same time reinforces to the consumer the coffee culture that is at the heart of the brand.

Similarly, Innocent has made itself the fastest growing business in the UK's food and drink sector by building a strong organizational culture that ensures its employees share its strategic vision. In their company headquarters, 'Fruit Towers' in West London, Innocent's young and irreverent culture is reinforced by a sign saying 'Burglars' on the front window and another saying 'People' on the door (Simmons, 2006). There is a 'wall of acclaim' beside the reception where consumer praises of the brand are proudly displayed. Employees engage in communal stretching exercises at the regular Monday morning meetings where everyone updates on sales and swaps stories across departments in an informal and relaxed atmosphere that often includes sitting on cushions on the floor. Winning the accolade of 'Top Employer of the Year – 2005', Innocent treats its employees generously in order to provide the right atmosphere for them to flourish and use their own creativity in their jobs.

Of course, from a more critical perspective, we are also right to be sceptical about such seemingly enlightened employer/employee relationships which can be regarded as a form of control, a kind of 'brainwashing'. They can even be seen as establishing a quasi-cult around the brand to ensure that employees internalize the brand values unquestioningly in order to appear more committed and authentic to the consumer. This in turn helps inscribe the brand into the 'life-world' of the consumer (Arvidsson, 2006, p. 43) as they interact with employees. In the next section we go on to consider the consumer aspects of brand culture in more detail.

BUILDING BRAND CULTURE FROM THE OUTSIDE

We have just explained above how a key aspect of brand culture is to ensure that a common vision unites employees. The other key building block of brand culture is how well the values that the organization embodies match what its customers are seeking. Employees and management may share a similar passion but if this is not also shared with the customer then the brand will be doomed to failure. It is now well recognized that consumers no longer seek just functional benefits from products and services, they seek meanings that help them construct and maintain their identities (Elliott and Wattanasuwan, 1998). By providing us with symbolic resources, brands present us with a multitude of possible ways to express ourselves and with which to gain the approval of our peers. They enable us to make a social statement about who we are or, just as often, who we would like to be (Table 5.1).

Table 5.1	Brand cultures and self-expression
I am a high achiever	Mercedes, Rolex, Hermes
I am on my way to the top	BMW, Tag Heuer, Armani
I am an individual	Apple, Swatch
I am a world citizen	British Airways, Benetton
I care about the environment	Co-operative Bank, Body Shop

Source: Goodchild and Callow (2001)

A brand's culture, its ethos in terms of core beliefs and values, can thus play an important role in consumers' identity projects. On account of this, many of the enduring brand cultures stand for social agendas as illustrated in Table 5.2.

Table 5.2	Brand cultures and their social agendas
Bodyshop	Ethically sources goods and environmental awareness
Benetton	Awareness of global issues such as AIDs, racism and poverty
The Mini	'Small is beautiful: mocking pretentions larger cars'
Apple	Against the totalizing uniformity of large corporations such as Microsoft and IBM
Harley Davidson	Being true to oneself – an outlaw image and disregard for convention

When we look at the brands in Table 5.2 we can see that they act as quasi-activists in the sense that they lead us in thinking differently about the world and ourselves (Holt, 2004). Heath and Potter (2005) see this as 'the rebel sell', arguing that it is rebellion, and not conformity, that drives desires in the marketplaces as we seek to differentiate ourselves from others. A good example of this is the Volkswagon Beetle that is remembered as an iconic rebel car in the 1960s and 70s when it was seen as a rejection of the values of mass society and the showiness of its larger competitors. This iconicity has been leveraged very successfully by VW in its popular relaunch of the Beetle in the late 1990s.

These social agendas, and the values they represent, can generate deep bonds with consumers who 'buy into them' both literally and metaphorically. The founders of Ben & Jerry's ice cream, Ben Cohen and Jerry Greenfield, have built a strong brand culture around a social and ecological conscience since they launched the brand in 1978. They continue this into the present with innovative developments such as their recent launch of a 'Fossil Fuel' ice cream which is accompanied by an invite to 'Help Lick Global Warming with Ben & Jerry's New Flavour'. This contributes to their 'Lick Global Warming' campaign which raises money for climate change research (Marketing Digest, 2007). They use sustainable dairy farming programmes ('caring dairy'), achieve a carbon neutral footprint (or 'hoofprint' as they like to refer to it!), and in 2006 launched the first Fairtrade vanilla ice cream. Their consistent commitment to a social agenda has developed a following of highly loyal consumers who see the company as caring for more than just commercial gain. Once again, as Arvidsson (2006) reminds us, we need to maintain a healthy scepticism over such actions. Creating social agendas in this way also enables large corporations to better infuse themselves through every aspect of our lives. It is often how they convince us that they are 'authentic'.

This perceived authenticity of corporate intention and responsibility is becoming increasingly more important to consumers. This is particularly relevant in terms of what Holt (2002) describes as the postmodern branding paradigm, which is 'premised upon the idea that brands will be more valuable if they are offered, not as cultural blueprints, but as cultural resources – as useful ingredients to produce the self as one so chooses'. As people chose brands that have the right meaning for them in terms of how they want to reflect their identity, they need to be confident that the brand is not going to let them down. Choosing brands that they can be sure will enhance their identity helps consumers minimize the purchase risk and, as we will see later in this chapter, they can become very disillusioned with the brand if they feel it has betrayed their trust.

Co-creation of Meaning with Consumers

As value shifts to experiences, the market is becoming a forum for conversation and interactions between consumers, consumer communities and firms. (Prahalad and Ramaswany, 2004, p. 5)

Nowadays brands must be seen to share, rather than manipulate, consumer's passions and emotions. Consumers' contribution to brand culture, and their role in co-creating meanings with marketers, should be acknowledged. A good example of this is Salomon who in 1994 had a traditional ski market image and found themselves excluded from the new opportunities presented by the snowboarding market (Cova and Cova, 2002). This market had its roots in the urban passion for skateboarding and was against everything that skiing represented, e.g. its upmarket and elitist associations. Salomon's overall approach in developing this market was 'to be humble' and not to attempt any overt commercial overtures to the boarders. They sought to develop rapport with the boarders by hanging out where they did and by spending time getting to know them. Salomon maintained a strong presence at the boarding parks and brought along boards to be tested without giving any pressures or incentives to buy. The aim was 'just to be there' and, in so doing, to become acquainted with the opinion leaders and gather feedback to develop the boards in line with what the boarders themselves wanted. Salomon made sure they were present in the right places, the places perceived by the boarders to be 'cool'. They advertised in the boarders' media, making use of trendy visual imagery that would make an impact. They also gave lots of financial support for contests and events. In 1996 Salomon launched its new snowboard production with no advertising, just physical presence and distribution through Pro-shops which were the boarders own distribution channels. By 1999 Salomon had risen to number three in the French snowboarding market.

As we see in this example of Salomon, the role of the consumer is changing to take a much more active part in the production of value. The firm and the consumer have traditionally been seen as having distinct roles: the role of the firm to create brands offering benefits; the role of the consumer (the target market) being to passively consume those brands, and taking no role in actual value creation around the brand. In Chapter 3 on postmodernism we highlighted the blurred boundaries between traditional binary divisions such as production/consumption. This blurring affects the role of the consumer. Because consumers want relationship with brands they can trust, and with whose values they can identify, they are now influencing much more directly the value systems that a brand embodies and that give it a unique culture. Accordingly to Fournier (1998), we can form relationships with brands that are just as fulfilling as the relationships we have with other people. On this same basis, however, we can put the same pressure on brands that we do on human relationships, and we can expect a lot from them! Consequently, marketers need to spend a lot of effort to co-create brand experiences with consumers, experiences that form a crucial part of building and maintaining brand culture. Through their website, Ben & Jerry's invite customers to suggest new flavours and even to ask for a discontinued flavour or product to be reinstated. This approach shows foresight and acknowledges the power that consumers now have to make demands on a brand. For example, Wispa was an iconic 1980s chocolate bar that was discontinued by Cadbury's in 2003. Thousands of consumers felt very strongly about this and used MySpace and Facebook to lobby Cadbury's for its return. Following this pressure from loyal customers, the bar was reintroduced in 2007. This is by no means an isolated incidence. Other successful campaigns by loyal communities surrounding a brand include the Fiat 500 (ceased production 1975) and the Raleigh Chopper (ceased production 1979) which were both recently relaunched (2004 and 2007 respectively).

CREATING ICONIC BRANDS

In Doug Holt's (2004) path-breaking book on cultural branding, he shows how brands become iconic. Icons are representational symbols that embody meanings that we admire and respect. They provide us with templates of what to value and how to behave. In ancient times icons were mainly religious figures (saints, gods, disciples and so forth) and stories about them were circulated mainly by word-of-mouth, passed down through generations in this way. Now, Holt argues, the circulation of cultural icons has become a key economic activity and takes place through mass communications (i.e. film, books, TV, sports, advertising, PR, etc.). Many icons are film stars such as James Dean and Marilyn Monroe, politicians such as John F. Kennedy and Martin Luther King, or sporting heroes such as Michael Jordan. These figures all represent certain kinds of stories, stories that convey 'identity myths' (Holt, 2004) that people use to address the anxieties and desires they have about their own identity. To illustrate, the 1950s rebel figure, James Dean, defied middle-class conventions of suburban family life and encapsulated the idea that a man could follow his own desires. This myth was especially appealing to the postwar American male who felt tied down by family responsibilities and the dull routine of working for a large and faceless corporation.

According to Holt, iconic brands are the ones that best know how to respond to key cultural tensions that are taking place in the wider sociocultural environment. A good example of this is Brand Beckham (Milligan, 2004). As a sporting celebrity, David Beckham is also a powerful brand that embodies core values of dedication, down-to-earth humanity and an impeccable sense of style. Proud of being a loving father, Beckham is well known for being in touch with his feminine side, changing his hair styles regularly and willing to be photographed in a sarong. The identity myth that he represents helps young men carve a path between the perceived 'sissiness' of the feminine, and the widespread disapproval of the 'brutish' masculine.

Companies can now be seen as competing in myth markets rather than product markets (Thompson and Haykto, 1997; Holt, 2004). Traditionally, myths make us aware of oppositions that they progressively mediate such as good/evil, life/death, science/nature, male/female and so forth; their tales take on life's big contradictions and the complexities of being human (Arnould, 2008). It is in this sense they speak across cultures and Fraser (1922/1985) has shown how similar myths and symbolic associations exist across very different religious beliefs. And so it is that commercial myths can also resonate with us at deep, unconscious levels. A successful brand creates a commercial myth that intersects with both historical and popular memory (Thompson and Tian, 2008; Arnould, 2008). Take, for example, the highly successful Magners Irish Cider Campaign that is single-handedly accredited with changing consumer attitudes to cider by transforming it into a fashionable drink. In order to do this, the Magners campaign very successfully taps into beer discourse in order to position and legitimize cider as a masculine and culturally empowering drink. This discourse is about 'challenge, risk and mastery – mastery over nature, over technology, over others in good natured "combat" and over oneself' (Strate, 1992, p. 82). However, a crucial aspect of the campaign's success is that it also draws on nostalgic, age-old images of the Irish male as being in touch with his deeply romantic self, thereby restoring a sense of the 'intense masculinity' that has become displaced and unfashionable in twenty-first century representations of masculinity. The nature/culture binary is central to the Magners campaign. Maclaran and Stevens' (2009) analysis of the Magners campaign illustrates how the Celtic soul that lies at its core is encouraging young men to negotiate a masculinity that restores ideals of manliness (culture) alongside a celebration of the feminine (nature). Thus, as a commercial myth, this conception of 'Magners Man' conveys a new mythic ideal that draws on many existing cultural myths to achieve its unique 'syncretic blending of narrative and imagistic elements' (Thompson and Tian, 2007).

WHEN THE BRAND ELUDES CONTROL

Identity myths thus have the power to forge deep bonds with consumers and they are often a crucial part of the relationship we have with a brand. Yet, similar to any meaningful relationship, people can feel very aggrieved when it does not go well. The fact that brands can engender deep emotions in us also means that we can become very dissatisfied if our trust is betrayed, or if we feel let down in some way. For example, when a well-known shopping centre in Dublin was radically refurbished, many consumers felt that they had lost a part of their heritage and were very unhappy with what the management had done to the centre. Some experienced such deep emotions over the changes that they swore never to return (Maclaran and Brown, 2005).

In the current business world it is almost impossible for a company to control its external brand image. Modern communication technologies, and in particular the internet, mean that there are very few corporate secrets and any discrepancy between a company's outward image and its internal one swiftly gets revealed. Consumers talk to other consumers all the time and with the use of email, web discussion groups and social networking sites, news can spread very quickly. Consumers also talk to employees and this brings us full circle, back to our previous discussions about the importance of good employee relations. Dissatisfied employees can set up their own web-sites to reveal home truths about their employer, both to other employees and consumers alike. There are a plethora of boycotting sites to be found on the web, each revealing various dissatisfactions and rallying others to join the boycott. Such actions can seriously damage a company's reputation. Because brand culture is organic, flowing as much from employees and customers, as from an organization's strategic vision, it can also be fragile and not easily controlled by marketers. Brand culture, therefore, can be adversely affected by negative associations just as easily as it can be enhanced by positive ones.

Many well-known brands have had their reputations severely tainted. Martha Stewart was convicted of illegal stock-trading in relation to her own media company. Perrier's crystal clear water with health-giving properties was contaminated with benzene. The energy company, Enron, was found guilty of accounting fraud. Indeed, transgressions of this nature have become so commonplace that terms such as 'brand rehabilitation strategy' and 'brand repair' are now in frequent use in relation to attempts to avoid irrep-arable damage to a brand's culture (Kahn, 2005). However transgressions do not always have to be damaging and sometimes they can form an intrinsic part of a brand's culture. Aaker et al. (2004) found that relationships with 'sincere' brands such as Coca-Cola, Ford and Hallmark, perceived to be tra-ditional and family-orientated, suffered after transgressions. Conversely, relationships with 'exciting' brands such as Virgin, Yahoo and MTV, per-ceived as more youthful and irreverent, showed signs of reinvigoration.

A brand does not always have to commit a transgression to acquire neg-ative connotations. Brand tainting can also occur because consumers' per-ceptions change. Recently there was criticism of the Bodyshop (BBC News, 2006) when L'Oreal took over the company. The Bodyshop was seen as joining the 'enemy' because L'Oreal is 26.4% owned by Nestlé which has been criticized for marketing powdered baby milk in developing countries. Sometimes the most powerful sources for brand tainting exist beyond the control of those who manage the brand, as, for example, with the symbolic associations that may emanate from particular consumer groups that use the brand. The red, white, black, and camel check that is synonymous with Burberry led to the brand becoming severely tainted in the UK where it is associated with a 'chav' image. This image is typified by Daniella Westbrook, the *EastEnders* soap opera star who gained notoriety for her cocaine addiction, and who is a major fan of the Burberry brand. In 2002 she and her baby were photographed, both dressed head to foot in Burberry check and with a matching pushchair. Because of negative associations such as these, the Burberry check has been downplayed in recent designs. Indeed, the baseball cap was discontinued by the company in 2004 in an attempt to distance itself from this marginalized 'chav' group. Interestingly, this tainting has not affected the brand's international markets where Burberry is still seen as an upmarket, very British brand.

Another threat of tainting comes from the many anti-branding movements and campaigns that have been gaining momentum. Works like Naomi Klein's *No Logo* (1999), one of the most influential anti-globalization texts, expose how branding techniques are grounded in a profit motive despite the many creative ways in which marketers may try to hide this through appeals to authenticity. In particular, Klein severely critiques such brands as Nike, The Gap, McDonald's, Starbucks, Shell and Microsoft, and highlights their many exploitative practices. In addition, successful brands often work to suppress competition in the marketplace. A good example of this is Microsoft whose software is on 80–90% of computers around the world (Lury, 2004). A dominant market position, such as Microsoft's, enables a brand culture to be diffused globally (see Chapter 12), with the risk that local cultures are eroded, or even extinguished, in its wake. 'Culture Jamming' has become a well-known method of resistance to the pervasiveness of brand culture, made famous by the activist magazine, *Adbusters*. Culture jamming involves transforming advertisements in an ironic way to critique the corporation behind the advertisement's message. Whereas originally these activities focused on the ways in which brands manipulated desires, now they are more likely to expose the hypocrisy 'between brand promises and corporate actions' (Holt, 2002, p. 85).

SUMMARY

In this chapter we have looked at the different facets of brand culture and explored its many influencing factors. Marketers are by no means the sole source for the meanings that surround a brand and that produce its overall culture. There are many organic influences that marketers cannot control as, for example, those that stem from organizational culture and employee perceptions of the brand. Consumers also play a major role and often co-create meanings which can be both positive and negative. The most successful brands built strong cultures that incorporate these organic influences and remain sufficiently flexible to adapt to changes in the macro environment. The best brands tell great stories with which we can identify. However, the more we look to brands to guide our beliefs and behaviours, the more they are likely to be held accountable. Activist movements against brands are likely to become more aggressive as brands play a bigger part in our everyday lives. In the future, as Holt (2002) has indicated, the most successful brands are likely to be those that provide us with the most creative cultural resources.

Case study: Building a Mini brand culture

Like the Volkswagon Beetle, the Mini is an iconic car that dates back to the rebel culture of the 1960s. Just like the mini-skirt and the Beatles, the little car is an enduring symbol of the 'swinging sixties'. The Mini was designed by the British Motor Corporation (BMC) in response to the increasing popularity of the smaller and fuel efficient German 'bubble cars'. Sir Alec Issigonis, the Mini's designer, has become a legend in his own right, famed for his innovative design that allowed both performance and space despite the limitations of size. Sir Alec's history intertwines with that of the Mini and many stories circulate around him that contribute to the Mini's brand culture and reinforce it as a triumph for British design. Fans relate how Pininfarina, a famous Italian carmaker, once asked Issigonis why he did not style the Mini a little. The reply that Issigonis made to this competitor's taunt has now become part of the Mini myth: 'It will still be fashionable when I'm dead and gone' (Beh, 2008).

The Mini was marketed as a fun car with a cheeky image. 'You don't need a big one to be happy', 'Happiness is Mini shaped' and 'Small is Beautiful' are some of its famous straplines. Its brand culture has evolved around this image, an image that made it 'cool' to drive a small, unpretentious car. In challenging prevailing notions of respectability, the Mini was very much a part of the countercultural movement that emerged during the 1960s. Heralding the idea of the 'rebel sell' that we have previously referred to, it stood for a youth culture that was hedonistic and fun-seeking. The Mini was continually associated with major celebrities throughout this decade. This enhanced its brand culture significantly, giving it celebrity status by association

FIGURE 5.1   *A customized 'Pittsburgh Steelers' Mini and proud owner*

with stars such as Peter Sellers, Ringo Starr, Britt Ekland, Lulu and fashion designer, Mary Quant. When Marianne Faithful drove to Mick Jagger's drugs trial in her Mini, and George Harrison's psychedelic Mini appeared in the Beetles' *Magical Mystery Tour*, the Mini's subversive connotations were enhanced (wikipedia.com). Well-known dare-devil racers such as Niki Lauder, Enzo Ferrari and Steve McQueen drove Mini Coopers. In 1969 three Minis featured as getaway cars in *The Italian Job*. The car chase that ensued, with its daring stunt-driving that included descending a set of steps, has become a classic. In 2003 three new BMW MINIs featured in a remake of this film.

INTERNET RESOURCES

An article by Bernard Cova: 'The Tribalization of Society and its Impact on the Conduct of Marketing'. http://visionarymarketing.com/articles/cova/cova-tribe-2001.html

The famous activist magazine, *Adbusters*. www.adbusters.org

The MINI car website. http://www.mini.co.uk/

Professor Jonathan Schroeder's video interview. http://www.revver.com/video/662442/jump-in-11-professor-jonathan-schroeder/

KEY READINGS

Arvidsson, A. (2006), *Brands, Meaning and Value in a Media Culture*. London: Routledge.

Like other iconic brands, the Mini addressed certain tensions in society at the right time. During the post-war 1950s in Britain and the USA, size was regarded as a marker of status and this was particularly so in the case of cars. The Suez crisis of 1956 meant that oil prices soared and the size–status equation came under pressure from the need for fuel economy. The Mini car addressed this contradiction and, at the same time, countered the postwar climate of continued austerity with its message that linked fun and size (Beh, 2008). The Mini symbolized a unique blend of hedonism, small size and Britishness, core values that consumers quickly responded to. They bought the Mini not just for its fuel-saving capacity, but also because they were buying into these core values. In doing so they were using the Mini to say something about their own identity: they were cool!

Over the years, although it was a mass produced car, the Mini brand culture evolved to include a highly individualistic element. This was aided by its many endorsements from celebrities who had specially designed models. It became the custom for individual owners to decorate their Minis in unique ways. Some painted union jacks on the roof or on the bonnet, while others painted colourful stripes or motifs on the bodywork. Still others kitted out the interior in fanciful décor, sometimes running a theme throughout the car's interior and exterior. This element of creativity and individual self-expression was added to the brand culture by consumers themselves and has now become an important part of the brand's evolving history.

The Mini car finally ceased production in 2000, having become a legend in its own right. A huge following of loyal fans around the globe still mourn its loss and remain committed to guarding the Mini's heritage. Many of them also deeply resent the launch of the new BMW MINI in 2001 (BMW bought the Mini brand as part of their takeover of Rover) and argue that it is not an authentic Mini. They perceive one of its core values, Britishness, to have been violated by association with a German manufacturer. In terms of its size also, the design of the new MINI can no longer be regarded as particularly small. There is thus a clash of brand cultures between the values of the old Mini and the new MINI which is still being played out in the marketplace. Many of the classic Mini clubs that exist will not permit new MINI owners to join and refuse to admit that the new model has any links to them. Despite this opposition, there can be no doubt that the launch of the new MINI has been highly successful. The new design has taken one of the Mini's core values, fun, and used this value very successfully in conjunction with the theme of individualization. As far as the new MINI manufacturer, BMW, is concerned, there is no disjuncture between the old Mini and new MINI and the brand has simply evolved. The new MINI website (http://www.mini.co.uk) invites customers to design their own MINI from hundreds of different combinations, alongside the claim that:

> Over the years MINI has changed. However the foundations of this small car, its character traits, have remained unchanged from its inception in the 1950s until today. Be it old Mini or the present-day MINI, people just can't stop talking about it.
>
> Because it's in the genes!

Holt, D.B. (2004), *How Brands Become Icons: The Principles of Cultural Branding.* Boston, MA: Harvard Business Press.

Schroeder, J.E. and Salzer-Mörling, M. (eds) (2006), *Brand Culture*. London: Routledge.

Thompson, C.J. and Arsel, Z. (2004), 'The Starbucks Brandscape and Consumers' (Anticorporate) Experiences of Glocal', *Journal of Consumer Research*, 31 (December), 631–649.

SEMINAR EXERCISES

Discussion Topics

1. Outline the three cornerstones of brand culture. Discuss which you think is the most important.

2. What are the different ways in which employees can influence a brand's culture during their interactions with customers? Thinking of your own experiences, identify an incident with an employee that has helped you form an opinion about a brand.

3. How do brands help us create and maintain our identities? Think of your own relationship with brands. What are your favourites and how do you think these are consistent (or not) with how you see yourself?

4. In what ways must brand culture be seen as 'authentic'? How does this concept relate to brands that you buy or admire?

Group Exercises

1. Take a brand of your choice and put together a presentation about its brand culture.

   (i) What do you think are the different influences on its brand culture?

   (ii) What are the brand's core values and how have these evolved?

2. Search through marketing magazines, newspaper reports and marketing websites to identify a recent case of brand tainting (other than those discussed in the chapter).

   (i) Document what happened to cause the tainting.

   (ii) How could this have been prevented?

   (iii) What should the brand do now to try and overcome the associations of tainting?

3. Investigate more about the classic Mini's history and compare this to the launch of the new BMW MINI.

   (i) Why is there a potential clash of brand cultures?

   (ii) How to you think this may be resolved in the future?

REFERENCES

Aaker, J., Fournier, S. and Brasel, S.A. (2004), 'When good brands do bad', *Journal of Consumer Research*, 31 (June), 1–16.

Arnould, E. (2008), 'Commercial mythology and the global organization of consumption', *Advances in Consumer Research* (forthcoming).

Arvidsson, A. (2006), *Brands, Meaning and Value in a Media Culture*. London: Routledge.

Balmer, J.M.T. (2006), 'Corporate brand culture and communities', in
J.E. Schroeder and M. Salzer-Mörling (eds), *Brand Culture*. London: Routledge,
pp. 34–49.

Beh, K.H. (2008), *'Unity in Diversity? Relationships in the Mini Brand Community'*.
Unpublished doctoral dissertation: De Montfort University.

Cova, B. and Cova, V. (2002), 'Tribal marketing: The tribalization of society and its
impact on the conduct of marketing', *European Journal of Marketing*, 36 (5/6),
595–620.

Elliott, R. and Wattanasuwan, K. (1998), 'Brands as symbolic resources for the
construction of identity', *International Journal of Advertising*, 17, 131–144.

Fournier, S. (1998), 'Consumers and their brands: developing relationship theory in
consumer research', *Journal of Consumer Research*, 24 (March), 343–373.

Fraser, J.G. (1922/1985), *'The Golden Bough: A Study in Magic and Religion'*.
New York: Macmillan.

Goodchild, J. and Callow, C. (2001), *Brands, Visions and Values*. Chichester: Wiley.

Heath, J. and Potter, A. (2005), *'The Rebel Sell: How the Counterculture Became
Consumer Culture'*. Chichester: Capstone Publishing.

Holt, D.B. (2002), 'Why do brands cause trouble? A dialectical theory of consumer
culture and branding', *Journal of Consumer Research*, 29 (June), 70–90.

Holt, D.B. (2004), *How Brands Become Icons: The Principles of Cultural Branding*.
Boston, MA: Harvard Business Press.

Ind, N. (2007), *Living the Brand: How to Transform Every Member of Your
Organization into a Brand Champion*. London: Kogan Page.

Kahn, B. (2005), 'Brand rehab: how companies can restore a tarnished image',
Knowledge@Wharton. http://knowledge.wharton.upenn.edu/article.
cfm?articleid=1279

Lury, C. (2004), *Brands: The Logos of the Global Economy*. London: Routledge.

Maclaran, P. and Brown, S. (2005), 'The center cannot hold: consuming the utopian
marketplace', *Journal of Consumer Research*, 32 (September), 311–323.

Maclaran, P. and Stevens, L. (2009), 'Magners Man: Irish cider, representations
of masculinity and the 'Burning Celtic Soul', *Irish Marketing Review*.
forthcoming

Marketing Digest (2007), 'Brand-ish opinion'. http://www.ameinfo.com/news/
Marketing_Digest/

Milligan, A. (2004), *Brand it Like Beckham: The Story of How Brand Beckham Was
Built*. Alderney: Cyan Publishing.

Prahalad, C.K. and Ramaswany, V. (2004), 'Co-creation experiences: the next
practice in value creation', *Journal of Interactive Marketing*, 18 (3), 5–14.

Schroeder, J.E. (2007), Video Interview with Professor Jonathan Schroeder. http://
www.revver.com/video/662442/jump-in-11-professor-jonathan-schroeder/

Schroeder, J.E. and Salzer-Mörling, M. (eds) (2006), *Brand Culture*. London: Routledge.

Schroeder, J.E. and Salzer-Mörling, M. (2006), 'Introduction to the Cultural Codes
of Branding', in J.E. Schroeder and M. Salzer-Mörling (eds), *Brand Culture*.
London: Routledge, pp. 1–12.

Schultz, M. and Hatch, M.J. (2006), 'A Cultural Perspective on Corporate Branding:
The Case of LEGO Group', in J.E. Schroeder and M. Salzer-Mörling (eds), *Brand
Culture*. London: Routledge, pp. 15–33.

Simmons, J. (2005), *My Sister's a Barista: How They Made Starbucks a Home Away From Home*. London: Cyan.

Simmons, J. (2006), *Innocent: Making a Brand from Nothing but Fruit*. London: Cyan.

Strate, L. (1992), 'Beer Commercials: A Manual on Masculinity', in S. Craig (ed.), *Men, Masculinity and the Media*. Newbury Park, CA: Sage, pp. 78–92.

Thompson, C.J. and Arsel, Z. (2004), 'The Starbucks Brandscape and Consumers' (Anticorporate) Experiences of Glocal', *Journal of Consumer Research*, 31 (December), 631–649.

Thompson, C.J. and Tian, K. (2008), 'Reconstructing the South: How Commercial Myths Compete for Identity Value through the Ideological Shaping of Popular Memories and Countermemories', *Journal of Consumer Research*, 34 (February), 519–613.

Thompson, C.J. and Haytko, D.L. (1997), 'Marketplace Mythology and Discourses of Power', *Journal of Consumer Research*, 31 (June), 162–180.

CHAPTER 6

Consumer Collectives

Nia Hughes

INTRODUCTION

Following on from Chapter 5, in this chapter we further develop our knowledge and understanding of the role of brands and cultural practice by exploring them in the context of consumption communities or collectives. This means that the level of analysis moves from individual to group, and from individual engagement to collective engagement. It also means that we must focus on new forms of voluntary social participation, and the ways in which they enhance individual experience.

Typically, participants might elect to be a part of a lifestyle grouping; or a subculture; or a consumer tribe; or a brand community; or a consumer micro-culture; or a resistance movement. This is an interesting phenomenon, given that in recent times, more established forms of social community (e.g. some traditional religious communities, neighbourhood communities) have often floundered. The breakdown of these traditional forms of community, based upon long-established social structures, is exemplified by growing patterns of individual consumption replacing joint, social consumption. Putnam (1995) notes the phenomenon of the lone tenpin bowler in America, an example of an individual consuming a service without the usual social participation that goes with it, possibly resulting in eventual loss of social capital (Bourdieu, 1984) and community ties. Different forms of capital are available to people in their daily lives: economic capital refers to the financial assets they can draw upon, whilst social capital refers to the 'features of social organization such as networks, norms, and social trust that facilitate co-ordination and co-operation for mutual benefit' (Putnam, 1995, p. 67).

Clearly, in this analysis a decline in both community spirit and social capital represents a negative trend in social life. However, this apparent breakdown of traditional social practices and interaction is balanced by the emergence of new forms of social participation, based upon consumption and brands. Therefore, rampant individualism in some consumption arenas has been matched by a growth in new forms of community in other arenas. Arguably, the new subcultures, tribes and brand communities are replacing the traditional socially structured community based upon established social class relations. We will return to this theme later in the chapter, but meanwhile we start by outlining a number of different consumer groupings and their distinctive practices and behaviours.

Subcultures emerge when a number of people interact with one another and innovate new forms of practice (Jenks, 1993), or different ways of doing, living and being. A subculture is defined by what is distinctive about subcultural members, but also by the degree of difference from mainstream culture and non-members. Increasingly, subcultures express themselves through cultural life, coalescing around brands and consumption. Hence it is instructive for marketers to gain some understanding of subcultural theory and practice. Individuals may subvert certain consumption objects out of the mainstream to use as symbolic resources for their everyday culture (as occurred with the subversion of the Burberry brand by 'chavs'). The subverted object, and its symbolic meanings, as understood by the lifestyle group or elective subculture using it, creates new forms of expression and facilitates identity formation. Willis (1978) argues that there is a continuous interplay, a homology, between the subcultural group's tastes and the style of things (objects, brands, people, texts) that together produce meanings for the subculture's members. Even within subcultures, there is space for the individual to negotiate distinctiveness through consumption practices (Kates, 2002).

In the twentieth century, two contrasting approaches to studying subcultures were prevalent (Thornton, 1997). Firstly came the sociological/anthropological approaches championed by the Chicago School researchers in the 1920s, which used participant observation to produce ethnographies of juvenile street gangs and criminally deviant groups. These studies represented the first systematic attempt to identify and understand subculture (Hebdige,1979). Subsequently, the Birmingham Centre for Contemporary Cultural Studies (CCCS) took a different approach to subculture, focusing instead on semiotics (the language of signs) and the reading of the 'texts' such as clothes, music, consumer goods in order to uncover symbolic meaning. These studies focused on the emergent style culture and wider cultural identifications of British working-class youth. Examples include Willis's (1977) seminal ethnographic study of young working-class school boys; Willis's (1978) study of motor-bikers; Hebdige's (1979) influential work on Italian scooter style and, in a rare example focusing on females, McRobbie's (1989) study of female teenyboppers.

In order to study any subculture, Hebdige (1979) stressed the need to identify how a subculture deviates from its wider cultural context, in an effort to identify the differences which have given rise to the subculture. Hebdige (1979) outlined the cyclical nature of the relationship between culture and subculture. There is an initial fracture away from the dominant culture followed by recuperation or re-incorporation, the latter involving two possible pathways. Subcultural signs may be converted into mass-produced objects acceptable to mainstream culture. The hooded sweatshirt came to be identified with badly behaved young men in the UK in the early 2000s, but the style soon became subsumed into mainstream fashion, commonly worn by fashionable middle-class women on their shopping trips to Waitrose. Secondly, subcultures are 'managed' and accepted by the mainstream, albeit labelled by the dominant groups as deviant or distasteful behaviour, until such time as the behaviour spreads to a wider cultural domain. The music industry offers several examples of cultural forms that began life as innovative subcultures that were initially rejected but subsequently embraced by the mainstream: from early rock and roll, through to punk music, through to rap and beyond. Hence a 'cycle leading from opposition to defusion, from resistance to incorporation, encloses each successive subculture' (Hebdige, 1979, p. 100). Subcultures may, in any case, be subject to a lifecycle effect, reaching a state of corruption that creates negative meanings in due course.

Subcultures of consumption are a subset of subcultural theory. The widely accepted definition of a subculture of consumption is that of Schouten and McAlexander (1995) who state that this is a distinctive subgroup of society that self-selects on the basis of a shared commitment to a particular product class, brand or consumption activity. Other characteristics of Schouten and McAlexander's (1995) subculture of consumption include: an identifiable, hierarchical social structure; an unique ethos, or set of shared beliefs and values; and unique jargons, rituals and modes of symbolic expression.

Because consumers choose to join such subcultures, they take a part in the creation of their own categories (Schouten and McAlexander, 1995), and identities, with subcultural membership setting boundaries in terms of behaviour and practices. Within this process, shared meanings are forged, and when they join the subculture, they hand over their identity, or some part of it, to the group (Celsi et al., 1993). A number of studies have illustrated how subcultures of consumption can emerge, in different ways, across a wide range of cultural contexts: Harley-Davidson bikers (Schouten and McAlexander, 1995); skydivers (Celsi et al., 1993); Mexican immigrants (Peñaloza, 1994); Barry Manilow fan club members (O'Guinn, 1991); sports card collectors (Baker and Martin, 2000); Star Trek fans (Kozinets, 2001); gay consumers (Kates, 2002).

However, subcultural theory is not without its critics. Nelson et al. (1992) have suggested that the use of the term 'subculture' in the context of (American) leisure activities is inappropriate, as leisure groupings do not exhibit sufficient experiential and social depth, and style, to demonstrate that they are a way of life. Another criticism, given that subcultural research is often concerned with exploring youth subcultures, is the difficulty of defining (or subsequently analysing) such groupings, which may be characterized by constantly shifting cultural affiliations such that group membership is highly fluid, with a high 'churn rate'. Although subcultures are undeniably important as a form of lifestyle grouping, or as enablers of social identity, membership of a subculture may, for some, play only a minor role in their everyday lives. On the other hand, Kates' (2002) ethnography of gay consumers shows that it is possible for subcultural consumption to pervade all aspects of members' lives, affecting all forms of their everyday consumption.

Holt (1997), in his critique of the use of the concept of a subculture of consumption, argues that the notion of subculture of consumption – as proposed by Schouten and McAlexander (1995) and others who followed in their tradition – is flawed because it overlooks the relevance of important social categories such as ethnicity, gender, social class and age. Also it suggests that lifestyles are shared individual rather than collective constructs. Holt (1997) goes on to deconstruct Schouten and McAlexander's analysis of Harley-Davidson bikers, arguing that what they were witnessing was a culturally charged object (the bike) with multiple meanings that vary across different people. Therefore the Harley-Davidson 'subculture of consumption' attracted a variety of different sub-collectivities who inscribed their own particular collective meanings upon the bike, articulated through differing consumption practices. To summarize Holt's argument: he claims that Schouten and McAlexander's observations were actually based upon a group that consisted of a number of subsets of smaller, class/age-homogenous groups which inscribed common meanings to the Harley-Davidson experience, but whose consumption practices were actually very different – they were, if anything, a number of different subcultures rather than a single one.

In comparison to classic subcultural theory, subcultures of consumption are not usually focused upon a particular set of common socio-economic circumstances. Members may exhibit diverse social positions, but be bound by their affiliation to a particular consumption activity, and enjoy collectively shared experiences. Indeed, highly distinct subsets of meanings may also emerge such that microcultures exist within the consumption subculture. In Thompson and Troester's (2002) study, the narratives that consumers recounted to each other about their consumption experiences in the context of natural health practices, allowed them to establish a common value system that made sense of their world. The shared narratives, shared practices and symbolic associations bound the participants together in a natural health microculture based upon a particular value system.

In order to avoid the problem identified by Holt (that is, Schouten and McAlexander's inference that subcultural theory is concerned with individual constructs), Kozinets (2001) proposed the use of the term 'culture of consumption'. He conceptualized this as an interconnected system of commercially produced images, texts and objects that particular groups use, which are subjected to the overlapping (perhaps conflicting) practices and identities of different cultural groups. For Kozinets (2001) this redefinition has the added benefit of discarding the implicit link between subculture and deviant behaviour, and also counters Nelson et al.'s (1992) criticism of leisure activities being classed as subcultures. Kozinets (2001) conducted extensive participant observation resulting in detailed interpretations of the Star Trek fan community. From this he offered a redefinition of the nature of culture, or subculture, in relation to the Star Trek community, offering detailed descriptions of the distinctive way of life and shared commitment.

Marker goods such as Star Trek memorabilia or Harley-Davidson bikes, indicate membership of the subculture and act as symbolic boundaries between subculture and mainstream culture. But these are porous boundaries. Just as subcultures may appropriate the meanings of brands and objects, so the media is influential in disseminating consumption meanings and shaping subcultural capital. Clearly, in the case of Star Trek fan clubs and conventions (Kozinets, 2001), the 'Star Trek culture of consumption' and the mainstream TV programme of Star Trek are inextricably linked. The boundary between subcultural meaning and the meanings intended by mass media must be negotiated, or contested. Not all meanings are of equal status (Kozinets, 2001), there is an array of meanings, including the preferred meanings as implicitly suggested and created by the originator-producer; and other meanings are added by the media, or by the subculture. Meaning must somehow be wrested from this repertoire of possibilities by each individual or cultural group.

NEO-TRIBES

Given the criticism of the concept of subculture, and its association with twentieth century modernist ideas on social structure and social class, perhaps a more fruitful line of enquiry is to focus on tribes and neo-tribes. Tribes have been of interest to anthropologists for many years, but the focus has tended to be upon remote or exotic or traditional tribes, where membership is ascribed, i.e. a person has not made a choice to join a specific group, they are born into it; they simply belong. Social anthropologists have also focused on the social structures of tribal society (which might produce social class hierarchies) and the ways in which objects might shape or enhance (our understanding of) social interactions.

Maffesoli (1996) relocated the concept of tribes in late twentieth century life, arguing that identity based upon social class had been replaced with other types of identifications such as interests and shared outlooks that are independent of one's social background. Therefore, individuals choose to join certain elective, rather than ascribed, tribes that reflect those interests and outlooks. For Maffesoli (1996), these are tribes that exhibit certain states of mind or a certain ambience, expressed through lifestyles, and appearance, rather than through rigid social divisions or organization. Focusing more closely on the consumption patterns of young consumers of urban dance music, Bennett (1999) draws upon Maffesoli's tribal concept to suggest a new framework based upon the term 'neo-tribe', the term 'neo-tribe', an entity that has highly fluid membership, and constantly shifting musical preferences. This goes some way to distinguish the neo-tribe from the subculture, as subcultural theory is focused more on social class as a fixed entity, in the traditional way, whilst the concept of neo-tribes is characterized by 'temporal gatherings' and 'fluid boundaries'. According to Bennett (1999), the socially static, fixed functions and relationships experienced within subcultural groups, that results in identity being 'given', are being replaced by socially fluid, unstable roles and relationships, within neo-tribes, that allow identity to be self-created. This development also marks the paradigm shift from modernist views of people, class and society to postmodernist views of looser sociality, populated by neo-tribes (Bennett, 1999) – new forms of social community that offer opportunities to enact particular lifestyles and practices.

Hetherington (1998) notes that membership of a neo-tribe is based upon elective and affective factors: for the individual, the tribe represents an empathetic and emotional space where meaning is chosen (i.e. elective) and where meaning is derived from feelings (i.e. affective) about objects and practice. The term proxemics describes the cultural and natural elements that characterize any particular situation: put simply, it is the neighbourhood, its aura and its affective connotations that make up the imperceptible situations which constitute our 'community network' (Maffesoli, 1996, p. 123). Clearly this is an important concept in any discussion of groupings based upon lifestyle, meanings and feelings. It seems that much of the satisfaction gained from group membership and collective consumption is dependent on the specific proxemics, or the dynamics of belonging to a specific group, a dynamism that goes beyond social class and structure.

BRAND COMMUNITIES

Muniz and O'Guinn (2001) define a brand community as a specialized, non-geographically bound community based upon a structured set of social relationships among admirers of a brand who may be physically distant to one another. This is in contrast to other forms of consumer collectives, that conceptualize consumption practice occurring in situations where close proximity is the norm, or where consumption by one person is evidenced by the gaze of another member of the group. Clearly, the focus on brands is critical in this form of collective consumption.

Of course, strong brand communities that are publicly critical of the brand manufacturer/producer, and which broadcast those criticisms online, present a threat to brand equity and to the brand marketer. Whilst marketers in their organizational roles seek to control brands, it is generally thought that brand communities spring up from within a consumer grouping. Increasingly, however, companies seek to monitor and control the brand community as well as the brand. Specialist agencies such as Smack Inc. in America can plan and execute 'fully integrated marketing strategies that help to develop your Brand Community': its website (smackinc.com) describes an example of its work in 'building a brand community around a brand commodity': Duck Tape, a form of sticky insulation tape used in home improvements.

Slater (2000) noted the strong influence of the Coca-Cola Brand Collecting Club members on the marketing strategy of the Coca-Cola company, the latter being anxious to keep club members happy, and making product changes in order to do so. If the criticism of a brand and a company is strong enough, it may lead to a consumer boycott: the Ethical Consumer website (ethicalconsumer.org) lists a plethora of consumer boycotts currently operating in English-speaking nations. Alternatively, brand criticism may coalesce around an anti-brand movement, as experienced by McDonalds: McDonaldsSucks.com.

Such is the strength of brand relationships that the consumer can experience love, passion, separation anxiety and emotional commitment with regard to their cherished brands (Fournier, 1998), and companies that make certain brands in their portfolios redundant may experience difficulty in persuading customers of those products to move on. Muniz and Schau (2005) noted that although the Apple company effectively abandoned the Apple Newton brand, a brand community nevertheless emerged: a consumer-created community that grew away from the marketer that fostered it. This Apple Newton brand community relishes the opportunity to be the underdog in the brand/consumer relationship, and to invest the brand (and their own consumption of the brand) with quasi-religious qualities. Muniz and Schau (2005) note the power of consumer narratives in allowing consumers to understand, structure and share their consumption experiences. Typically, members of the Apple Newton brand community position themselves as a persecuted minority, in relation to non-brand admirers and indeed the Apple company. Brand community members perceive themselves as the enlightened ones: the ones who kept the faith; who survived adverse conditions; and who paved the way for a brand resurrection.

COUNTER CULTURES AND RESISTANCE GROUPINGS

Taste allied to identity can act as a powerful mechanism for brand interactions and collective consumption. However, it is not just taste that unifies consumers but also distaste, where the concept of negative self emerges: the sense that something is 'just not me'; or 'so not me' (Banister and Hogg, 2001). The strength of the distaste, communicated and shared with others, may form a platform for consumer resistance, for boycotts, and for the formation of counter cultures.

'Culture jamming' is the phenomenon by which those who have distaste for certain companies or brands go on to hijack the modes of communication used by those brands. This often involves collective action against the conformity of brands and mainstream culture and communications. Interestingly, however, Heath and Potter (2004, p. 99) suggest that it is rebellion, not conformity, that has for decades been the driving force of the marketplace, and that counter-cultural critics of the consumer society (see Chapter 5 on *Adbusters*, and Naomi Klein's *No Logo*), and culture jammers, focusing as they do on the notion of conformity, are missing the target:

> *Countercultural theorists would like to think that their rebellion is merely a reaction to the evils of the consumer society. But what if countercultural rebellion, rather than being a consequence of intensified consumption, were actually a contributing factor?*

This could occur, claim Heath and Potter (2004), if enough people were driven by the need to compete with one another in order to achieve distinction (here we hark back to Bourdieu's ideas) and thus to rebel against conformity. In this analysis, it is rebellion that drives the consumer society, not the conformity suggested by many counter-cultural movements. Similarly, Hetherington (1998, p. 5) notes that fringe and mainstream activities tend to mingle after a while: 'It is not only that so-called alternatives become part of the mainstream but that alternatives draw on the mainstream as well.'

SHARED LIFESTYLES

In a study based in a university town in Pennsylvania, Holt (1997) identified four social-class-based lifestyles characterized by the social and geographic breadth of their cultural frameworks of taste: urban working-class service users, rural working-class service providers, upper middle-class highly educated cosmopolitans and middle-class neo-traditionalists. Echoing Bourdieu's (1984) concept of distinction, Holt (1997, p.339) claims that consumption patterns are socially meaningful in that they exist in opposition to comparable alternatives, therefore lifestyles are 'symbolic boundaries that create what is distinctive about a particular consumption pattern by placing this pattern in relation to other significant alternatives'. Holt argues that, traditionally, lifestyle analysis aggregates consumers into groups but then treats consumption patterns as belonging to individuals due to the presence of dominant traits or value systems that structure an individual's consumption in particular ways. On the other hand, Holt's (1997, p.341) poststructuralist lifestyle analysis treats consumption patterns as the consequence of several interlocking collectivities working together: as a result, 'collective consumption patterns exist as tendencies for members of a collectivity to enact similar consumption practices'. Clearly this has some similarities to Kozinets's (2001) culture of consumption

An important aspect of any new lifestyle co... .. 'ty, or brand community or subculture is that they involve elect.. .. that is, the association is voluntarily chosen by the indiv.. .. .. .oulsory. These are a new form of consumption community, ... ticipation is consciously chosen rather than passively re.. .. ordained social structures and traditional social comm... .. .. 'rands are increasingly a means by which individuals ca.. .. 'nst the tastes of their parents and against the values .. .. .m culture.

A plethora of consumption-related online communi... .. .n established in recent years (see also Chapter 11), using forum.. .. as bulletin boards, newsgroups, e-mailing lists, online games and chat .ooms. Some of these communities operate via asynchronous time-delayed discussions (e.g. email) where communication styles are likely to be information-based, factual and technical (Kozinets, 2002). More dynamic are the communities operating in real-time, where according to Kozinets (2002), community members engage in more social and relational styles and behaviours, in an environment that facilitates more real-life engagement and communications. Participants in online communities may of course belong to more than one; they may even adopt different identities in each community as well as having a different identity (or identities) offline. This, of course, is part of the playfulness that we associate with postmodern consumption: the ability to create different selves and to display multiple identities.

Online communities in the form of social networking sites have proliferated since the early 2000s, and may encompass a number of different types of collectives, from subcultures to brand communities to resistance groupings. By 2008, Facebook had enlisted some 59 million users since its launch in 2004 (Hodgkinson, 2008). Clearly this presents a very enticing prospect for advertisers and it is therefore hardly surprising that the site now includes 'FacebookAds' which allow brand marketers and manufacturers to 'participate' in the Facebook community, through advertising. However, signs of resistance are already being shown by a minority of Facebook users, leading to a petition called 'Facebook! Stop invading my privacy' (Hodgkinson, 2008). It seems likely that Facebook, the organization, will increasingly find itself regulating and policing the activities of the members in order to provide a suitable environment for corporate marketers to reach their target audiences.

Case studies: Three types of consumer collectives

1 Lower mill estate

Whilst there are many examples of lifestyle subcultures based upon sport and leisure, a more recent phenomenon is the emergence, in the UK, of middle-class lifestyle groupings whose purpose is to downshift to simpler ways of living, of eating and of going on holiday, such that daily family existence creates only a low carbon footprint. Alongside this 'new' way of living is the rejection of mainstream ideas about life that are based upon overtly expensive lifestyles. The practices adopted by such middle-class families demand different forms of consumer collectives, and hence different shared practices. One particular example is the Lower Mill Estate in the Cotswolds, which offers those who can afford it the opportunity to buy a second (holiday) home, in a safe, purpose-built, secluded, rural location. This traditional model of a family holiday attracts a specific demographic: affluent, middle-class, young-middle-age couples with children, who are drawn to the relatively closed and safe community lifestyle, affordable only to those who already have similar lifestyles and incomes – in other words, 'people like us'. In that sense, they are a self-selected group based upon already-common social and cultural capital; a particular culture of consumption based upon shared and individual practices. This consumption space offers the potential for participants to enact a traditional middle-class holiday, with their children experiencing an Enid Blyton-style childhood of innocent adventures and cream teas. This is a middle-class phenomenon that seems to arise in response to the challenges of life in the 2000s, a time where excess and waste have become unfashionable, and where the qualities of thrift and austerity, at every level of existence, are socially sanctioned.

2 A typical collectors' club

Around one-third of the UK population can be classed as a collector (Pearce, 1998), and collectors clubs abound in the UK and in the USA. They may operate as online communities or they may operate more traditionally as a monthly club meeting. The clubs typically form around objects that might be deemed to be low culture (such as hatpins, old picture postcards, 1960s glass, coins, stamps, militaria). Collectors' clubs are often run in a formal fashion, with membership fees, guest speakers, special events at Christmas, nights out in the summer and other social events. This programme of activity requires that individuals adopt roles to enable the club to operate. Typically, a club president will be elected each year who provides leadership and ensures that procedures are followed. There may also be a secretary who acts as the central contact for all members, who books speakers and social events, and who sets and circulates the agenda for the monthly meeting. Finally, a treasurer will be responsible for book-keeping and administration of members' monies. These roles are taken very seriously but other less formalized roles also exist: the elder statesman role conferred upon the past president (usually but not exclusively a male role); the social duty of providing tea and coffee at the club meeting (usually but not exclusively a female role). Evidence seems to show that in the UK, collecting is an activity that cuts across social class, and is popular with all socio-economic groupings (Pearce, 1998). However, the

CONCLUSION

Clearly, individuals have a significant degree of freedom to create their individualized identity through consumption, but the key message of this chapter is the extent to which individual preferences and lifestyles are constrained or empowered by the influence of 'others', directly or indirectly. These will usually be consumer collectives that the individual has elected to join, and there may be a constellation of collectives to which each individual belongs. Bourdieu (1984) goes further, arguing that individuals demonstrate certain enduring dispositions, in the way that they consume different categories of products and services in their own life. Thus forming a process, age profile is skewed toward the middle-aged or young-middle-aged sector of the population. The notion of a collecting subculture has, however, been very firmly rejected by Pearce (1998), who argues forcefully that in her study of UK collecting practices there was no evidence of any real subcultural factors relevant to collectors and collecting: collectors were simply proportionally representative of the population as a whole, merely a segment or a minority group of the whole, and not a separate caste with personal or social defining characteristics.

3   MMOGs (massively multi-player online games)

Real life and virtual life, and thus real communities and online communities, can become inextricably linked, as has occurred in the activity known as 'gold farming'. In many online games such as 'World of Warcraft' and 'Star War Galaxies', a player needs to acquire an online currency (gold) by performing, successfully, a number of menial, boring, low-skilled tasks, which are nevertheless necessary, but very time-consuming. A player who can acquire gold quickly may use that as currency to buy equipment or resources (e.g. a virtual horse) which allows faster progression to higher playing level, where more stimulating and demanding tasks are to be found that require more sophisticated skills. The fastest way to bypass the low-level tasks is simply to acquire gold by other means, such as buying it from other players. The going rate at the time of writing was £39.99 (real currency) for 5000 gold pieces, or virtual currency (Mostrous, 2008). In his recent report on gold farming,

Heeks (2008) describes how a vast virtual economy has grown, based upon the real-world activity of acquiring in-game currency (gold). He also notes that this is a world that operates under the radar of public attention, and indeed under the radar of mainstream media and marketers. He claims that this market, like the sale of digital pornography (another form of online community), is an example of liminal ICT work, that operates at the threshold, or even below, what is deemed socially acceptable and legally permissible.

Indeed, the demand for gold in the online community is such that 'gold farmers' have emerged whose role in (real) life is to recruit employees (typically young Chinese men) who will then spend hours at the computer, performing the low-level tasks that earn online gold (Mostrous, 2008). The gold can then be sold by the employer (the gold farmer) to online gamers – for real money, that generates enough profit to pay the real-world workforce a real-world wage. Clearly this structured community is a microcosm of the real-life economy, but it also creates an online hierarchy, a distinction in social position between: (1) players, who do the higher-level tasks, i.e. more challenging 'work', as part of their leisure time; (2) the supporting community of workers, who are employed to do low-level unskilled work, albeit online; and (3) the gold farmers who are the intermediaries, employing the workers and supplying gold to the players. So, perhaps unsurprisingly, online communities yield social structures and social characters not dissimilar to those found in traditional community life. It is possible to link these differing levels of engagement, and different collectives, with different positions on Maslow's (1954) hierarchy of needs, and indeed with different socio-economic positions and access to resources.

or habitus, by which our own social, cultural and parental background gives us the disposition to make certain consumption choices in certain ways. Therefore, logically, if we are conditioned, as individuals, by our cultural capital and social capital (that is, our cultural tastes and our social networks and contacts), then the extent of our freedom to make consumption choices is perhaps more constrained than we realize. Through habitus, we perpetuate the existing class structure because we inherit our enduring dispositions from the previous generation – our parents, and from their/our background. We then pass these same dispositions on to the next generation, our children. Clearly, this analysis is deterministic, and underplays the effects of social mobility and of consciously acquired tastes: the tastes that we shape for ourselves, for instance, through brands. It also underplays the tastes that emerge through our membership of consumer collectives and elective groups, although such collectives may not necessarily be social-class neutral.

This chapter started with a discussion of important theoretical concepts that underpin subsequent ideas about the formation, experience and practices found in consumer collectives. We continued by exploring some of the alternative forms of consumption communities that emerge, noting lifestyle effects, subcultures, brand communities and consumer tribes as significant concepts by which to analyse these consumption communities, and the collective nature of their consumption. The chapter concluded with the work of Bourdieu (1984) and Holt (1997), suggesting that we cannot ignore the underlying (and insidious) social class influences and class lifestyles that may shape the consumption patterns of individuals. As such, the individual consumer needs to be socially and culturally contextualized, but this presents a challenge to the notion of the agentic, independent, postmodernist consumer.

INTERNET RESOURCES

Brand community website. http://www.ducktapeclub.com

Brand Management Agency, Smack Inc. http://www.smackinc.com/news.cfm

Center for Communication and Civic Engagement, University of Washington. http://depts.washington.edu/ccce/polcommcampaigns/CultureJamming.htm

Culture jammers' website. http://www.abrupt.org/CJ/

The Ethical Consumer organization and its list of current boycotts. http://www.ethicalconsumer.org/Boycotts/currentUKboycotts.aspx

The Guardian. http://www.guardian.co.uk/technology/2008/jan/14/facebook

Lower Mill Estate. http://www.lowermillestate.com/press08/Times%20Magazine%20Aug%2030-08.htm

KEY READINGS

Cova, B., Kozinets, R.V. and Shankar, A. (eds) (2007), *Consumer Tribes*. Oxford: Butterworth-Heinemann.

Gelder, K. (ed.) (2007), *Subcultures*. London: Routledge, Volumes I, II and II.

Muniz, A.M. and Schau, H.J. (2005), 'Religiosity in the abandoned Apple Newton brand community', *Journal of Consumer Research*, 31 (4), 737–747.

SEMINAR EXERCISES

Discussion Topics

1. What criteria would you use to decide whether a particular group was a tribe, or a subculture, or some other type of consumer collective? Apply these criteria to the three examples

of groupings in the case study, and explore how well the concepts fit the situations.

2. Discuss the social networking practices and interactions that emerge through membership of Facebook (or a similar site). Are these individual practices or collective practices? Do they lead to fundamentally different behaviours than are conducted offline? Do proxemics matter in this context? Is this an example of a new form of cultural activity?

3. Discuss how relevant you think the concept of social class is in the consumption of goods and services, nowadays. Identify goods and services where you think class is very important and others where it is not important.

4. Are brand communities simply a top-down extension of corporate branding strategies (driven by marketers), or are they spontaneous communities that emerge from the consumption needs and practices of consumers?

Group Exercises

1. Drawing upon the group's experiences, create a two-dimensional map of the various consumer collectives occupied by students. Use intersecting or separate circles to show relationships between different spheres of influence, and use arrows to suggest the directions of influence.

2. Conduct a debate on Heath and Potter's (2004) perspective of counter-culture. Before the debate, spend some time researching counter-cultural ideas and theories.

3. Each group member should use the library and search engines to gather evidence on two brands and their brand communities. You should take a critical perspective upon the differences between the brand community members and the corporate marketing messages in the ways that they discuss and represent the brand. Share your findings with other group members, and assess whether any trends emerge.

REFERENCES

Baker, S.M. and Martin, M.C. (2000), 'The meaning of exchange in a sports card subculture of consumption', *Research in Consumer Behaviour*, 9, 173–196.

Banister, E. and Hogg, M.K. (2001), 'Mapping the negative self: From "So not me" to just not me', in *Advances in Consumer Research XXVIII*. Valdosta, GA: Association of Consumer Research, pp. 242–248.

Bennett, A. (1999), 'Subcultures or neotribes? Rethinking the relationship between youth, style and musical taste', *Sociology*, 33 (3), 599–617.

Bourdieu, P. (1984), *Distinction: A Social Critique of the Judgement of Taste*. Harvard, MA: Harvard University Press.

Celsi, R.L., Rose, R.L. and Leigh, T.W. (1993), 'An exploration of high-risk leisure consumption through skydiving', *Journal of Consumer Research*, 20, 1–23.

Cova, B., Kozinets, R.V. and Shankar, A. (eds) (2007), *Consumer Tribes*. Oxford: Butterworth-Heinemann.

Fournier, S. (1998), 'Consumers and their brands: developing relationship theory in consumer research', *Journal of Consumer Research*, 24 (4), 343–372.

Gelder, K. (ed.) (2007), *Subcultures*. London: Routledge, Volumes I, II and II.

Heath, J. and Potter, A. (2004), *Nation of Rebels: Why Counterculture became Consumer Culture*. New York: Harper Collins.

Hebdige, D. (1979), *Subculture: The Meaning of Style*. London: Methuen.

Heeks, R. (2008), *'Current Analysis and Future Research Agenda on "Gold Farming": Real-world Production in Developing Countries for the Virtual Economies of Online Games'*. Working Paper No. 32. University of Manchester: Institute for Development Policy and Management.

Hetherington, K. (1998), *Expressions of Identity: Space, Performance, Politics*. London: Sage.

Hodgkinson, T. (2008), 'With friends like these …', *The Guardian*, January 14.

Holt, D. (1997), 'Poststructuralist lifestyle analysis: conceptualizing the social patterning of consumption in postmodernity', *Journal of Consumer Research*, 23 (March), 326–350.

Jenks, C. (1993), *Culture*. London: Routledge.

Kates, S.M. (2002), 'The Protean quality of subcultural consumption: an ethnographic account of gay consumers', *Journal of Consumer Research*, 29 (December), 383–399.

Kozinets, R.V. (2001), 'Utopian Enterprise: articulating the meanings of Star Trek's culture of consumption', *Journal of Consumer Research*, 28 (June), 67–88.

Kozinets, R.V. (2002), 'The field behind the screen: using netnography for marketing research in online communities', *Journal of Marketing Research*, 39/1 (February), 61–72.

McRobbie, A. (ed.) (1989), *Zoot Suits and Second-Hand Dresses: An Anthology of Fashion and Music*. London: Macmillan.

Maffesoli, M. (1996), *The Time of the Tribes*. London: Sage.

Maslow, A.H. (1954), *'Motivation and Personality'*. New York: Harper Row.

Mostrous, A. (2008), 'Busy computer warriors pay faraway geek mercenaries to fight their battles for them', *The Times*, August 20.

Muniz, A. and O'Guinn, T. (2001), 'Brand community', *Journal of Consumer Research*, 27 (March), 412–432.

Muniz, A.M. and Schau, H.J. (2005), 'Religiosity in the abandoned Apple Newton brand community', *Journal of Consumer Research*, 31 (4), 737–747.

Nelson, C., Treichler, P. and Grossberg, L. (1992), 'Cultural studies: an introduction', in L. Grossberg et al. (eds), *Cultural Studies*. New York: Routledge, pp. 1–22.

O'Guinn, T. (1991), 'Touching greatness: the Central Midwest Barry Manilow Fan Club', in R. Belk (ed.), *Highways and Buyways*. Provo, UT: Association of Consumer Research, pp. 102–111.

Pearce, S. (1998), *Collecting in Contemporary Practice*. London: Routledge.

Peñaloza, L. (1994), 'Border crossings: a critical ethnographic exploration of the consumer acculturation of Mexican immigrants', *Journal of Consumer Research*, 21 (1), 32–55.

Putnam, R.D. (1995), *Bowling Alone: The Collapse and Revival of American Community*. London: Simon and Schuster.

Schouten, J. and McAlexander, M. (1995), 'Subcultures of consumption: an ethnography of the New Bikers', *Journal of Consumer Research*, 22 (June), 43–61.

Slater, J.S. (2000), 'Collecting the real thing: a case study exploration of brand loyalty enhancement among Coca-Cola brand collectors', in S.J. Hoch and R.J. Meyer (eds), *Advances in Consumer Research*, vol. 27. Provo, UT: Association for Consumer Research, pp. 202–208.

Thompson, C. and Troester, M. (2002), 'Consumer value systems. Postmodern fragmentation: the case of the natural health microculture', *Journal of Consumer Research*, 28 (March), 550–571.

Thornton, S. (1997), 'A general introduction', in K. Gelder and S. Thornton (eds), *The Subcultures Reader*. London: Routledge.

Willis, P. (1977), *Learning to Labour*. Farnborough: Saxon House.

Willis, P. (1978), *Profane Culture*. London: Routledge and Kegan Paul.

CHAPTER 7

Gender and Consumer Behaviour

Lydia Martens

INTRODUCTION

The concept of gender was brought into academic usage to stand for the cultural manifestations of biological sexual differences. Human beings are born with a set of sexual organs and a body which is both shaped and regulated by hormones. However, what it means to be 'a woman' or 'a man', and 'a boy' or 'a girl' is a cultural accomplishment that has its roots both in the way gender is structurally present in our society (for instance, through the gendering of positions in the labour market), and in the way gender is 'done' on an everyday level through the way we talk, walk and interact with others (West and Zimmerman, 1987). The domain of consumer culture is not immune to this for, as pointed out by Bristor and Fischer, 'gender is a pervasive filter through which individuals experience their social world, and consumption activities are fundamentally gendered' (1993, p. 519).

But what does it mean to say that 'consumption activities are fundamentally gendered'? Well, we have all heard of the common stereotypes: of women enjoying shopping and being style managers of their homes and families, even taking it upon themselves to dress their husbands! Men, on the other hand, are portrayed as abhorring shopping and avoiding the shopping mall. Yet, equally pertinent is the ferocious male consumer of sex, alcohol and expensive sports cars – *à la* James Bond – not to mention the popular and enduring *Playboy* magazine, which has had men reach out for the top shelf of the supermarket magazine rack for decades now. Whilst such popular images clearly contradict one another, questioning the very notion of the consumer as a female persona, they have had a clear impact on directions in consumer behaviour research, which operated for some time with the presumption that the shopper was a female subject (Catterall et al., 2005, p. 491). However, Bristor and Fischer's statement really points us to the breadth of applicable interest areas. For it is important not only to explain how we have come to live in a world where the consumer has historically become constructed as female, but also how gender imagery and portrayals of femininity and masculinity are utilized in the broad range of sales discourses evident in consumer culture. It is also important to consider how consumption practices constitute one group in a broader range of ongoing social practices through which people construct and give voice to their gender identification. Before moving on to discuss these three concerns, this chapter will consider different ways in which gender and consumer behaviour may be theorized. Again, this suggests the breadth of this area of consumer behaviour.

FEMINISM AND CONSUMPTION

Gender has really made its presence felt in different social science disciplines as a consequence of the incorporation of feminist politics and thinking into academic agendas; a shift that has been marked from the 1970s onwards. The argument presented here is that in order to comprehend gender and consumer behaviour theoretically, it is necessary to consider not only the interrelationship between theories of gender and consumer behaviour, but also the influence feminism has had in shaping social and cultural agendas in different discipline areas. For whilst it is clear that gender is of central importance when thinking about the nature of consumer culture and the patterning of consumer behaviour, it has paradoxically not received the level of scholarly attention one might expect. To cite Jonathan Schroeder, in his introduction to a special issue on Consumption, Gender and Identity in *Consumption, Markets and Culture*: '... gender rarely plays a central role in framing research, with notable exceptions, of course; but generally gender has become a boutique item in the mainstream mall of consumer research' (2003, p. 1). In addressing why this might be the case, a first observation is that the discipline of marketing and consumer behaviour has not been peculiar in this respect! Cultural sociologist Celia Lury has already argued in 1996 that theories of consumption could benefit from being more gender informed, and whilst *Consumer Culture* illustrates the centrality of gender in consumer behaviour, this challenge has not really been taken on board in a major way by most scholars of consumption and consumer culture.

There have been some attempts at explaining this paradox, from within the field of marketing and consumer behaviour (see e.g. Catterall et al., 2005) and outside it (see Casey and Martens, 2007a; Martens, 2009), and it is useful to consider them briefly here. In the introduction to our edited collection on gender and consumption, for instance, we talk about the fact that feminist interest in consumption-related themes has been rather peculiar (Casey and Martens, 2007b) and, in fact, historically somewhat hesitant. Tracing this back to early second wave feminist texts, and especially the popular piece *The Feminine Mystique* by Betty Friedan (1963), it is possible to see how consumer behaviour came to be negated as an area of feminist interest. Unlike other domains of social life, therefore, feminist scholars have not been hammering on the door of consumer behaviour scholarship to argue for the inclusion of gender into the research agenda, and it has thus been easy for gender to be ignored in mainstream consumer behaviour. The latter is picked up by Catterall and her colleagues (2005), who bear witness to the fact that marketing and consumer behaviour studies have not been completely immune to feminist ideas and input, with the 1990s in particular featuring some common feminist questioning of male biases in the discipline. But the title of their paper, 'Postmodern Paralysis', connects with another important development. For if early second wave feminism ignored gender and consumer behaviour, their argument is that more recently, feminist work around consumer behaviour has become influenced too much by trends in postmodern theorization, leaving it essentially without a critical focus. Within this context it may be useful to observe that a consumer behaviour agenda did make it through the 'feminist backdoor', so to speak. Through the cultural turn in social theory during the 1980s, in which feminists played a central role, they addressed a multitude of 'popular' cultural phenomena, from fashion (Wilson, 1985) and the soap opera (Ang, 1985) to girls' magazines (McRobbie, 1991), and more recently, to such post-feminist formulations as Meryl Storr's (2003) *Latex and Lingerie*, which provides a comprehensive ethnographic analysis of the Ann Summers' party. It is probably true that the theoretical contribution feminisms may make to gender and consumer behaviour in the future lies in the critical and questioning edge it brings to the scholarly enterprise. In order to hold onto this critical approach, it will be important that perspectives from different disciplinary areas and different formulations of feminism are brought together in new and eclectic ways. In this way we may hope to gain insight not simply into the gratifying, pleasurable and fantastical draws of consumerisms, but also into how such consumerism connects with a complexity of local and global material inequalities, suggesting that the contents of the purse and the power this wields varies significantly between different types of people across the globe.

THEORIZING GENDER AND CONSUMPTION

Having said that, let us now consider what it might mean, as suggested by Lury (1996), to make approaches to consumer behaviour more gender informed. One manner in which the study of gender and consumption has been approached is through a comparison of patterns of consumption between men and women. An example of this is Colin Campbell's (1997) work on the differences in shopping practices between men and women, and the analysis by Irene Cieraad (2007) into the 'gender' differences in the appearance and contents of children's bedrooms. When empirical consumer research shows that 'women' and 'men', or 'boys' and 'girls' do it differently, or that there are some interesting gender facets to the consumption practices under investigation, the next step in the enquiry should be how those differences or facets may be explained. This requires recourse to theories of consumption and gender, which explain not only how consumer behaviour is patterned and how consumers and entrepreneurs make consumption practices culturally meaningful, but also how gender shapes those patterns and meanings, and vice versa, how consumption patterns and meanings shape gender culture. In addition, it is important to recognize that theoretical perspectives 'grow' through empirical reflection upon the world; there is thus always a symbiotic relationship between empirical findings and theoretical interpretation and development.

Elizabeth Silva's (2007) chapter, entitled 'Gender, Class, Emotional Capital and Consumption in Family Life', is an interesting example on how theoretical insights may 'grow' as a consequence of empirical reflection. In her chapter, she draws on the story of *one* family, which participated in a project on the uses and consumption of technology in the home. The research encounter is an accomplishment between Silva, as middle-class social researcher, and the working class mother/wife/woman/consumer research participant, representing 'her family'. The researcher is quickly drawn into (physically and discursively) what turns out to be the research participant's main and major domestic pride and glory; her new, grand and splendid looking kitchen. As this is not a well-to-do family, Silva points to the contradiction of this luxurious and large kitchen positioned 'in the centre' of this otherwise rather 'common' home. After some encouragement from Silva, the woman somewhat reluctantly tells the story of the recent purchase and installation of this kitchen. This is a story which exudes the admirable qualities of the prudent and knowledgeable consumer, with the acquisition of excellent bargains and the considerable savings made in the kitchen's installation. The manner in which the story of the kitchen unfolds could be explained using a Marxian theoretical interpretation, where the female domestic consumer turns into the producer of her home, attempting in true 'Capitalist' fashion to hide the true relations of labour behind the family's accomplishment; the work, the planning and the budgeting that went into 'making *her* dreams come true'. There is, of course, a class story in this work, and Silva quite rightly utilizes Bourdieu's (1984) work on *Distinction*, which offers an explanatory framework for understanding how the selections made by consumers reflect their socially constituted taste, as well as the contents of their purse and what may be achieved with this over time in terms of generating status and distinction in everyday life. This could perhaps have been supplemented with an analysis of the contemporary pressures consumers face to consume more with, as Juliet Schor (1998) conceived it, people aspiring to consume with a focus 'upwards' rather than the 'traditional' pattern of 'doing like the Joneses'.[1]

Yet, Silva takes a micro-level approach, which focuses on a specific family and their technological consumption patterns and decisions, and she is particularly interested in how gender operates alongside class in explaining the specific consumption patterns in this family. And there is a gender dimension here, as it soon turns out that whilst the new large four-wheel-drive car outside the front door is 'his', the new kitchen is rightfully 'hers'; a truism constituted both mentally and practically through agreement and collaboration between the spouses. Thus whilst the kitchen is 'her project', it has been achieved through the constructive partnership between husband and wife. Theoretically, Silva here builds up a feminist critique of Bourdieu's tri-fold theory of economic, social and cultural capital as central to explaining competitive consumption practices, by arguing that these gender dimensions in consumption practices require the inclusion of 'emotional capital' into the analytical framework. 'Emotional' capital is an interesting theoretical concept, as it points to the value that a woman's domestic management brings to a family's overall capital, allowing them to 'consume' in ways not otherwise possible. Without the ingenious efforts of Silva's female participant, there would likely not have been a kitchen, and perhaps not even a large four-wheel-drive car.

Another lucid example of the symbiotic relationship between empirical insight and theoretical application in relation to gender and consumption may be found in the article 'Barbie girls versus sea monsters: Children constructing gender' by Michael Messner (2000). As was the case for the last example, Messner's paper does not take us into retailing space, nor do we directly encounter purchasing decisions. This is a story about the ways in which the cultural artefacts of the marketplace, in this case the Barbie doll, become resources for girls in their construction of group practices, and how, through the interaction between groups of boys and girls at the opening ceremony of the local soccer club, children actively construct gender. So, whilst Silva's account attempts to theoretically work through how gender implicates consumption theory, in Messner's work we find an example of how the consumption practices (interpreted here as 'use' rather than 'purchase') of children may be understood by thinking through gender theory.

This article has an autobiographical tone, as Messner was present at the opening ceremony as the proud father of a young son, who was about to join

---

[1] In case this needs clarification, 'doing like the Joneses' was an expression used in the 1950s and 60s to describe how consumers tried to 'keep up' with the consumption patterns of their neighbours. If we agree with Schor, the 'world of reference' consumers used at this time was rather smaller than it is today.

the soccer club. Messner's starting point is the description of an 'incident' during the ceremony. The team of girls that are at the centre of the incident are lined up, alongside the other teams, donning their soccer clothes and a mascot; a life-sized Barbie, dressed in green and white stripes, just like the girls. Whilst the teams are lined up alongside one another waiting for the ceremony to start, the girls start chanting songs and dance around their mascot. The boys, whose team is called Sea Monsters, stand alongside the girls, also waiting for the ceremony to start. When they eventually notice each other looking onto the girls' performance, they start to show their displeasure by shouting anti-Barbie slogans at them. After the ceremony, when the teams are again lined up, and the girls continue their dance and song routine, the boys start making incursions into the girls' team. Parents observing the incident note that 'girls will be girls, and boys will be boys'.

In response, Messner points to the inherently social nature of the incident, explaining how it may be understood by making recourse to three theoretical approaches to gender; gender structure, gender culture and gender performance. Within these three dimensions lies the interaction between, what in sociology is known as, the relationship between structure and agency. Messner is keen to reject the idea that all that happened during the incident was girls and boys *performing* gender, insisting that it is by no means an accident that it came about in the way it did. He discusses each dimension of gender in some detail. In relation to gender structure, he comments on the way in which the soccer organization is itself gendered, discussing for instance, the gender division between volunteer coaches and managers at the club, as well as the fact that the football teams are gender segregated, with boys and girls being separated into gender specific teams from the young age of five. However, it is in relation to gender culture that Messner touches on the ongoing debate within feminism about the impact and significance of Barbie culture. Connecting this with our earlier discussion of useful ways in which feminist perspectives may be incorporated into consumer behaviour research, Messner shows that one can hold onto the structural factors that envelop children's gendered practices, whilst at the same time allowing for their agency.

In summary, the domain of gender and consumer behaviour is marked by a specific historical trajectory of feminist engagement. This has resulted in a long-lasting silence on consumer behaviour, reflected for instance in the absence of consumption related articles in some of the major journals reporting on developments in feminist and gender studies (e.g. *Signs*, *Gender and Society*). On the other hand, in more recent work by 'post-feminist' scholars, there are signs of an absence of feminism's critical edge, leading to an overemphasis on the role of consumerism in a set of self-focused identity practices, at the expense of analyses that illustrate the 'wider picture'. However, thinking about the role and place of feminism is only part of the story in our concern here with gender and consumer behaviour. Thus, in addressing

Lury's (1996) suggestion that consumption theory could benefit from greater input of insights from gender theory, two examples have been considered here which illustrate how theoretical interpretation in this area has been furthered through the symbiotic relationship between theoretical conjecture and empirical reflection. Both reflect the above concerns of engaging critically with the wider picture, with Silva's work being an excellent example of the ways in which class and gender merge in important ways in a comprehension of consumer choices and the development of a consumer persona in the female respondent of her study. Messner, on the other hand, offers a creative interlinking of theoretical perspectives of gender performativity and gender structure/culture, suggesting that constructions of gendered selves happen within the context of structural forces that demarcate the boundaries of what is possible and what is not. Let us now proceed by returning to the three themes, which as suggested earlier, provide insight into the broad domain of gender and consumer behaviour, starting with the question how the consumer became historically constructed as a female subject.

GENDER AND THE DEVELOPMENT OF CONSUMER CULTURE

De Grazia's and Furlough's (1997) edited collection, *The Sex of Things*, has been instructive for bringing gender more to the forefront of historical work on consumer culture. Whilst historians (e.g. McKendrick et al., 1983; Campbell, 1987) have been keen to explain the development of 'demand' for goods and services as capitalism developed into the main force shaping industrializing societies, De Grazia and her colleagues consider how gender mapped onto this process. Their arguments are nuanced in part because industrialization was a long and drawn out process, and consequently, historians of different time periods have particular stories to tell. David Kuchta's (1996) chapter on men and fashion, for instance, makes it clear that men were visible consumers during the eighteenth and nineteenth centuries. Yet, the rise of the early department store in the middle of the nineteenth century is instructive for illustrating how the feminized consumer became a more consolidated social and cultural persona at this time, and it is worthwhile to consider briefly how that came about.

The first department stores opened up in Paris, New York and Chicago in the middle of the nineteenth century. The well-known Parisian store Au Bon Marché, for instance, which inspired Emile Zola's (1883) novel *Au Bonheur des Dames* (The Ladies' Delight) and intrigued modernist scholars like Walter Benjamin, opened in 1852 (Miller, 1981) containing within its 'borders' a broad range of 'goods departments' that sold, amongst other things, 'fashionable articles, especially clothes and other objects that could improve the female "look" or the male appearance' (Learmans, 1993, p. 83).

As department stores became a more established feature in the inner cities of industrializing countries, purposely designed stores were build that featured large show windows, and that had interiors so lush, luxurious and exuberant that some have compared them with cathedrals or palaces (e.g. Crossick and Jaumain, 1999). New technologies for displaying the goods on sale enabled entrepreneurs to entice customers in, and showing them their goods in the most desirable way possible (Williams, 1982; Leach, 1984). Needless to say, the early department store was remarkable because, by utilizing the latest technologies and developments on offer in this progressive modernity, it introduced brand new ways of marketing and retailing goods.

Gender was evident in these early stores in diverse ways. Whilst the customers where overwhelmingly well-off ladies of leisure, for whom these new stores offered a welcome new public space in which they could spend time away from their homes without risking their reputations, the stores were typically owned by male entrepreneurs and staffed by women from the lower middle and working classes. Judy Giles (2004) talks about the intriguing transformation in the relationship between women of different classes these stores instigated; whereas traditionally, the interaction in the service relationship had been one of the dominant lady and her subservient domestic female servant, the lower class female shop assistant employed in the early department store held stylistic knowledge and thus power which could be unnerving to the upper class female customer. However, the development of retailing culture also brought forth a number of new professional occupations in which middle class women found jobs. Gender pervaded the very organization of these new retailing spaces, and the assumed priority of the female customer, and the department store's efforts to avoid male embarrassment when making purchases meant that male goods departments were frequently situated in the basement (Reekie, 1993). The upper reaches of the stores contained all sorts of female 'conveniences', including 'lavish lounges and rest rooms, well-stocked reading rooms, writing rooms with complimentary stationary and pens, restaurants with live musicians, post offices, beauty salons, nurseries, meeting rooms for women's groups, delivery services, and repair services ...' (Benson, 1979, p. 205), all of which illustrate the eagerness of early department store owners to create a retailing space to attract well-to-do ladies of leisure.

Whilst we may lament the fact that these features are no longer present in the contemporary department store, it is through the theme of shoplifting that the gender dimensions of Victorian nineteenth century life become apparent, and with it, the consolidation of the consumer as female subject. Shoplifting, known in the nineteenth century as kleptomania, 'store-itis' or 'mal du mall', was a social puzzle in the sense that the thieves in question were in fact well-to-do ladies, who were perceived as easily able to afford the often relatively cheap articles which they stole (Abelson, 1989a, 1989b). Historians have been drawn by this nineteenth century 'social problem', in part because Victorian society had a habit of medicalizing the behaviour of women which was apparently incomprehensible. Kleptomania; the irresistible need to steal in women, was thus conceived of as a mental disorder, a form of hysteria that some women suffered from. Yet, one of the difficulties of hind-sight is that it never was clear, not now nor during the nineteenth century, how extensive the problem of kleptomania actually was. As this opens the possibility that it was not so widespread, the phenomenon has thus been explained by seeing it as symptomatic of the growing social unease around the development of these new retailing practices and spaces in a society which was rather traditional in outlook and simply 'not used' to it. Shopping thus came to be conceived of as a disruptive force in the cultural fabric of society. The process of making sense of this new retailing culture mapped onto gender in the sense that the powerful medical and cultural discourses associated with it construed 'shopping' as something that 'women' did within the context of wider debates about the specific malleable and impressionable nature of the female subject (Camhi, 1993; Whitlock, 2005).

SELLING GENDER

It must be clear by now that gender and consumer behaviour is a broad area of studies, tapping into a range of theoretical perspectives with a breadth of substantive areas to consider. Thinking 'from the past to the present', as we did above, is also useful for considering the ways in which gender has been 'sold' over time. Historians have been keen observers of marketing practices in relation to gender. Take for instance Vinikas' (1992) *Soft Soap, Hard Sell* and Sivulka's (2001) *Stronger than Dirt*. Both provide interesting insight into the revolution in bodily cleanliness we experienced during the twentieth century; a process which, if not actively stimulated by the marketing of products like soaps and mouthwashes, was certainly 'actively' accompanied by such discourses. The soap brands discussed by Vinikas and Sivulka are not unfamiliar to us; Lifebuoy, Palmolive, Ivory, Fairy and Lux are all still in the market place today, and whilst in terms of their contents, these products will have changed over time, the same is no doubt the case for the stories marketers have told about these products. Of course, the twentieth century has been a hugely significant period for the development of marketing itself, made possible for example by concomitant developments in media, which created useful spaces for marketers to tell their stories in such diverse settings as films, radio and later television, magazines and newspapers, and in due course, on bill boards and buildings. Then, as now, marketers usually tapped into some pertinent aspect of everyday culture to sell their ware, offering their product as the facilitator for improving or perfecting the task in hand. Thus soap sales discourses in the early part of the twentieth century were formulated around the cultural 'need' to secure a mate, both for men and for women. Romance featured prominently in advertisements which stipulated that the desirable feminine and masculine body could be created through changed cleanliness practices. For women this meant that washing with the right soap would give softness of skin, replace 'offending' bodily smells with the floral scent of the soap, and create that dainty perfection for which Bette Davies was purportedly so famous (Sivulka, 2001, p. 207). Interestingly, similar injunctions were made to men, suggesting that BO[2] could stand in the way of maintaining a successful relationship with a woman (Sivulka, 2001, p. 187).

Marketing discourses have also been salient in the development of that other prominent twentieth century female persona, the housewife. The housewife and her alter ego, the breadwinner, were the epitomic icons of the ideology of separate spheres, which arguably re-emerged in the postwar years to generate a cult of domesticity (Palmer, 1989). Palmer traces the decline in domestic servants which meant that middle class women ended up doing 'their own' housework. This transformation was a stimulus for the invention of many new and different types of commodities, which were sold not only as aids in housework (like the vacuum cleaner), but that also symbolized the shift in 'the home' as a site for stylistic and leisure consumption. Women's magazines must be recognized as salient vehicles for the communication and promulgation of home fashions, in addition to providing an advisory forum for how best to tackle a breadth of domestic challenges (Martens and Scott, 2005). According to Giles (2004), the housewife was a 'uniform' and classless persona precisely because marketers could for the first time unite women from different backgrounds under the same banner; that of their shared domestic responsibilities. In advertisements of the time, which may be viewed by opening the pages of women's magazines from the postwar years, she was portrayed in the same manner; as an immaculate and always smiling woman, often in high heels and with a 'dainty' white apron, donning well-groomed wavy hair. Sometimes she was accompanied by her husband, for instance when larger purchases like a washing machine needed to be made. Picturing the housewife in the middle of her family meant a reiteration of her role as the caretaker and 'servant' of the household. The housewife was also without doubt the shopper of the family. It was to her, Mrs Consumer, that marketers targeted a diversity of domestic products to help furnish and maintain the home (Rutherford, 2003). It was this same persona that Friedan, and second wave feminists following in her wake, reacted against in such a vehement and negative manner, as the world was about to change in terms of the assumptions made almost automatically in relation to gender roles in society.

---

[2] Body Odour.

Case study: Doing gender, doing consumption – a study of the consumption of sex

Thinking through the consumption of sex is interesting because, in contradistinction to the common assumption of the consumer as female, with respect to this form of service provision, gender roles have traditionally been seen as operating 'the other way round', with 'men' typical in their role as consumers and women in the role of 'woman-as-commodity' (Roberts, 1998). Prostitution is argued to be the oldest 'commercial' exchange relationship between men and women, invariably shrouded in degrees of secrecy because of its socially questionable nature (Grenz, 2005). Pornography, on the other hand, is a somewhat newer phenomenon, which has grown in prevalence and visibility with the rise of mass media, and concomitantly, of second wave feminism, which has offered vehement critiques of the ways sexual portrayals of women are demeaning and oppressive (Dworkin, 1981). It seems that as we have moved into contemporary society, sex and commerce have combined in new ways to confront everyday life in rather more explicit ways than was the case in the past. In today's society, representations of sex and bodies are used in various guises in advertising, in newspapers and magazines, on TV and in films, and it is probably true to say that boundaries of what is acceptable and what not are continuously shifting. Let us therefore consider how the 'sexualization of culture' (Attwood, 2005) is in fact also a sexualization of consumer culture.

Three salient and interconnected facets are part of the story: the diversification of the market for sex products and services; the consolidation of a consumer attitude and rationalization amongst male consumers of sexual services; and the targeting of sexual products at women. Starting with the first theme, the transformation in the relationship between sex and commerce was already implied in my comments above on pornography. It is also apparent in Bernstein's account of the market for sexual services targeted at men:

During the last 30 years, demand for commercially available sexual services has not only soared but become ever more specialized, diversifying along technological, spatial and social lines. The scope of sexual commerce has thus grown to encompass: live sex shows; all variety of pornographic texts, videos, and images, both in print and on line; fetish clubs; sexual 'emporiums' featuring lap-dancing and wall-dancing; escorts agencies; telephone and cyber-sex contacts; 'drive-through' striptease venues; and organized sex tours of developing countries (2001, pp. 392–3).

This ready supply, overwhelmingly by women[3] (though no doubt organized in important ways by male entrepreneurs), using their bodies in diverse ways in the cash nexus connects, peculiarly enough, with our earlier theoretical discussion on the extension of Bourdieu by feminist theorists. Whilst Silva (2007) attempted to broaden the gender applicability of Bourdieu's theories by arguing for the inclusion of emotional capital, Beverley Skeggs (1997) focuses on how women use their bodies as a form of capital. This partly explains the prominence of body enhancement products and practices in our contemporary consumer culture, though evidence from the merchandise of the early department store warns us against exaggerating the novelty of this phenomenon. Thinking about the body as a form of capital moves different contemporary phenomena closer together. Thus, the use by women of their bodies in the production of pornographic imagery is perhaps not so different from the female celebrity, who also extensively capitalizes on her body and appearance, or, for that matter, the Victorian woman, who not only uses her appearance to make a good 'match' but then moves on to be the walking proof of her husband's wealth by self-decoration practices (Veblen, 1953). Sadly, the material need to utilize the body in this way has given rise to the global sex worker (Ehrenreich and Hochschild, 2003), and her predicament appears in stark contrast to the seemingly frivolous pursuits of sexual pleasures in our contemporary society.

Whilst the diversification Bernstein talks about is clearly targeted at men, Attwood emphasizes the different ways in

---

[3] However, we should not ignore the way young men and transvestites utilize their bodies in similar ways to women!

which women are now also increasingly drawn into the market for sexual products.

> *Women are increasingly targeted as sexual consumers. … Women's consumption of sexual commodities is regarded as a huge growth area, and erotic products – most notably lingerie and sex toys – are increasingly visible in the West End, the high street and the virtual world of the Internet. (2005, p. 392)*

This raises the question whether the traditional demarcation between 'man-as-sex-consumer' and 'woman-as-commodity' is shifting, and in what ways. To answer that question, let us turn briefly to their arguments.

Bernstein discusses the ways in which the men, who took part in her study, illustrated a contemporary consumer disposition in relation to their use of commercial sexual services; men thus positioned themselves very much as consumers in their research encounter with her. According to Bernstein, her research suggests a crucial shift from 'a relational to a recreational model of sexual behaviour, a reconfiguration of erotic life in which the pursuit of sexual intimacy is not hindered but facilitated by its location in the marketplace' (2001, p. 397). Paying for such services had 'the benefit' of making the sexual encounter clearly bounded, devoid of the expectation for 'more', even though the men also engaged the fantasy that the engagement provided an 'authentic interpersonal connection' (2001, p. 402). Exchanging money for sex was also seen by the men as an equal exchange, in which neither party was exploited. Interestingly, they also assumed the right to be a sex 'consumer', with the associated right to make choices and introduce variety into their consumption practices. Bernstein's male research participants therefore 'do consumption' very much according to the contemporary image of the sovereign consumer, and in so doing, they participate in the production of a gendered consumer domain which positions women in contradictory ways.

By contrast, Attwood (2005) and Storr (2003) question how women and female participation in sexual practices are 'portrayed' in this process of sexual commoditization. The popular and much discussed rabbit vibrator is highlighted by Attwood as an example of the incorporation of ideas from second wave feminism (sisters are doing it for themselves) into female sexuality. It prefigures a more active female sexuality and a more prominent presence of clitoral pleasures. Meryl Storr, on the other hand, is not so optimistic in her conclusions of the Ann Summers Party. She discusses the varied bodily and social pleasures 'to be had' at the party, with games, banter, teasing, joking and the copious consumption of sweets all making it 'the ultimate girls' night in'.[4] Yet, against this backdrop of agentive female homo-sociality, she identifies the party's 'organizational regime' as prioritizing phallus centred, vaginal penetrative heterosexual sex, which emphasizes the female body as passive and receptive of sexual pleasures (2003, p. 135) and which illustrates the rejection of homosexuality. The Ann Summers Party is therefore also a gendered consumer experience and like Bernstein, Storr sketches a picture which illustrates the connections between gender and the disparate positions 'men' and 'women' are allotted in contemporary society.

Today, it is possible to see some similarities and also some differences in the ways gender is sold in consumer culture. Romance certainly continues to be a major theme through which entrepreneurs lure customers, though arguably there has been a shift from the dainty romanticism of the interwar years towards much more sexually explicit imagery and insinuations, leading, as the case study illustrates, to what some have termed the sexualization of culture (Attwood, 2005). Whilst it is impossible to provide a comprehensive overview of recent trends in marketing practices here, one remarkable trend must certainly be the development of niche marketing, which targets specific (lifestyle) groups of consumers. Interestingly, men

---

[4]This is the title of chapter 2 in her book.

are increasingly addressed as consumers in their own right, and women are demarcated by age, interest and socio-economic background. However, regardless of whether you look into men's lifestyle magazines (which incidentally are a relatively recent and new literature genre for men) or consider magazines and products targeted at Tweenage girls, you are confronted with specific and often quite strong messages about femininity and masculinity; in short, recommendations on how to 'do self' by 'doing gender' (Jackson et al., 2001; Russell and Tyler, 2002).

INTERNET RESOURCES

Article written by John Crawford Brown on the early department store in 1921.
   http://www.oldandsold.com/articles14/new-york-34.shtml

Course descriptor on Gender and Consumer Culture by Dr Richard Wilk.
   http://www.indiana.edu/~wanthro/498syl05.htm

KEY READINGS

Casey, E. and Martens, L. (eds) (2007), *Gender and Consumption: Domestic Cultures and the Commercialization of Everyday Life*. Aldershot: Ashgate.

Catterall, M., Maclaran, P. and Stevens, L. (2005), 'Postmodern paralysis: The critical impasse in feminist perspectives on consumers', *Journal of Marketing Management*, 21, 489–504.

Scanlon, J. (ed.) (2000), *The Gender and Consumer Culture Reader*. New York: New York University Press.

Schroeder, J.E. (ed.) (2003), Special Issue on 'Consumption, gender and identity', *Consumers, Markets and Culture*, 6 (1) 1–4.

SEMINAR EXERCISES

Discussion Topics

1. The notion that the consumer is female is a common contemporary stereotype. How is this stereotype reflected in: (i) consumer practices; (ii) the construction of the early department store; and (iii) consumer behaviour scholarship? In what respect is the stereotype negated?

2. Drawing on your reading of the early department store, develop a proposal for how theoretical perspectives of gender and consumption may be brought together in an explanation of how gender is prevalent in this domain of consumption.

3. Discuss, by making reference to the sexualization of consumer culture, how: (i) sex is sold to consumers in gendered ways; (ii) sex is used in marketing practices; (iii) consumers 'do gender' through their consumption of sex services and products.

Group Exercises

1. Select a distinct area of consumer practices (e.g. department store shopping, visiting the supermarket, celebrating Christmas or Thanksgiving) and put together a presentation on how gender shapes this practice. As part of the presentation, discuss whether, if you engage in the practice yourself:

    (i) You partake in the gendered dimensions of those practices,

    (ii) You do so consciously, and

    (iii) Whether there are aspects of the gendered organization of the practice that you question and challenge.

2. Identify ONE women's and ONE men's lifestyle magazine. Peruse one issue of each magazine before coming to class and decide which advertisement reflects an interesting take on gender and sexuality. Within the group, present your advertisements and provide a rationale for your selection. Then compare the advertisements, drawing out:

    (i) How the advertisements of the women's and men's lifestyle magazines differ.

    (ii) Whether there are similarities.

    (iii) In what ways gender and sexuality are connected in the advertisements.

3. Select ONE of your most favourite goods/articles/items. Discuss:

    (i) If at all, how your gender identity is connected with this item.

    (ii) How items 'like this' are sold to consumers.

    (iii) Reflect on whether your gender association with the item is connected with the ways the item is sold.

REFERENCES

Abelson, E. (1989a), 'The invention of kleptomania', *Signs*, 15 (1), 123–143.

Abelson, E. (1989b), *When Ladies Go A-Thieving: Middle-class Shoplifters in the Victorian Department Store*. Oxford: Oxford University Press.

Ang, I. (1985), Watching Dallas: Soap Opera and the melodramatic imagination. London: Methuen.

Attwood, F. (2005), 'Fashion and passion: marketing sex to women', *Sexualities*, 8 (4), 392–406.

Benson, S.P. (1979), 'Palace of consumption and machine for selling: the American department store, 1880–1940', *Radical History Review*, 21 (Fall), 199–221.

Bernstein, E. (2001), 'The meaning of the purchase: desire, demand and the commerce of sex', *Ethnography*, 2 (3), 389–420.

Bourdieu, P. (1984), *Distinction: A Social Critique of The Judgement of Taste*. London: Routledge and Kegan Paul.

Bristor, J. and Fischer, E. (1993), 'Feminist thought: implications for consumer research', *Journal of Consumer Research*, 19, 518–536.

Camhi, L. (1993), 'Stealing femininity: department store kleptomania as sexual disorder', *Differences*, 5 (1), 26–50.

Campbell, C. (1987), *The Romantic Ethic and the Spirit of Modern Consumerism*. Oxford: Basil Blackwell.

Campbell, C. (1997), 'Shopping, Pleasure and the Sex War', in P. Falk and C. Campbell (eds), *The Shopping Experience*. London: Sage, pp. 166–176.

Casey, E. and Martens, L. (eds) (2007a), *Gender and Consumption: Domestic Cultures and the Commercialization of Everyday Life*. Aldershot: Ashgate.

Casey, E. and Martens, L. (2007b), 'Introduction', in E. Casey and L. Martens (eds), *Gender and Consumption: Domestic Cultures and the Commercialization of Everyday Life*. Aldershot: Ashgate, pp. 1–11.

Catterall, M., Maclaran, P. and Stevens, L. (2005), 'Postmodern paralysis: the critical impasse in feminist perspectives on consumers', *Journal of Marketing Management*, 21, 489–504.

Cieraad, I. (2007), 'Gender at play: décor differences between boys' and girls' bedrooms', in E. Casey and L. Martens (eds), *Gender and Consumption: Domestic Cultures and the Commercialization of Everyday Life*. Aldershot: Ashgate, pp. 197–218.

Crossick, G. and Jaumain, S. (eds) (1999), *Cathedrals of Consumption: The European Department Store 1850–1939*. Aldershot: Ashgate.

De Grazia, V. and Furlough, E. (eds) (1996), *The Sex of Things: Gender and Consumption in Historical Perspective*. Berkeley: University of California Press.

Dworkin, A. (1981), *Pornography: Men Possessing Women*. London: Women's Press.

Ehrenreich, B. and Hochschild, A.R. (2003), *Global Woman: Nannies, Maids, and Sex Workers in the New Economy*. London: Granta Books.

Friedan, B. (1963), *The Feminine Mystique*. London: Gollancz.

Giles, J. (2004), *The Parlour and the Suburb: Domestic Identities, Class, Femininity and Modernity*. Oxford: Berg.

Grenz, S. (2005), 'Intersections of sex and power in research on prostitution: a female researcher interviewing male heterosexual clients', *Signs*, 30 (4), 2091–2113.

Jackson, P., Stevenson, N. and Brooks, K. (2001), *Making Sense of Men's Magazines*. Oxford: Polity Press.

Kuchta, D. (1996), 'The making of the self-made man: class, clothing and English masculinity, 1688–1832', in V. de Grazia with A. Furlong (eds), *The Sex of Things: Gender and Consumption in Historical Perspective*. Berkeley: University of California Press, pp. 54–78.

Leach, W. (1984), 'Transformations in a culture of consumption: women and department stores 1890–1925', *Journal of American History*, 71 (September), 328–342.

Learmans, R. (1993), 'Learning to consume: early department stores and the shaping of modern consumer culture (1860–1914)', *Theory, Culture and Society*, 10, 70–102.

Lury, C. (1996), *Consumer Culture*. Cambridge: Polity Press.

Martens, L. (2009), 'Feminism and the critique of consumer culture, 1950–1970', in S. Gillis and J. Hollows (eds), *Feminism, Domesticity and Popular Culture*. Oxon: Routledge, pp. 33–47.

Martens, L. and Scott, S. (2005), 'The unbearable lightness of cleaning: representations of domestic practice and products in *Good Housekeeping* magazine (UK) 1951–2001', *Consumers, Markets and Culture*, 8 (4), 379–402.

McKendrick, N., Brewer, J. and Plumb, J.H. (1983), *The Birth of a Consumer Society: The Commercialization of Eighteenth-century England*. London: Hutchinson.

McRobbie, A. (1991), *Feminism and Youth Culture: From 'Jackie' to 'Just Seventeen'*. Basingstoke: MacMillan.

Messner, M.A. (2000), 'Barbie girls versus sea monsters: children constructing gender', *Gender & Society*, 14 (6), 765–784.

Miller, M. (1981), *The Bon Marche: Bourgeois Culture and the Department Store, 1869–1920*. Princeton: Princeton University Press.

Palmer, P. (1989), *Domesticity and Dirt: Housewives and Domestic Servants in the United States, 1920–1945*. Philadelphia: Temple University Press.

Reekie, G. (1993), *Temptations: Sex, Selling, and the Department Store*. London: Allen & Unwin.

Roberts, M.L. (1998), 'Gender, consumption, and commodity culture', *American Historical Review*, 103 (3), 817–844.

Russell, R. and Tyler, M. (2002), 'Thank heaven for little girls: "Girl Heaven" and the commercial context of feminine childhood', *Sociology*, 36 (3), 619–637.

Rutherford, J.W. (2003), *Selling Mrs. Consumer: Christine Frederick and the Rise of Household Efficiency*. Athens: University of Georgia Press.

Scanlon, J. (ed.) (2000), *The Gender and Consumer Culture Reader*. New York: New York University Press.

Schor, J. (1998), *The Overspent American: Upscaling, Downshifting and the New Consumer*. New York: Harper Collins.

Schroeder, J.E. (ed.) (2003), 'Guest editor's Introduction: Consumption, gender and identity', *Consumption, Markets and Culture*, 6 (1), 1–4.

Silva, E. (2007), 'Gender, class, emotional capital and consumption in family life', in E. Casey and L. Martens (eds), *Gender and Consumption: Domestic Cultures and the Commercialization of Everyday Life*. Aldershot: Ashgate, pp. 141–157.

Sivulka, J. (2001), *Stronger than Dirt: A Cultural History of Advertising Personal Hygiene in America, 1875 to 1940*. New York: Prometheus Books.

Skeggs, B. (1997), *Formations of Class and Gender: Becoming Respectable*. London: Sage.

Storr, M. (2003), *Latex and Lingerie: Shopping for Pleasure at Ann Summers Parties*. Oxford: Berg.

Veblen, T. (1953), *The Theory of the Leisure Class*. London: George Allen and Unwin.

Vinikas, V. (1992), *Soft Soap, Hard Sell: American Hygiene in an Age of Advertisement*. Iowa: Iowa State University Press.

West, C. and Zimmerman, D.H. (1987), 'Doing gender', *Gender & Society*, 1 (2), 125–151.

Whitlock, T.C. (2005), *Crime, Gender and Consumer Culture in Nineteenth Century England*. Aldershot: Ashgate.

Williams, R.H. (1982), *Dream Worlds: Mass Communication in Late Nineteenth Century France*. Berkeley, CA: University of California Press.

Wilson, E. (1985), *Adorned in Dreams*. London: Virago.

CHAPTER 8

Ethical Debates in Marketing

Elizabeth Parsons

INTRODUCTION

Marketing ethics remains a topic of vigorous debate. As the key form of communication between organizations and the general public, marketing is subject to a significant amount of societal scrutiny. Marketing also plays a central role in organizational attempts to engender the values of commitment, trust and loyalty amongst employees, customers and the public. While marketing ethics have been a cause for concern for some time, recent developments in new communications technologies, coupled with the opening up of previously closed economies in the transformation of some countries to free market systems, have undoubtedly exacerbated ethical challenges. Examples of this can be seen in the controversial promotion of cigarettes in developing countries, and in the case of Nestlé who were accused of misleadingly promoting milk formula in developing countries as better for babies than mothers' milk. However, as Brenkert (2008, p. 4) observes, 'we harbour, as a society, a deeply divided consciousness over marketing'. Many of those living in developed countries readily embrace the array of goods that are the consequence of the efficient operation of markets, at the same time some feel a sense of unease at the cost of this abundance. This chapter first considers the definition and scope of research on marketing ethics. This is followed by a discussion of the role of marketing ethics in contemporary society. In particular it explores how marketing ethics might offer practical guidelines to both organizations and the individuals working within them. The chapter then examines some ethical criticisms of marketing practice including: marketing research; advertising; and product and brand management. In closing, the chapter draws together these debates in a case study which explores the marketing of cosmetics.

MARKETING ETHICS: A DEFINITION AND SCOPE

Surprisingly few authors offer an actual definition of marketing ethics. Drawing from Aristotelian moral philosophy for inspiration, Gaski observes that marketing ethics could be considered as 'standards of conduct and moral judgement applied to marketing practice' (1999, p. 316). Murphy et al. open this out to include institutions themselves, defining marketing ethics as 'the systematic study of how moral standards are applied to marketing decisions, behaviours and institutions' (2005, p. xvii). However, ethical standards typically vary from one institutional environment to the next and from one culture to the next, which makes a universal application of a set of ethical marketing codes problematic. Complications also emerge from differing perspectives on ethics. In this respect Laczniak et al. (1995) found that the views of American consumers and CEOs differed widely, with consumers being far more pessimistic than CEOs about the ethical climate of businesses.

Defining the scope of marketing ethics is also difficult, as the literature on marketing ethics is both complex and extensive. At several intervals over the past thirty years scholars have made attempts to summarize and review this body of work. Murphy and Laczniak (1981) locate initial debate on marketing ethics in the 1930s, although they observe that more significant developments occurred in the 1960s (i.e. Bartels, 1967). This latter work was largely concerned with highlighting a general, global approach to marketing ethics. It was not until the 1970s that work began to focus on specific issues such as marketing research, consumer issues, managerial issues and marketing education issues. In their recent review Nill and Schibrowsky (2007) observe that the volume of research on marketing ethics has recently been increasing quite dramatically. They attempt to classify the series of topics that have been covered in research on marketing ethics (Table 8.1). In exploring these topics they observe a lack of work on pricing and discrimination. They also find a worrying reduction of publications on marketing ethics in the top journals, leading them to surmise that marketing ethics is 'no longer an integral part of marketing discourse' and that, instead, it has 'evolved into a specific sub-discipline' (2007, p. 272).

WHAT ROLE FOR MARKETING ETHICS?

The role marketing ethics ought to play, both in relation to the individual and the organization, has been a key topic for debate. Authors have questioned the extent to which marketing ethics might offer guidelines to marketers (Gaski, 1999; Smith, 2001). They have also been concerned with how theories of marketing ethics might translate into application (Robin

Table 8.1 Topical areas of marketing ethics	
	Issues related to:
Functional areas	Product Price Placement Promotion
Sub-disciplines of marketing	Sales Consumers/consumption International marketing Marketing ethics education Marketing research Social marketing Internet marketing Law and ethics
Specific ethics related topics	Ethics and society Ethical decision-making models Ethical responsibility towards marketers' stakeholders Ethical values Norm generation and definition Marketing ethics implementation Relationship between ethics and religion Discrimination and harassment Green marketing Vulnerable consumers

Source: Nill and Schibrowsky (2007, p. 258)

and Reidenbach, 1987, 1993; Smith, 1995; Thompson, 1995). In addressing these issues, studies have been undertaken from two key perspectives: the normative approach, which aims to prescribe ethical standards and offer guidelines regarding marketing practice; and the positive approach, which aims to describe and understand ethical practices through empirical work. Before exploring these perspectives, however, it is useful to summarize their underpinning philosophies, these being primarily deontological and teleological theories.

Deontological Theories

Deontological theories focus on the behaviours of the individual, specifically the principles used to arrive at the ethical decision. Murphy and Laczniak (1981, p. 252) give the example of Kant's categorical imperative as a deontological theory 'that persons should act in such a way that their maxim for action could be a universal law'. In this perspective the focus is on the behaviour itself and actions are judged by their inherent wrongness or rightness. As Hunt and Vitell observe, 'For deontologists the conundrum has been to determine the "best" set of rules to live by' (1986, p. 6). The principles for these rules may come from a range of sources such as the family, religion, politics, etc.

Teleological Theories

By contrast teleologists place emphasis on perceived outcomes rather than behaviours. They propose that individuals should make judgements based on an evaluation of the likely consequences of their actions. Teleological theories differ however on the issue of whose good one ought to promote:

- *Ethical egoism* suggests that individuals should act in their own interests, i.e. choose an act that results in the most favourable consequences for the individual.

- *Utilitarianism* strives to produce the greatest good for the greatest number of people. Here, an act should be judged on an evaluation of the balance of good consequences over bad consequences it provides for all individuals (Hunt and Vitell, 1986, pp. 6–7).

Although this discussion of the two sets of theories is a simplification, it is important to understand their principles, as they provide the basis for most normative work, and some positive work, on marketing ethics.

A Normative Role for Marketing Ethics

Authors working from a normative perspective have been concerned to provide a series of recommendations regarding marketing practice (Laczniak, 1983; Laczniak and Murphy, 1985, 1993, 2006; Smith and Quelch, 1993; Chonko, 1995; Murphy et al., 2005). These recommendations are concerned with 'what marketing organizations or individuals ought to do or what kinds of marketing systems a society ought to have' (Hunt, 1976, p. 20). Laczniak and Murphy, in describing normative marketing ethics, observe that 'exchange, because it is *social*, must have its outcomes evaluated in terms of fairness or rightness on all marketplace parties' (2006, p. 154). In examining the role of ethics in marketing management, Smith (1993) observes that the marketing manager often has little direct authority and has to rely on the co-operation of other functions within the organization. This means that marketing managers are typically exposed to a range of competing pressures. Chonko (1995) explores how marketing professionals might deal with unethical behaviour. In his evaluation it seems that whistle blowing (or threatening to blow the whistle), and negotiation, are potentially the most advantageous courses of action. He also usefully identifies some reasons why professionals sometimes engage in unethical behaviour. The first issue is diffusion of responsibility, where elaborate organizational structures mean that responsibility is so diffuse that accountability is difficult to pinpoint. A second issue is rationalization, through which wrong decisions can often easily be explained away. Chonko observes that four commonly held beliefs about behaviour might facilitate this:

- A belief that the behaviour is within reasonable ethical and legal limits – that is, the behaviour is *not really* immoral or illegal.

- A belief that the behaviour is in the best interests of the individual, the organization, or both – the individual would somehow be *expected* to undertake the behaviour.

- A belief that the behaviour is *safe* because it will never be found out or published, the classic crime and punishment issue of discovery.

- A belief that because the behaviour helps the organization the organization will *condone* it and even protect the individual who engages in the behaviour (Gellerman, 1986, cited in Chonko, 1995, p. 114).

A key issue is that managers are not aware that marketing ethics can be learnt. Instead they seem to think that ethics are merely a product of their upbringing, religious beliefs and social circle. To this end theorists (particularly normative theorists) are at pains to develop marketing ethics education at business school level. As Laczniak and Murphy observe:

> *The role of relativism and the attitude that all marketing practices are flexible depending on circumstance and personal opinion – views often expressed by business students – seem overstated given the articulated norms and values of marketing professionals, as well as specific codes developed through the consensus of peer practitioners (2006, p. 171).*

They argue further that these codes ought to be taught in business schools, although students should be taught to improve the ethical cultures of their organizations rather than merely to preach ethics (2006, p. 172). To try and bridge the gap between seemingly abstract codes of ethics and the everyday decisions that marketing managers face, Laczniak and Murphy have developed a set of perspectives to guide marketing activity. Their seven basic perspectives (BP) are as listed below:

- BP1: Ethical marketing puts people first.

- BP2: Ethical marketers must achieve a behavioural standard in excess of the law.

- BP3: Marketers are responsible for whatever they intend as a means or ends as a marketing action.

- BP4: Marketing organizations should cultivate better (i.e. higher) moral imagination in their managers and employees.

- BP5: Marketers should articulate and embrace a core set of ethical principles.

- BP6: Adoption of a stakeholder orientation is essential to ethical marketing decisions.

- BP7: Marketing organizations ought to delineate an ethical decision-making protocol. (Laczniak and Murphy, 2006, p. 157)

Laczniak and Murphy observe that taken in isolation these perspectives are difficult to apply. For example, in the societal perspective in BP1 – whose interests ought marketers to put first? – they suggest that this can be addressed by referring to BP6, the adoption of a stakeholder orientation. They highlight a series of further relationships between the perspectives and suggest that while each basic perspective is a useful guideline in itself, they work together to form a holistic approach to marketing management. Overall, in taking a normative approach to marketing ethics, Murphy et al. (2005, p. 47) chart a middle path between ethical theory, individual judgement and societal standards:

> *In the final analysis, ethics still requires considerable prudential judgement that comes from the intuition of the marketing manager (hopefully, grounded in virtue ethics), but it is tempered by a knowledge of ethical theory as well as corporate, industry and societal standards.*

A Positive Role for Marketing Ethics

While normative approaches to marketing ethics have traditionally held sway, positive approaches to marketing ethics have recently become increasingly popular. Over the years, authors have developed a series of frameworks in order to better understand ethical decision-making in marketing (Ferrell and Gresham, 1985; Hunt and Vitell, 1986; Thompson, 1995). The most widely used of these frameworks has undoubtedly been Hunt and Vitell's (1986, 2006) 'General Theory of Marketing Ethics'. The model attempts to 'explain the decision-making process for problem situations having ethical content' (1986, p. 5). Since publication, the framework has been applied in a range of contexts, with most authors finding significant support for the model (Mayo and Marks, 1990; Hunt and Vasquez-Parraga, 1993; Menguc, 1998; Vitell et al., 2001).

In their 'General Theory of Marketing Ethics', Hunt and Vitell recognize that, when making decisions, marketers draw on both teleological and deontological evaluations and, thus, they build both of these elements into their model (Figure 8.1). They observe that the cultural, industry and organizational environments, as well as past personal experiences, impact upon the individual's perception of the ethical problem. These factors also impact on the perceived alternatives available to them. They suggest that both a

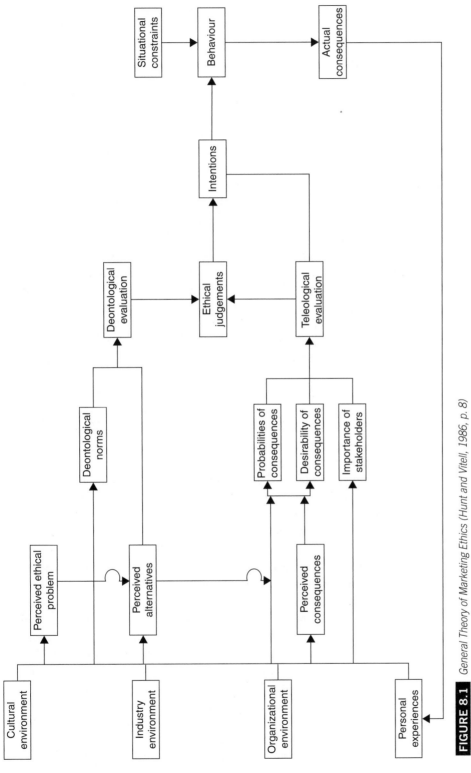

FIGURE 8.1   *General Theory of Marketing Ethics (Hunt and Vitell, 1986, p. 8)*

deontological and teleological evaluation of these alternatives takes place. In the deontological evaluation, they posit that the individual evaluates alternatives against a set of norms including personal values and beliefs. They also observe that these norms include specific beliefs such as 'deceptive advertising, product safety, sales "kickbacks," confidentiality of data, respondent anonymity and interviewer dishonesty' (1986, p. 9). In the teleological evaluation, four constructs are considered, these include '(1) the perceived consequences of each alternative for various stakeholder groups, (2) the probability that each consequence will occur to each stakeholder group, (3) the desirability or undesirability of each consequence, and (4) the importance of each stakeholder group' (1986, p. 9). They also note that individuals will differ in the stakeholder groups they identify and the relative importance of these.

The key part of the model is the combination of these two sets of evaluations. The model posits that 'an individual's ethical judgement (for example, the belief that a particular alternative is the most ethical alternative) is a function of the individual's deontological evaluation (i.e. applying norms of behaviour to each of the alternatives) and the individual's teleological evaluation (i.e. evaluating the sum total of goodness versus badness likely to be produced by each alternative)' (1986, p. 9). Hunt and Vitell then introduce an intentions construct, 'the likelihood that any particular alternative will be chosen' (1986, p. 9), which intervenes between ethical judgement and actual behaviour. They argue that intentions may often differ from ethical judgements due to the influence of teleological evaluations. For example, an individual may reach a conclusion regarding the most ethical course of action but choose another course due to preferred consequences, either to themselves, or perhaps to the organization. In these cases the individual may well feel guilt depending on their individual ethical norms and beliefs. The action taken is also dependent on situational constraints, such as opportunities, and these may also result in behaviours that do not match intentions and ethical judgements. Hunt and Vitell also include a learning construct, the 'actual consequences' of the chosen alternative. These actual consequences feed back into personal experiences and, therefore, highlight the possibility that individuals may, to an extent, become conditioned by their organizational context, i.e. through the operation of punishments and rewards. It is important to note that the cultural, industry and organizational environments, and past personal experiences, as well as affecting the perceived ethical problem and alternatives available, also affect deontological norms, perceived consequences, probability of consequences, desirability of consequences and importance of stakeholders. Thus the model takes account of situational and contextual factors both in the formulation of the problem and the resulting action or behaviour.

Thompson (1995) introduces a further model of marketing ethics arguing that 'the current models of marketing ethics do not sufficiently address the multitude of contextual influences that, from a contextualist perspective, are intrinsic to ethical reasoning' (1995, p. 177). While there is not space here to adequately describe Thompson's contextualist model, an overview of its key components is useful in understanding some critiques of earlier perspectives on marketing ethics. In particular Thompson highlights the 'multiplicity of cultural meaning and value systems' and the fact that the marketing agent is 'culturally situated'. He posits that culturally shared beliefs influence marketing managers' identification of ethical issues, interpretations of the relevant community of stakeholders and evaluations of marketing actions (Thompson, 1995, pp. 183–185).

ETHICAL CRITICISMS OF MARKETING PRACTICE

The marketing practices undertaken by organizations have been criticized for a range of reasons. Three sets of functions of particular contemporary concern are explored below.

Marketing Research and Segmentation

Marketing research is one of the key interfaces between an organization and its public. However, because it relies on collecting personal information from individuals it is open to abuse. The potential ethical pitfalls of marketing research are numerous, both the practices of data collection and the subsequent use of this data present ethical challenges. Murphy et al. highlight a series of issues relating to the professional conduct of market researchers that includes: the duty not to engage in deceptive practices; the duty not to invade privacy; and the duty to manifest concern for respondents (2005, pp. 52–57). In actuality, using the data collected, organizations have been accused of inappropriate stereotyping and the passing on of personal details to other organizations. Data can also easily be manipulated and/or presented in a particular light to tell the story the organization wants to tell. Statistics are well known to be powerful agents in creating arguments because in general people tend to believe them.

The general public in the UK are now so used to requests for their personal information that they often fail to question the use to which this data will actually be put. Personal details are requested in relation to a wide variety of circumstances, ranging from returning goods to a store, to completing guarantees for goods purchased, and applying for store loyalty cards. This also applies to a range of occasional services, from hotel stays, to visiting the hairdresser, or taking the car to the garage. This is in addition to the range of financial and home services which hold details about their customers from credit card, pension, insurance and mortgage companies, electricity, gas, internet and telephone providers. In fact, there are undoubtedly hundreds of organizations that hold data about each one of us. Some individuals would say that this is not a problem. It is a problem, however, when data is used to the consumer's disadvantage, as, for example, when organizations pass details on to other service and goods providers, or bombard individuals with promotional telephone calls, post, emails and text messages. These messages can be very carefully tailored to the individual. By linking purchase histories with personal details, organizations build up a relatively clear picture of the consumers' daily lives, not only their age, gender, occupation and place of residence, but also what they eat and drink, and even the personal hygiene products they use.

This fine grained targeting becomes more of an issue where vulnerable segments are involved. Indeed, a study by Smith and Cooper-Martin (1997) found significant public disquiet over the ethics of some targeting strategies. Vulnerable groups might include children, teens, older consumers and those which Murphy et al. term 'market illiterates' (2005, p. 74). This last group includes those that for one reason or another are not familiar with the workings of the market, this may be due to cultural illiteracy (i.e. in the case of immigrants), but it may also be due to poor access to educational and financial capital. However, Baker et al. point out that 'consumer vulnerability is multi-dimensional, context specific and does not have to be enduring' (2005, p. 128). They refute the commonly held assumption that some individuals, because of membership in a particular group, are always vulnerable, and observe that all individuals may experience vulnerability at some point in their lives due to family death, illness, etc.

Advertising

Advertising is the area of marketing activity which has attracted the most criticism over the years. Research suggests that consumers innately distrust advertising. A review of consumer surveys on beliefs about advertising since the 1930s found that '70% think that advertising is often untruthful, it seeks (perhaps successfully) to persuade people to buy things they do not want, it should be more strictly regulated, and it nonetheless provides valuable information' (Calfee and Jones Ringold, 1994, p. 236). Broadly speaking, advertising has been criticized on two levels: at the micro level the content and type of some messages has been cause for concern, and at the macro level the wider effects of advertising on society have been questioned.

On the micro level, advertisements have been criticized for excessive portrayal of violence, the use of sex and profanity and the elicitation of negative emotions such as shock, fear and guilt (LaTour and Zahra, 1988; Huhmann and Brotherton, 1997; Dahl et al., 2003). In general authors warn against some of the outcomes of using negative emotions in advertising. For example, LaTour and Zahra (1988) express concern for the consumer's psychological well being in the case of fear appeals. Advertising to vulnerable groups such as children, the elderly and those on low incomes has also been a target for criticism. Authors have expressed concern about young consumers, in particular young children's ability to comprehend and interpret advertising (Moore, 2004). They also observe that the blurring of advertising and leisure entertainment makes it particularly difficult for even older children to distinguish between what is, and what is not, an advert (Lindstrom and Seybold, 2003). Carrigan and Szmigin (2000) address the issue of advertising and ageism, arguing that elderly consumers are substantially discriminated against, not only by being marginalized generally in marketing activity, but also by being negatively stereotypically portrayed in advertisements. Advertisements have also been accused of promoting increased levels of anxiety and insecurity in society because they typically encourage processes of social comparison against idealized images. The negative influence of advertising on young women's body image has been a particular cause for concern, and the use of very thin models in fashion advertising has been blamed for an increased incidence of anorexia amongst this group (Fay and Price, 1994).

On the macro level the key issue for critics is the role that advertising might play in manipulating consumers. Packard's (1957) book *The Hidden Persuaders* is often cited in this context. Packard explores the subliminal techniques used by advertisers to manipulate consumer expectations and desire for products and services. More recently, Pollay (1986) posits that 'Advertising is without doubt a formative influence within our culture'. He goes on to conclude that scholars 'see it as reinforcing materialism, cynicism, irrationality, selfishness, anxiety, social competitiveness, sexual preoccupation, powerlessness and/or a loss of self respect' (1986, p. 18). A key strand in subsequent debate about the role of advertising in society is whether it merely reflects a pre-existing reality or whether it actually moulds this reality. In response to Pollay's trenchant critique of the negative effects of advertising Holbrook observes that 'most advertising appears to mirror or reflect rather than to mould or shape the values of its target audience' (1987, p. 100).

Product and Brand Management

Murphy et al. (2005, p. 82) identify a series of ethical issues in relation to product and brand management. In particular, they ask 'what *degree of disclosure* does a product manager owe consumers who will be using the organization's branded product? and what responsibilities do product managers and retailers have related to the *social ramifications* of their products?' The issue of social responsibility becomes obvious when we think about potentially harmful products such as alcohol, tobacco and fast foods.

One of the central ethical issues in relation to harmful products is misleading and deceptive advertising. This has been a particular problem in the tobacco industry where several lawsuits have been filed, accusing the industry of deceptive marketing practices, which have led to mistaken beliefs about smoking. A series of cases have been made against tobacco manufacturers, attempting to hold them responsible for injury, premature death or medical expenses related to tobacco use. Concerns have also been raised over marketing cigarettes to young people. Several studies have observed that adolescents are particularly susceptible to both tobacco and alcohol advertising (Hastings and Aitken, 1995; Pollay et al., 1996). In this respect, the infamous Joe Camel campaign has been the subject of much debate, with commentators arguing that the cartoon character directly targeted the youth market (Calfee, 2000; Cohen, 2000). In an attempt to revive flagging sales, R.J. Reynolds introduced the Joe Camel cartoon character in 1988. As a result of the controversy that followed, the company agreed to cease using the character in 1997. However, Calfee (2000) observes there is little evidence that the campaign did actually precipitate an increase in youth smoking. He also observes that the 'idea' that the advertisements were targeted primarily at underage smokers travelled far and fast in the popular press, government and the public health community. Arguing that, in this respect the campaign fostered a positive outcome, observing: 'This putative role for Joe Camel appears to have substantially increased the level of public and political support for the most important anti-smoking activities of the 1990s' (2000, p. 179).

Questions have also been raised regarding manufacturers' and retailers' responsibilities in relation to unhealthy (and fast) foods. Debate has raged in the context of a rising obesity problem in the adult population, but more worryingly, the child population, in the UK and US. A series of lawsuits have been filed against fast food restaurants in which litigators have tried to draw lessons from the successes of tobacco litigation. The central argument has been that the information provided regarding the nutritional value of fast food products is misleading, leading to overconsumption and eventually, obesity. Allegations have also been made that fast food is addictive. However, as Robinson et al. (2005, p. 305) observe in their analysis of a recent lawsuit against McDonalds, 'those who try to hold food companies legally liable for the costs associated with obesity have a difficult road ahead'. Instead they recommend alternative approaches, such as social marketing, as a solution to combat obesity (see Stead et al., 2007).

The question remains as to what extent manufacturers and marketers might be held responsible for the effects of their products on society. Overall it appears that the key elements in the marketing of potentially harmful products relate to addiction, deception and duty to warn. The first of these is very difficult to militate against, but in relation to the last two issues, deception and duty to warn, perhaps the key issue is one of information and, in particular, the type and level of information provided on packaging and in advertising. Undoubtedly manufacturers have come a long way in this respect. Many fast food retailers and restaurants now produce detailed breakdowns of the fat and nutritional content of their foods for customers. Cigarette and tobacco packaging also contains significant health warnings, and alcohol advertising (in the UK at least) comes with warnings regarding sensible drinking.

Case study: The marketing of cosmetics

Female beauty is a major cultural and financial industry in Western democratic countries. Advertising spend in the cosmetics industry is proportionally higher than in any other sector. Perhaps, then, it is not surprising that ethical breaches occur with some regularity in an industry that is so fiercely competitive and where the stakes are so high. The case study below explores two key ethical elements of cosmetics marketing: deceptive advertising and consumer manipulation.

Deceptive advertising: realistic claims?

The bold claims of cosmetics manufacturers have been the cause for much controversy over the years. Claims such as skin rejuvenation and repair, improved elasticity, smoothing of wrinkles and the reduction of fine lines are routinely made by the industry. One of the key elements in the industry's advertising strategy is the language of science. Cosmetics advertisements often call upon the authority of scientific research for 'proof' that their products are effective. However consumers can easily be misled by this scientific 'jargon' (Sims, 2007). For example, the cosmetics company Olay gives the following description of their anti-ageing skin care product in their online advertising:

> Regenerist reclaims the lifted look of your youth. Phase 1 is specially formulated to ignite cellular regeneration and infuse skin with repairing moisture. Phase 2 helps fill wrinkles with polishing micro-powders and hydrating moisture. The high concentration of peptide-B3 complex also improves skin's moisture barrier, giving you stronger skin structure and a more youthful glow

Another cosmetics company, Avon, offers the following description of their Anew Alternative skin cream:

> For the first time, we can encourage skin to fight the ageing process using Glycation-Reversing Technology. This breakthrough formula helps reverse existing damage and rebuild its support structure. Helps reverse the signs of ageing, restores youthful contours and redefines facial features

The language used here is a careful mixture of scientific sounding terms such as 'Glycation-Reversing Technology'

'Sci-fi' jargon that spreads confusion over skin creams

By **Paul Sims**

COSMETIC firms are misleading women over the effectiveness of skincare creams with incomprehensible scientific jargon, it was claimed yesterday.

The consumer group Which? accused companies including L'Oreal and Garnier of baffling consumers into buying their products.

Television adverts are filled with references to pentapeptides, lipopeptides and hyaluronic acid and claim products will 'refuel surface skin cells' resulting in a 'dewy glow'.

But after posing as a customer and contacting three companies for a better explanation, Which? said the 'evidence' to back up the claims is confusing – even to a trained scientist.

It said: 'Pentapeptides, hyaluronic acid and omega 3 might sound impressive, but scratch beneath the surface of the glossy cosmetic adverts and the claims of some companies don't make a whole lot of sense.'

The consumer magazine said it approached customer services at Olay Regenerist, Garnier Nutritionist Omega Skin and L'Oreal Derma Genesis and asked how its ingredients actually worked on the skin.

They showed the results to Sense About Science, a charity that promotes understandable science, which claimed customers are being 'fobbed off'.

After reading Which?'s transcripts, the scientists said they

CLAIM AND COUNTER-CLAIM

Olay Regenerist claim: 'Pentapeptides are fragments of molecules. They're found naturally throughout the body so they originate from the body.'

Fact: 'Laboratory-made pentapeptides may be chemically indistinguishable from those that occur naturally, but they're not extracting them from real cells.'

Garnier Nutritionist claim: 'Lipopeptides are a natural stimulant that helps the skin.'

Fact: 'Certain lipopeptides can be potent stimulants – of the immune system. But you cannot really link stimulation of the immune system with skin rejuvenation.'

were no wiser about how pentapeptides, lipopeptides or omega 3 managed to 'help with the signs of ageing' or 'improve the appearance of your skin'.

Dr Aarathi Prasad, for the charity, said: 'They are taking the real science out of context so it becomes bad science.

'The words sound cutting edge and are psychologically tantalising, but it's potentially more sci-fi than solid science.

'The words are not clear-cut, even to scientists.

'They imply an effect, but they don't really hold up to scrutiny.'

A spokesman for L'Oreal said: 'Each ingredient is developed specifically for a functional benefit and often represents many years of research.

'Some are established dermatological ingredients and some are developed by L'Oreal scientists and are given names which reflect their molecular origin.

'Hyaluronic acid is, in fact, widely recognised by dermatologists as a high-powered hydrating ingredient which is naturally present in the skin, and which helps lock moisture in the skin.'

p.sims@dailymail.co.uk

Reproduced with permission of Daily Mail

and complex ingredients such as 'peptide-B3 complex'. These phrases are used alongside the active terminology of fighting, polishing, hydrating, repairing, redefining, reversing and restoring. Impressive results are also claimed such as a 'stronger skin structure and a more youthful glow'.

The industry has made questionable claims not only in relation to its advertisements but also its labelling. For example sunscreen makers have been accused of making misleading health claims on their labelling which over-inflate the sun protection abilities of their products. This is a particular problem in products designed for use on young children. In fact the power of language is central to the cosmetics industry's promotional efforts. In the UK, the Advertising Standards Agency has reprimanded the manufacturers of skin care creams for using misleading terminology in their advertising campaigns, making assertions, such as 'the home alterative to surgery' and 'steering hearty cells to the base of wrinkles'. The use by skin care manufacturers of science to bias the opinion of consumers regarding their products might easily be seen as exploitative, in particular by taking advantage of the poor scientific and technological knowledge of the population. A second issue relating to deception is perhaps more straightforward with some cosmetics manufacturers digitally manipulating advertising images, airbrushing out skin imperfections, lengthening eye lashes and enhancing eye colour. Recently two major cosmetics manufacturers in the UK (Rimmel and L'Oreal) were censored by the Advertising Standards Agency for using false eye lashes on models in their advertisements for mascara.

Consumer manipulation: playing on anxieties?

Although individual advertisements might be charged with making unrealistic claims and inflating the properties of products, taken as a whole these types of advertisements also impact significantly on wider consumer society. Cosmetics advertising relies on the consumer's desire to look young and attractive and plays a role in setting the tone and extent of these desires. One of the most powerful techniques of persuasion used in cosmetics advertising is the suggestion that a sense of improved self esteem will result from using the products. As Reventós observes 'Hidden beneath the glamorous ideals in beauty ads there are subtexts that play on women's anxieties and feelings of inadequacy, while promising a sense of self-worth' (1998, p. 32). To this end, the industry promotes a range of problems, many of which women did not even know they had, such as pale skin or thin eye lashes, and to which they are offered the ideal magical solution. As Reventós suggests 'many beauty ads appeal specifically to our sense of magic, to the "Cinderella" syndrome: the magic of personal transformation that is part of the imaginative life of most women' (1998, p. 34).

Whilst relying on men and women's anxieties surrounding appearance, these advertisements arguably play a role in actually impacting upon our everyday practices of personal hygiene. For example, women and some men are now generally persuaded that having a 'skin care routine' involving several different products is now essential for

healthy and attractive skin. Of course, this takes time as well as costing money. There is a similar trend in hair care products where manufacturers have created a number of product niches based on new hair styling techniques such as straightening, curling and colouring hair. An array of gels, mousses, creams, lotions and serums have emerged, each one creating a different hair fashion. The cosmetics industry (as have many other industries) has relentlessly pursued a policy of niche product diversification and extension. Sales of these products rely on creating a consumer need for a wider array of products. Another way in which manufacturers have achieved this, is by dividing the body up into an increasing number of discrete zones and persuading the consumer that each zone requires a different type of cosmetic product. For example, skincare products are sold in the form of eye creams, as well as neck and face creams. Research suggests that the ingredients in these creams do not differ very significantly between product types, and that in fact the main way in which they differ is through price and packaging size.

Who is responsible?

The Advertising Standards Authority (ASA) is the chief regulator of advertising in the UK. The mission of the agency is to 'apply the advertising codes and uphold standards in all media on behalf of consumers, business and society' (ASA website). The main principles of these codes are that advertisements should not mislead, cause harm or offend. Recently the ASA surveyed 445 cosmetic advertisements appearing on television, radio, direct mailings, online, on posters and in the press. In assessing the advertisements, using the ASA codes, they found that 32 (7%) represented obvious breaches of the codes. Three of these 32 advertisements were investigated by the ASA after receiving complaints and all three were found to be unacceptable. The survey found that the key problems were 'unsubstantiated cumulative beneficial effect claims and physiological claims for skin creams for women' (Advertising Standards Authority, 2007, p. 2). Within the cosmetics category advertisements for skin creams were a particular cause for concern, with a breach rate of 19 per cent.

INTERNET RESOURCES

The Academy of Marketing – 'Marketing and Ethics Special Interest Group'. http://www.academyofmarketing.info/ethicssig/sigethics.cfm

Advertising Standards Authority. http://www.asa.org.uk/

The American Marketing Association – statement of ethics. http://www.marketingpower.com/AboutAMA/Pages/Statement%20of%20Ethics.aspx?sq=ethics

The Market Research Society's code of conduct. http://www.mrs.org.uk/standards/codeconduct.htm

KEY READINGS

Brenkert, G. (2008), *Marketing Ethics*. Oxford: Blackwell.

Hunt, S.B. and Vitell, S.J. (2006), 'The general theory of marketing ethics: A revision and three questions', *Journal of Macromarketing*, 12 (26), 143–153.

Laczniak, G.R. and Murphy., P.E. (2006), 'Normative perspectives for ethical and socially responsible marketing', *Journal of Macromarketing*, 12 (26), 154–177.

Robin, D.P. and Reidenbach, E. (1993), 'Searching for a place to stand: Toward a workable ethical philosophy for marketing', *Journal of Public Policy and Marketing*, 12(1), 97–105.

SEMINAR EXERCISES

Discussion Topics

1. Discuss the pros and cons of taking a deontological approach versus a teleological approach to decisions surrounding marketing ethics.

2. Using examples discuss the extent to which you think manufacturers and marketers might be held responsible for the effects of their products on society.

3. Discuss the importance of ethics in marketing research. Identify the ethical factors that need to be taken into consideration at each stage of research design, data collection and the reporting of findings.

4. 'Marketing creates unnecessary needs and wants.' Discuss the ethical implications of this statement. To what extent do you agree with it?

Group Exercises

1. Using one of the examples below prepare a presentation summarizing the key ethical debates in the case concerned. Use real

life examples from marketing magazines, newspaper reports and marketing websites to illustrate your discussion.

(i) The promotion and sale of unhealthy or harmful products.

(ii) The targeting of vulnerable segments in advertising campaigns.

(iii) The invasion of consumer privacy through intrusive marketing practices.

2. Look up the Advertising Standards Association's (ASA) top ten most complained about advertisements in their annual report (this can be found on their website). For each advert discuss:

(i) Why the advert might be seen as unethical.

(ii) Which groups you think the advert is most likely to offend.

(iii) Whether or not you agree with the ASA's ruling and why.

3. Consider the following scenario (adapted from Lund, 2000, p. 334):

Sarah Jones is the marketing manager of a large building company. She is designing an advertisement for a new housing development her company is about to start building. The development is located in a low area which has flooded in the past. The company has recently done some work to reduce the danger of flooding in the future. The fact is that if a flood occurs, the homes are still likely to be flooded with up to five feet of water.

Identify the alternatives available to the marketing manager.

For each of these alternatives:

(i) Identify the stakeholders that would be affected.

(ii) Identify the probable consequences of the decision for each stakeholder group.

(iii) Identify the desirability of these consequences for each stakeholder group.

Given the above considerations identify which alternative you would choose and why.

REFERENCES

Abela, A.V. and Murphy, P.E. (2008), 'Marketing with integrity: Ethics and the service-dominant logic for marketing', *Journal of the Academy of Marketing Science*, 36 (1), 39–53.

Advertising Standards Authority (2007), *Compliance Report: Cosmetics Advertising Survey*. London: ASA.

Baker, S.M., Gentry, J.W. and Rittenburg, T.L. (2005), 'Building understanding of the domain of consumer vulnerability', *Journal of Macromarketing*, 25 (2), 128–139.

Bartels, R. (1967), 'A framework for ethics in marketing', *Journal of Marketing* (January), 20–26.

Brenkert, G. (2008), *Marketing Ethics*. Oxford: Blackwell.

Calfee, J. (2000), 'The historical significance of Joe Camel', *Journal of Public Policy and Management*, 19 (2), 168–182.

Calfee, J.E. and Jones Ringold, D. (1994), 'The 70% majority: Enduring consumer beliefs about advertising', *Journal of Public Policy and Marketing*, 13 (2), 228–238.

Carrigan, M. and Szmigin, I. (2000), 'Advertising in an ageing society', *Ageing and Society*, 20, 217–233.

Chonko, L. (1995), *Ethical Decision-making in Marketing*. Sage: Thousand Oaks, CA.

Cohen, J.B. (2000), 'Playing to win: Marketing and public policy at odds over Joe Camel', *Journal of Public Policy and Marketing*, 19 (2), 155–167.

Dahl, D.W., Frankenberger, K.D. and Manchanda, R.V. (2003), 'Does it pay to Shock? Reactions to shocking and non-shocking ad content among university students', *Journal of Advertising Research*, 43 (3), 268–280.

Fay, M. and Price, C. (1994), 'Female body shape in print advertisements and the increase in anorexia nervosa', *European Journal of Marketing*, 28 (12), 5–18.

Ferrell, O.C. and Gresham, L.G. (1985), 'A contingency framework for understanding ethical decision-making in marketing', *Journal of Marketing*, 49 (summer), 87–96.

Gaski, J. (1999), 'Does marketing ethics really have anything to say? A critical inventory of the literature', *Journal of Business Ethics*, 18 (3), 315–334.

Gellerman, S.W. (1986), 'Why "good" managers make bad ethical choices', *Harvard Business Review* (July/August), 85–90.

Hastings, G.B. and Aitken, P.P. (1995), 'Tobacco advertising and children's smoking: A review of the evidence', *European Journal of Marketing*, 29 (11), 6–17.

Holbrook, M.B. (1987), 'Mirror, mirror, on the wall, what's unfair in the reflections on advertising?', *Journal of Marketing*, 52 (July), 95–103.

Huhmann, B.A. and Brotherton, T.P. (1997), 'A content analysis of guilt appeals in popular magazine advertisements', *Journal of Advertising*, 26 (2), 35–45.

Hunt, S.B. (1976), 'The nature and scope of marketing', *Journal of Marketing*, 40 (July), 17–28.

Hunt, S.D. and Vasquez-Parraga, A. (1993), 'Organizational consequences, marketing ethics and salesforce supervision', *Journal of Marketing Research*, 30 (February), 78–90.

Hunt, S.B. and Vitell, S.J. (1986), 'A general theory of marketing ethics', *Journal of Macromarketing*, 6 (5), 5–16.

Hunt, S.B. and Vitell, S.J. (2006), 'The general theory of marketing ethics: A revision and three questions', *Journal of Macromarketing*, 12 (26), 143–153.

Laczniak, G.R. (1983), 'Framework for analyzing marketing ethics', *Journal of Macromarketing*, 6 (3), 7–18.

Laczniak, G.R., Berkowitz, M., Brooker, R. and Hale, J. (1995), 'The ethics of business: Improving or deteriorating?', *Business Horizons*, 38 (1), 39–47.

Laczniak, G.R. and Murphy, P.E. (1985), *Marketing Ethics: Guidelines for Managers*. Lexington, MA: Lexington Books.

Laczniak, G.R. and Murphy, P.E. (1993), *Ethical Marketing Decisions: The Higher Road*. Toronto: Allyn and Bacon.

Laczniak, G.R. and Murphy, P.E. (2006), 'Normative perspectives for ethical and socially responsible marketing', *Journal of Macromarketing*, 12 (26), 154–177.

LaTour, M.S. and Zahra, S.A. (1988), 'Fear appeals as advertising strategy: Should they be used?', *Journal of Services Marketing*, 2 (4), 5–14.

Lindstrom, M. and Seybold, P.B. (2003), *Brandchild: Remarkable Insights into the Minds of Today's Global Kids and their Relationships with Brands*. London: Kogan Page.

Lund, D.B. (2000), 'An empirical examination of marketing professionals' ethical behaviour in differing situations', *Journal of Business Ethics*, 24, 331–342.

Mayo, M. and Marks, L. (1990), 'An empirical investigation of a general theory of marketing ethics', *Journal of the Academy of Marketing Science*, 18 (2), 163–171.

Menguc, B. (1998), 'Organizational consequences, marketing ethics and salesforce supervision: Further empirical evidence', *Journal of Business Ethics*, 17 (4), 333–352.

Moore, E.S. (2004), 'Children and the changing world of advertising', *Journal of Business Ethics*, 52 (2), 161–167.

Murphy, P.E. and Laczniak, G.R. (1981), '*Marketing ethics: A review with implications for managers, educators and researchers*', *Review of Marketing*. pp. 251–266. Chicago: American Marketing Association.

Murphy, P.E., Lacinak, G.R., Bowie, N. and Klein, T. (2005), *Ethical Marketing*. Upper Saddle River, NJ: Pearson Prentice Hall.

Nill, A. and Schibrowsky, J.A. (2007), 'Research on marketing ethics: A systematic review of the literature', *Journal of Macromarketing*, 27, 256–273.

Packard, V. (1957), *The Hidden Persuaders*. London: Longmans, Green.

Pollay, R.W. (1986), 'The distorted mirror: Reflections on the unintended consequences of advertising', *Journal of Marketing*, 50 (April), 18–36.

Pollay, R.W., Siddarth, S., Siegel, M., Haddix, A., Merritt, R.K., Giovino, G.A. and Eriksen, M.P. (1996), 'The last straw? Cigarette marketing and realized market shares among youths and adults, 1979–1993', *Journal of Marketing*, 50, 1–16.

Reventós, D.M. (1998), 'Decoding cosmetics and fashion advertisements in women's magazines', *Cuardernos de Filologia Inglesa*, 7 (1), 27–39.

Robin, D.P. and Reidenbach, E. (1987), 'Social responsibility, ethics and marketing strategy: Closing the gap between concept and application', *Journal of Marketing*, 51 (January), 44–58.

Robin, D.P. and Reidenbach, E. (1993), 'Searching for a place to stand: Toward a workable ethical philosophy for marketing', *Journal of Public Policy and Marketing*, 12 (1), 97–105.

Robinson, M.G., Bloom, P.N. and Lurie, N.H. (2005), 'Combating obesity in the courts: Will lawsuits against McDonalds work?', *Journal of Public Policy and Marketing*, 24 (2), 299–306.

Sims, P. (2007), 'Cosmetic firms mislead women over skin creams with si-fi jargon', *Daily Mail*, December 21.

Smith, C. (1995), 'Marketing strategies for the ethics era', *Sloan Management Review*, 36 (summer), 85–97.

Smith, C. (2001), 'Ethical guidelines for marketing practice: A reply to Gaski and some observations on the role of normative ethics', *Journal of Business Ethics*, 32 (1), 3–18.

Smith, C. and Quelch, J. (1993), *Ethics in Marketing*. Homewood, IL: Irwin.

Smith, N.C. (1993), 'Ethics and the marketing manager', in N.C. Smith and J.A. Quelch (eds), *Ethics in Marketing*. Homewood, IL: Irwin, pp. 3–34.

Smith, N.C. and Cooper-Martin, E. (1997), 'Ethics and target marketing: The role of product harm and consumer vulnerability', *Journal of Marketing*, 61 (July), 1–20.

Stead, M., McDermott, L. and Hastings, G. (2007), 'Towards evidence-based marketing: The case of childhood obesity', *Marketing Theory*, 7 (4), 379–406.

Thompson, C.J. (1995), 'A contextualist proposal for the conceptualization and study of marketing ethics', *Journal of Public Policy and Marketing*, 14 (fall), 177–191.

Vitell, S., Singhapakdi, A. and Thomas, J. (2001), 'Consumer ethics: An application and empirical testing of the Hunt–Vitell theory of ethics', *Journal of Consumer Marketing*, 18 (2), 153–178.

CHAPTER 9

Sustainable Marketing and the Green Consumer

Caroline Miller

INTRODUCTION

This chapter considers the green consumer and sustainable marketing which is a term that appears to be paradoxical. Marketing is defined by Kotler et al. as, 'a social and managerial process by which individuals and groups obtain what they need and want through creating and exchanging products and value with others' (Kotler et al., 2008, p. 7) and sustainability means, 'Meeting the needs of the present without depleting resources or harming natural cycles for future generations' (www.cdc.gov/healthyplaces). With the current growth in population in many third world countries and the rise of consumerism in many developed countries sustainability and marketing seem in contradiction with each other (Table 9.1).

Marketing is a business function which has been criticized for fuelling consumption and encouraging materialism by stimulating wants as a means of satisfying human needs. Organizations benefit financially by providing products to meet consumer demand. Society is also considered to benefit by rising consumer spending as customers get what they want, organizations make profits and grow, creating employment. Materialism is seen as good because it is considered to promote economic growth and therefore it is seen to signify development which is understood as progress. Economic growth is usually measured by Gross Domestic Product per capita so countries that produce less are seen as less developed and to have made less progress (Bartelmus, 1994). Yet, Grove and Kilbourne (1994) suggest that marketers may promote materialistic values as positive in the short term but that this increased consumption of material goods will have long term deleterious effects. Daly and Townsend (1993) and Georgescu-Roegen

Table 9.1 Contrasting the sustainability and conventional marketing mindsets. Adapted from Peattie (2009)

Perspective	Sustainability thinking will require greater	Existing marketing thinking provides
Timeframe	Multi-generational futurity	Present, short-/mid-termism
Key objective	Promotion of welfare	Gratification
Guiding principle	Equity	Consumer sovereignty
Focus on addressing	Needs of communities (particularly of the poor)	Wants of individuals (particularly of the rich)
Worldview emphasizing	Global preservation and conservation	Global consumption and production systems
Setting	Environmental limits	Economic hyperspace

(1993) consider that if we continue to pursue progress through economic growth using finite resources such as water, oil and forests to fuel this then eventually it will lead to disaster:

> The world is warming up. As we burn up the planets coal, oil and gas reserves, and cut down its remaining forests, greenhouse gases are pouring into the atmosphere. The delicate balance of atmospheric gases that sustains life is thickening, trapping more and more heat and irreversibly changing our world ... an average temperature rise of around 1.3 degrees centigrade above pre-industrial levels is already inevitable and will bring with it some terrible impacts worldwide (www.greenpeace.org.uk).

The implications for people and for organizations are huge. Organizations will no longer be able to sustain production because nature will not be able to keep pace with consumer culture. 'During the 1990's the Newfoundland cod fishery collapsed sending a ripple of warning to fisheries across the world. It has not shown any signs of recovery. Its failure alerted fisheries round the world to the issue of conservation and sustainability' (Raffael, 2004, p. 2). Because of a shortage of raw materials (like coal or wood or fish), products may become too expensive for consumers because as non-renewable resources become scarce they will increase in price (we have already seen this with oil and food). Ultimately if global warming starts to affect human life then organizations face the depletion of their market, and people may face a future not with an unhealthy obsession with things but with difficulty in the acquisition of the necessities to sustain human life (water, clean air, food).

This chapter discusses how marketing activities have been blamed for current inequalities between the rich and the poor, using up natural resources, creating pollution and contributing to human and environmental decline. We examine the ways in which organizations can fulfil the wants and needs of the present whilst considering the requirement to conserve natural resource for future generations. We chart the struggle that organizations and consumers have between behaving responsibly for the benefit of everyone in the long term or in choosing short term gain. Regulation legislation and government initiatives are shown to have positive and negative impact upon how firms behave, we explore the managerially focused aspects of this through green marketing, identifying target markets and the green consumer, whilst also looking at the ethical implications of unsustainable marketing decisions. We then look at the potential for sustainability as well as the difficulties facing sustainable marketing in the future.

THE BIRTH AND EVOLUTION OF SUSTAINABLE MARKETING

Meadows (1972) and Woodhouse (1992) suggest that if population growth, industrialization, food production, resource depletion and pollution continue unchanged, 'then the limits to growth on the planet would be reached in the next one hundred years' (Woodhouse, 1992, p. 98). Meadows (1972) and Woodhouse (1992) show concern with the depletion of natural resources but also with the after effects of consumption – disposal, which is seen to be one of the main causes of pollution.

Organizations have been blamed for much of this pollution to the environment by the green movement who have drawn our attention to: pumping out emissions from oil and coal and gas into the air; disposal of chemical and nuclear waste; dangerous pollutants released into our streams, rivers and oceans; and the despoilment of our habitat with non-biodegradable packaging.

Pezzey (1992) in a paper, entitled 'Sustainability: An Interdisciplinary Guide', lists a range of effects linked to human economic activity:

1. Depletion of renewable resources (forest, fish, land and sea mammals).

2. Depletion of known reserves of non-renewable energy and minerals.

3. Depletion of non-renewable stock of genetic diversity (some plants and animals may become extinct) and soil (through erosion).

4. Severe problems of local and transient pollution in industrialized countries.

5. Problems of cumulative pollution (smog, acid rain, ozone depletion, greenhouse gases, global warming).

6. Wide growing inequalities between the rich and the poor.

7. Increased rates of change.

Environmental decline has been documented and discussed since the beginning of the Industrial Revolution, though limitations to economic growth as a result of resource shortages and pollution were not seen as problematic until the publication of Rachel Carson's (1962) book *Silent Spring* which demonstrated how human interaction with the environment was negative and likely in the long term to be significant (Kilbourne, 2004). Carson (1962) explained how insecticides accumulated in the food chain, eventually reaching toxic levels, killing birds and mammals, and provided evidence of invisible long term systemic damage. In 1985 a hole in the ozone layer was discovered during the British Antarctic Survey (for information on the hole in the ozone: www.antarctica.ac.uk). It was believed to have started in the 1930s as a result of using aerosols, refrigerant gas and cleaning fluids containing chlorofluorocarbons (CFCs – also known as freon). This depletion of the ozone was thought to be the cause of air pollution, acid rain, the greenhouse effect and global warming and has also been linked to increased levels of eye problems, skin cancer and damage to the immune system in humans.

'International concern resulted in the setting up of the United Nations World Commission on Environment and Development (the Brundtland Commission)' (Woodhouse, 1992, p. 98), who submitted a report entitled 'Our Common Future' (WCED, 1987), which set out concerns regarding environmental degradation, resulting in recognition that environmental and economic development issues should be treated with equal importance. The Brundtland Commission's definition of sustainable development is: 'Development that meets the needs of the present without compromising the ability of future generations to meet their own needs' (WCED, 1987, p. 42). Woodhouse (1992) suggests that there are three interpretations of sustainable development:

1. Neo-liberal View – 'The environment is natural "capital". The services derived from air, water, soil, biological diversity and recreation (the countryside etc.), depend on maintaining those environmental "assets" intact or renewing them' (Woodhouse, 1992, p. 111). This can lead to debt equity swaps where agencies like the World Wildlife Fund settle part of the debt of a country in order to control conservation of threatened ecological resources. It has been denounced as a form of neo-colonialism.

2. Populist View – 'The need for priority in development to be given to securing "sustainable livelihoods" for the poorest groups within communities' (Chambers, 1988 in Woodhouse, 1992, p. 113). Local communities reclaim economic control of their resources (Fairtrade), or local trade for local needs. There is some scepticism that local manufacturers have the ability to maintain production without outside support and so could be regarded as unsustainable.

3. Interventionist View – 'This view emphasizes international co-operation' (Woodhouse, 1992, p. 114), usually through

Table 9.2	Significant steps and setbacks: toward sustainable marketing
1962	Publication of Rachel Carson's book *Silent Spring* which shows how insecticides enter the food chain killing birds and mammals
1971	United Nations Anti Desertification Plan
	United Nations Tropical Forest Action Plan
1985	Hole in the ozone discovered by British Antarctic Survey
1986	Brundtland Report *Our Common Future* (WCED, 1987)
1987	United Nations environmental programme set out to measure and reduce use of CFCs
1990	Montreal Protocol to stop using CFCs by 2000
1990	1st Earth Summit (Rio) Publication of Agenda 21 – Governments commit to pursue sustainability
1991	Backlash against 'green marketing' – confusion and reluctance – consumers fail to engage with green products
1997	4th International Framework Convention on Climate Change
	Introduction of the Kyoto Protocol
2002	2nd Earth Summit (Johannesburg)
2005	Kyoto Protocol was ratified by 55 countries and became a legally binding treaty to cut greenhouse gas emissions
2007	Kyoto Protocol supported by 175 parties

international environmental treaties enforced by international agencies like the United Nations. The first treaty of this sort was the Montreal Protocol to eliminate the use of CFCs. There can be conflict as some countries fight to defend affected industries.

It was from the Brundtland Report (1987) that the idea of sustainable development was borne and hence some significant steps toward sustainable marketing (Table 9.2).

SUSTAINABLE MARKETING AND CORPORATE RESPONSIBILITY: SOME AMBIGUITIES

Peattie (2006) considers that moving industries and economies towards an environmentally and socially sustainable future will indeed be a challenge for marketers. Though sustainable development has its advocates there are also arguments against the need for change toward sustainability. Peattie (2006) offers the following rationale as argument against sustainability:

- Threats to the environment are considered to be exaggerated.

- Lack of scientific consensus on environmental issues like global warming means the need for change to sustainable development is seen as unproven. A Pew survey conducted in January 2007 registered a growing awareness among Americans of rising average temperatures, but little agreement on its cause. '... advertisers are not allowed to make reference to the view that human economic activity causes global warming because there is still scientific debate about it' (Grande, 2007, p. 16).

- Technological advances in how we make and dispose of products will make the need for change unnecessary.
- Sustainable development will disadvantage poorer countries.

Sustainability is often met with suspicion and distrust, particularly by developing countries as much global environmental change is seen to have been caused by rich countries which have already gone through a process of industrialization (Turner, 1993). It is the wasteful consumption, conspicuous consumption (Veblen, 1899) and materialistic lifestyle of industrialized nations that has put stress on the resources of developing countries. 'It is the view of some elements in the United Nations that poor countries are growing poorer because they are "exploited" by the global trading system' (United Nations Development Programme, 1992, Ch. 4). It is not surprising that many people in organizations are not interested in corporate social responsibility as defined in the document Corporate Social Responsibility: A Government Update which states:

> *Today, corporate social responsibility goes far beyond the old philanthropy of the past – donating money to good causes at the end of the financial year – and is instead an all year round responsibility that companies accept for the environment around them, for the best working practices, for their engagement in their local communities and for their recognition that brand names depend not only on quality, price and uniqueness but on how, cumulatively, they interact with companies' workforce, community and environment. Now we need to move towards a challenging measure of corporate responsibility, where we judge results not just by the input but by its outcomes: the difference we make to the world in which we live, and the contribution we make to poverty reduction. (Brown, 2004, p. 2)*

Companies often do not seek to engage in activities that have positive effects on the environment, society or promote public welfare because they are driven by short term profit and fear that this type of activity will have a negative affect on the bottom line. 'Being environmentally sustainable is a tricky business and companies need to conduct a thorough appraisal of all aspects of their business if they want to claim to be truly green. A company's environmental impact spans its greenhouse gas emissions, its use of natural resources, the effect of its products on the natural world, and the effect of its employees' (Harvey, 2007, p. 1). Peattie and Crane (2005) consider that commentators try to oversimplify the 'win–win' opportunities linked to change and that this is not surprising as companies would be more reluctant to engage in socially responsible activities if they were framed as complex, difficult and as involving compromise.

REGULATION/LEGISLATION

As environmental and welfare concerns have grown over the last decade it has become harder for people in organizations to resist taking responsibility for their actions especially when they are faced with accepting their responsibility, or alternatively with the threat of regulation and legislation. Political parties are becoming increasingly proactive in their stance toward sustainable development as David Cameron has made it clear that, 'As a government [you should be] trying to get business to face up to its responsibilities and behave responsibly, and if that doesn't work then there is always the threat of regulation and legislation at the end of it' (Parker, 2008, p. 2). Pezzey (1992) considers that it would be better for the process of sustainable development if people were less materialistic, avoided binge–purge cycles of consumption and moved houses and jobs less often but, as this would often run counter to an individual's best interests and Western notions of freedom and mobility, then policies or regulatory controls are needed to apply economic disincentives. The type of practice Pezzey (1992) suggests putting in place comprises:

- reducing the power of the mass media;

- taxing advertising and other mean of propagating materialism;

- tax increases on individual transport and telecommunications to discourage transience and dispersion;

- the use of public education to discourage materialism;

- encouraging people to adapt to lower standards of living.

Some of these policies have already been put into place. Congestion charges were introduced into London in 2003 to try to reduce the amount of traffic creating fumes (other cities have developed similar schemes like Stockholm, Singapore and Milan):

From March 13 2008, bills for cars falling in tax bands C to F will increase by £5 for a 12 month tax disc. Tax bands A and B remain the same at zero and £35 respectively, while motorists forking out for band G tax will see their bill increase to £400 … From April 2010, many new car buyers will have to pay a special "first year rate" tax, which Chancellor Alistair Darling says will encourage buyers to choose greener cars … Cars which emit less than 100 g/km of CO_2, such as the Volkswagen Polo Bluemotion and Seat Ibiza Ecomotive will remain tax exempt … The Chancellor also announced a tax cut for drivers of alternative-fuel cars in 2009, which range from £15 to £20, however from 2010 this discount will be a £10 flat rate (www. autotrader.co.uk).

Organizations as well as individuals are affected by environmental regulation. For a taste of how environmental regulations affect businesses in the UK visit www.envirowise.gov.uk where you can see how The Clean Air Act (1993), The Environmental Protection Act (1990), Control of Pollution Act (1989), Controlled Waste Regulations Act (1992) and other regulations and controls affect organizations.

Environmental taxes often hurt the very people they are put into place to protect (the poor), for example the high cost of fuel for cars and for heating has a greater impact on the lives of the poor, as do schemes like increased tax charges on older more polluting cars and garbage disposal charges. Governments are often reluctant to regulate because they fear that environmental legislation will in some way affect their pursuit of economic growth. Laws and regulations governing industrial practices affecting the environment are often criticized by organizations as the heads of these organizations complain they have to invest hundreds of thousands of pounds to put in pollution control equipment or in finding alternative sources of power. Owners of organizations (particularly smaller businesses) resent and often try to resist regulation, as they claim that absorbing the cost of imposed charges to protect the environment or the people living in it makes them less competitive.

GREEN MARKETING

Many organizations who start out in an environmentally responsible manner are finding that it has a positive affect on profits. 'Paul Rowley knowledge transfer co-ordinator at the centre for Renewable Energy at Loughborough University and co-founder of the energy advice web site Greenenergy 360. org said ... There are two real advantages for a small business becoming green. One is branding and marketing advantage. The other is the impact on the bottom line' (Bridge, 2008, p. 17). A positive relationship was also found by Wokutch and Spencer (1987) between corporate social responsibility and financial performance.

More and more companies are incorporating profit-centred activities with environmentally friendly practices. For example, Shell are now building a new GTL (Gas to Liquid) plant in Qatar which is capable of producing cleaner GTL fuel in an attempt to improve the problem of growing city air pollution (Shell DVD – Clearing the Air, 2008). Shell are practising environmental sustainability, producing profits whilst also attempting to improve living conditions and maximize life quality. Other organizations, like Wrap and Heinz, have joined forces in a project of product stewardship, redesigning materials used in can ends and bodies in order to reduce the impact of the product on the environment not just in its lifetime but also in order to reduce its effect as waste (www.iema.net).

Business Ethics Magazine annually rates companies and lists the top 100 socially responsible organizations. In 2007 the top ten best corporate citizens were: Green Mountain Coffee Roasters Inc., Advanced Micro Devices Inc., Nike Inc., Motorola Inc., Intel Corporation., International Business Machines Corporation, Agilent Technologies Inc., Timberland Company, Starbucks Corporation and General Mills Inc. (www.business–ethics.com). The concept of sustainability underpins green marketing. Kotler et al. (2005) suggest there are four levels of environmental sustainability:

1. *Pollution control/prevention* – cleaning up waste after it has been created or minimizing waste through green marketing programmes or by developing safer biodegradable or recyclable products and/or packaging.

2. *Product stewardship* – minimizing all environmental impacts throughout the full product life cycle (designing products which are easier to recover, reuse or recycle).

3. *New environmental technologies* – investing in research and development to pre-empt fully sustainable strategies, for example developing environmentally biodegradable washing products which also wash on a low temperature hence making energy savings.

4. *Sustainability vision* – develops a framework to show how the company's products, service, processes and policies comply with pollution control/prevention, product stewardship and new environmental technologies.

Unfortunately, some companies practise green marketing at the most basic level. McDonagh and Prothero (1997) infer that companies may be inadvertently engaging with green marketing on a simplistic level because there are so many meanings and issues related to environmentalism (such as sustainability, animal conservation, human rights, planet conservation, fair trade, organic trade, corporate social responsiveness ...) that green marketing becomes much more complex than the term may at first suggest.

Crane (2000) suggests that there has been a significant backlash against green marketing. Organizations in the 1990s were thought merely to have paid lip service to green marketing in order to make profits from rising consumer concerns regarding the environment following tragedies such as the Bhopal chemical poisonings (1984), Chernobyl's fatal radioactivity release (1986) and the Exxon Valdez oil spill (1989).

Green marketing was also discredited because of underperforming products, products made from re-cycled material were seen as inferior, overzealous promotion campaigns, inexact science (terms such as biodegradable, recyclable and environmentally friendly – were unproven) and legislation was inconsistent. There was no scientific proof that these 'environmentally friendly' products had any more positive effects on the environment than their predecessors, but companies were making money and enhancing their reputations as caring organizations based on these spurious claims.

THE GREEN CONSUMER

'There [was also] considerable evidence to suggest that the much vaunted consumer concern for the environment and concomitant desire for green products had not subsequently translated into purchase behaviour' (Crane, 2000, p. 280). In an article in the *Financial Times*, William Young, a lecturer in environment and business at Leeds University's School of Earth and Environment, said, 'Sustainability is a tendentious catch-all term with a certain political flavour and its own contradictions. It is hardly surprising, therefore, that the public at large is confused or indifferent'. Hutchins and Young (2005) also go on to suggest, 'There is no green consumer' which seems to be supported by the findings of a study undertaken by the National Consumer Council who admits that their research shows that '70 percent of the population do not know what the term means, and only 19 percent of consumers say they would welcome information on sustainable lifestyles' (Hutchins and Young, 2005, p. 6).

However, Dobscha and Ozanne (2001) consider that consumers who are concerned about the environment are obscured by the managerialist focus of literature which reports on green marketing. In their article on women seeking ecologically friendly solutions they followed McDonagh and Prothero (1997) in finding that women seeking eco-friendly solutions were having an impact upon current marketing practices. As individuals increasingly seek to live a life in harmony with nature consumption necessarily gets relegated to second place (for more on eco-feminism see www.greenspirit.org.uk and www.the greenfuse.org). As a conservation attitude, rather than a consumption attitude, is adopted and individuals opt for voluntary simplicity building anti-materialist/anti-consumption communities (like Ashley Vale[1]), ecologically friendly marketers are faced with considering the true environmental costs of all their decisions.

> *An ecologically friendly marketplace would include pricing that estimates environmental costs, less packaging and the use of more recyclable materials, advertising that has environmentally accurate information, and bulk purchasing to reduce packaging. More radical forms of eco-markets would encourage less consumption, local products and markets. And systems of barter ... (Dobscha and Ozanne, 2001, p. 210)*

---

[1] A brown site near Bristol which has been redeveloped by a not-for-profit community group, creating a sustainable housing project.

Yet, too often green marketing is seen by organizations as a marketing tool by which companies merely adapt their product to suit demand for environmentally friendly products (for example – dolphin friendly tuna, eco-friendly washing powder, fair-trade goods). Carrigan et al. suggest that companies get caught up in, 'What is desired by consumers' (Carrigan et al., 2005, p. 483) but that they may not be necessarily questioning what is good for them. As the market is becoming increasingly aware of issues relating to sustainability, 'marketers are finding it harder to ignore the "ethics gap" between what society expects and what marketing professionals are delivering' (Laczniak, 1993 in Carrigan et al., 2005, p. 490).

There are many examples of customers rejecting technically excellent products because of the environmental harm caused in their production or disposal (for example, Nike experienced boycotts when they used sweatshop labour). Individuals may choose to eat fair trade chocolate because they are concerned that coco farmers in developing countries get a fair day's pay for their labour. Harrison, Newholm and Shaw suggest that consumers may reject products because they have, 'political, religious, spiritual, environmental social or other motives for choosing one product over another … Ethical purchasing, is therefore, a very broad expression embracing everything from ethical investments (the ethical purchasing of stocks and shares) to the buying of fair trade products, and from consumer boycotts to corporate environmental purchasing policies' (Harrison et al., 2007, p. 2). In their book entitled *The Ethical Consumer*, Harrison , Newholme and Shaw develop a useful typology of ethical consumer practices which range from boycotting unethical companies, positive buying of eco-friendly products to conserving rather than consuming as practised by the eco-feminists discussed earlier.

Pre 1980 many organizations were offering products to what was considered a niche market at an inflated cost to the consumer, but, as more people became environmentally savvy, organizations have worked hard to stratify what was once believed to be an homogenous green market into, 'shades of green segments' (Roper Starch Worldwide, 1996). For example, the market was divided into True Blue Greens, Greenback Greens, Sprouts, Grousers and Basic Browns, with True Blue Greens most likely to purchase green products and Basic Browns being completely disinterested (for discussion of the difference between these segments see Fuller, 1999, pp. 334–337).

Peattie and Crane (2005) feel that disillusionment with green marketing stems from the consumer's distrust of organizations because of five failed manifestations of green marketing:

1. *Green spinning* – Reputation management through PR, not dialogue, by organizations who are targets of criticism (usually those in 'dirty' industries such as oil, chemicals, pharmaceuticals, automotive).

2. *Green selling* – A post-hoc promotion of environmental features of an existing product (there is usually no product development).

A promotional campaign vaunts the product's desirable green features to push sales. Very often these green features are unproven and theses types of claims have led to a consumer who is cynical and suspicious.

3. *Green harvesting* – Companies gain economies by reducing packaging or through energy saving efficiencies. Savings are not passed on to the consumer. Although the green product may cost the company less to produce, they sell at a premium to cash in on consumer interest in green products.

4. *Enviropreneur marketing* – There are two types: Boutique Enviropreneur products, here small start-up firms focus on bringing innovative green products to market (The Bodyshop, Calico Moon, Ectopia). Corporate enviropreneurs, by contrast, offer organized ranges alongside their regular products (Sainsbury, Boots).

5. *Compliance marketing* – Organizations limit environmental initiatives to planned or expected regulation. They usually use compliance to promote their newly adopted green credentials.

All five categories previously mentioned are, according to Peattie and Crane (2005), examples of false green marketing or greenwashing. Greenwashing is described by John Grant (2007) in his book *The Green Marketing Manifesto* as putting a lettuce in the window of your butchers shop and declaring you now cater for vegetarians.

As Dax Lovegrove, head of business and industry relations at World Wildlife Fund, points out: 'A lot of oil and gas companies talk about alternative energies and offsetting, but this distracts from the real issue because their industry is about sucking oil out of the ground ... the rhetoric has to match the reality of what a company is doing to address sustainability issues, as opposed to tinkering around the edges or communicating a red herring' (Grande, 2007, p. 16).

One of the major challenges for marketing lies in how it can help to move organizations and industry sectors towards a more environmentally sustainable path.

Organizations that practise green marketing in a truly socially responsible manner are considered by Peattie and Crane (2005) to exhibit four important characteristics. They are:

1. *Customer facing* – They undertake market research into customer wants, needs, attitudes and beliefs and knowledge. They research the needs of the company's other stakeholders and consider their impact upon future generations of customers.

2. *Have a long-term perspective*.

3. *Fully use company resources* – 'Actions or policies of any part
   of the company or its supply chain do not compromise the eco-
   performance of products' (Peattie and Crane, 2005, p. 265).

4. *Innovative* – In market structures and supporting services as well
   as product and product system technology, this means considering
   renting rather than selling products, improving product longevity,
   offering service and maintenance, reducing environmental impact
   through disposal by buying back and/or recycling.

An example of a company that put green marketing into practise through
implementing environmentally sustainable programmes and committing
fully to corporate social responsibility is Svenska Cellulosa Aktiebolaget
(SCA) who are featured in the case study at the end of this chapter.

THE POTENTIAL AND LIMITATIONS OF SUSTAINABLE MARKETING

Kilbourne (2004) acknowledges the limitations of sustainable marketing
particularly in Western societies. He suggest that it is likely to have mini-
mal impact because the underpinning philosophy which drives sustainability not only, runs counter to the tenants of marketing (Table 9.1), but also
contradicts the dominant social paradigm (collection of norms, beliefs, values and habits) (Kilbourne, 2004) predominant in Western industrialized
society (individualism, capitalism, etc.).

> *Within capitalism, for example economic growth is a necessary*
> *condition for the accumulation of capital ... The superordinate goal*
> *of society must, therefore, be consistent with and produce economic*
> *growth. One natural choice for this goal is the material conception*
> *of progress, or the accumulation of material wealth ... Because*
> *capitalism does not produce high levels of social justice ... it plays no*
> *part in capital accumulation ... (Kilbourne, 2004, p. 195)*

In addition to this, individuals, organizations and countries have pluralistic
views on the need for environmental sustainability and differing objectives
and abilities where economic, social and environmental protection/conserva-
tion are concerned. For example, poorer countries often have to exploit their
resources often exporting to richer nations to meet survival need or to pay
debts. Whilst exploiting these resources may meet short term survival needs,
it may be sewing the seeds for long term impoverishment as a result of environmental degradation. Sustainability cannot be about balancing economic
growth with environmental protection, pitting society and its wants and
needs against nature. Whichever perspective wins out the result can only be
a pyrrhic victory. As McDonagh and Prothero suggest, true sustainability can

Case study: Svenska Cellulosa Aktiebolaget (SCA) (sources: SCA Annual Report 2007, SCA Sustainability Report 2007, www.sca.com)

Svenska Cellulosa Aktiebolaget (SCA) is a company which develops, produces and markets personal care, tissue, packaging and forest products (toilet tissues, diapers, feminine care or sanitary products, incontinence products, publication papers and solid-wood products), and which operates in more than ninety countries. Sustainability is an integrated part of SCA's business activities as SCA not only wants to create shareholder value but chooses to do this in a way that contributes to a good environment for future generations as well as economic prosperity for current stakeholders.

Responsibility for the environment and corporate social responsibility (CSR) issues are based on SCA's core values: respect, responsibility, excellence and a commitment to openness and transparency, and is managed by the Group's Senior Management Team (The Sustainability Council). The Environmental and CSR Committees prepare sustainability policies, principles, targets and action programmes through an internal dialogue process involving environmental networks and CSR workgroups within the organization and externally with the communities they serve and with other stakeholders. External governance consists of a number of laws where the Swedish Companies Act is the foundation, the company's policies and procedures are also influenced by the Swedish Code of Corporate Governance, Stockholm stock exchange rules and regulations and Swedish accounting legislation. In many cases, SCA goes beyond just abiding by legislation and regulations. SCA encourages an ongoing dialogue with its stakeholders. Shareholders contribute at the annual general meeting, customers and consumers are reached through regular surveys and are invited to share their opinions on visit days, employees feedback through regular meetings and surveys, suppliers through relationship management and close monitoring, investors at analyst meetings and society in general as SCA publicly debates issues in the communities within which they operate. SCA co-operate with various NGOs including the World Wide Fund for Nature. SCA has four sustainability targets, three of which are environmental targets (efficient use of water,

reduction of carbon dioxide emissions, ensuring responsible use of raw materials) and the fourth focuses on compliance with SCA's Code of Conduct (Figure 9.1).

The company has been involved in environmental and social issues since its foundation in 1929. Early initiatives focused on investment in the building of churches, houses and general infrastructure in the communities within which it operated. More recent initiatives range from a project which is a joint development with Norweigan Statkraft to build wind turbine power parks in Northern Sweden to produce green electricity, investments in new combustion plants to reduce carbon dioxide emissions and to use production waste as fuel and so reduce other forms of pollution, responsible forestry – so setting aside felling in order to conserve and to maintain biological diversity (e.g. leaving stumps of trees to create habitats for insects and birds and conserving storm resistant pines to create conditions for large birds of prey to nest), using waste as a potential energy resource rather than sending it to landfill already mentioned (EU Directive on waste states landfill to be cut by 65% by 2015).

Every year SCA gets actively involved in projects designed to improve the every day lives and health of women around the world. In 2007 SCA supported the Dignity!Period. Campaign (www.actsa.org) launched by Action for Southern Africa which highlighted the plight of women in Zimbabwe where due to hyperinflation (amongst other things) women could no longer afford to pay for sanitary towels. SCA donated 250,000 packs of Bodyform sanitary products and generated a further £50,000 in donations. SCA also participates in a variety of activities and initiatives to raise support for and awareness of research and education into various forms of cancer. Other examples of community involvement include:

- Sponsorship of different sports and activities to raise awareness of incontinence in order to reduce social stigma associated with the condition.

- SCA sent medical personnel to help in 2007 when Mexico suffered severe flooding in the Tabasco

Target 1

More efficient use of water

How?

- Reduce consumption
- Reduce organic content in effluent water

Target 2

Reduce emissions of carbon dioxide

How?

- Transition from fossil fuels to biofuels
- Use alternative energy production: investment in wind power, Soda recovery boiler
- Energy savings through the internal programme ESAVE

Target 3

Responsible use of raw materials

How?

- Assess suppliers so raw material not from controversial sources: No illegally harvested timber, timber from forests with high conservation values, timber harvested in violation of human rights/affects indigenous peoples

- Manages forests according to forestry stewardship councils' international forestry management standards

Target 4

Compliance with SCA's code of conduct

How?

- Human rights assessment of sites to limit exposure to corruption and human rights abuse

- Continuous improvements in health and safety performance

- Rapid detection of legionella

- Respect for human rights – supports principles of UN Declaration of Human Rights

- Community involvement

FIGURE 9.1 *SCA's code of conduct. Source: SCA Sustainability Report www.sca.com*

region. They also donated personal care products, rubber boots, rainwear, torches, uniforms, insect repellent and medicines.

- SCA partnered with an international pharmaceutical company to educate women in Central America about the risks of cervical cancer.

SCA's high standards of corporate social responsibility attract investments, 'The proportion of investments in SCA shares which in some respect have sustainability as a criteria rose from 5 to 10% between 2004–2007' (SCA Annual Report, 2007, p. 53), and awards – second in the World's Greenest Company survey carried out in *The Independent* (2007). SCA was ranked among the Global 100 Most Sustainable Corporations in the world by the British consulting firm Innovest. SCA is also convinced that the group's sustainability initiatives improve its ability to compete when tendering for profitable contracts. The company has recently won a contract to supply Wembley Stadium with tissue for all their toilets.

More information about SCA's sustainability work can be found in the 2007 Sustainability Report which is available on www.sca.com.

only be achieved, 'along holistic principles ... Window-dress[ing] green strategies by company marketing departments will ultimately fail and embarrass if they are not backed up by an integrated approach throughout the whole organization' (McDonagh and Prothero, 1997, p. 385). What we need to rethink is the culture-nature nexus – to engender, 'a less is more attitude ...' (Kilbourne, 2004, p. 202) changing individuals, organizations, countries norms, beliefs, values and habits as consistently as possible with each other to try and engender widespread social responsibility for long term change.

CONCLUSION

In this chapter we have illustrated how sustainable marketing is a paradoxical term. Trying to balance conservation and consumption is not only a challenge for organizations but also for individuals. People are often irresponsible in trying to satisfy their wants and needs. Be it in borrowing too much for that shiny new car which incidentally may impoverish an individual's life in other areas and which in ten years time will probably be rotting on a scrap heap, or in selling slightly dodgy products to enhance an organization's bottom line without thought to the consequences. It is still not clear if green marketing has been as successful for the planet as it has been for many organizational balance sheets, but many people seek eco-friendly solutions. Companies may be trying to fulfil consumer wants and needs without a thought for the future but increasingly companies are being forced to face the consequences of their actions and are being coerced to consider ethics first rather than last. Sustainability may be highly difficult and complex to put into practice at an individual and at an organizational level, nevertheless the potential of sustainability for the future could be huge if every individual contributed in a community of practice which focused on protection, preservation and conservation rather than capital accumulation and consumption.

INTERNET RESOURCES

ACTSA. Action for South Africa. www.actsa.org
British Antarctic Survery. www.antarctica.ac.uk
Corporate social responsibility. www.mallenbaker.net/csr/index.html
Global 100 Sustainable Companies. www.global100.org
The Green Consumer. www.greenconsumerguide.com, www.gdrc.org
The green fuse – environmental philosophy. www.the greenfuse.org
Greenpeace. www.greenpeace.org.uk
GreenSpirit. www.greenspirit.org.uk
Legislation and regulation. www.envirowise.gov.uk
Sustainable marketing website. www.csr.gov.uk
The World Wildlife Fund. wwf.org.uk

KEY READINGS

Banerjee, B. (2007), 'Managing sustainability', in S. Linstead, L. Fulop and S. Lilley (eds), *Management and Organization A Critical Text*. Houndmills: Palgrave Macmillan, pp. 155–181.

Clegg, S., Kornberger, M. and Pitsis, T. (2008), 'Managing sustainability: ethics and corporate social responsibility', in *Managing Organizations: An Introduction to Theory and Practice*. London: Sage Publications.

Hart, S.L. (1997), 'Beyond greening: Strategies for a sustainable world', *Harvard Business Review*, January/February, 66–76.

Kangun, N. (1974), 'Environmental problems and marketing: saint or sinner?', in J.N. Sheth and P.L. Wright (eds), *Marketing Analysis for Societal Problems*. Urbana: University of Illinois Press, pp. 250–270.

Thompson, J. (1995), 'Sustainability, justice and market relations', in R. Eckersley (ed.), *Marketing the State and the Environment*. London: Macmillan.

Van Dam, Y.K. and Apeldoorn, P.A.C. (2008), 'Sustainable marketing', in M. Tadajewski and D. Brownlie (eds), *Critical Marketing*. Chichester: John Wiley.

SEMINAR EXERCISES

Discussion Topics

1. Discuss the positive and negative aspects of both materialism and environmentalism.

2. Consider some of the paradoxes and ambiguities which relate to sustainable marketing and discuss in your groups.

3. Woodhouse (1992) suggests there are three interpretations of sustainable development (neo-liberal view, populist view, interventionist view). Discuss the positive and negative aspects of each interpretation.

4. What are the main benefits of, and problems for, organizations and individuals of corporate social responsibility and sustainable marketing?

Group Exercises

1. Using the SCA case study as a template for a company that practises corporate social responsibility and commits to sustainable marketing, identify a company of your choice that you think is as committed to these issues as SCA.

   (i) Justify your choice by detailing characteristics which you consider show it to be a truly green organization.

(ii) Try to identify targets that the company has set toward sustainable development and describe how it aims to meet these targets.

(iii) Consider the benefits and problems for the organization of your choice of implementing CSR/sustainability programmes.

(iv) What things do you think this company could do in the future to enhance its reputation as responsible and ethical?

2. Each student should identify a number of organizations that allegedly practise green marketing. Try to identify those that are:

(i) Green spinning.

(ii) Green washing.

(iii) Green selling.

(iv) Green harvesting.

(v) Enviropreneur marketing.

(vi) Compliance marketing.

(vii) Justify your distinctions.

3. Take a product of your choice which you consider may not be environmentally friendly and consider how to develop a sustainable marketing programme for this product.

(i) Consider how you will meet the needs of your customer and the environment.

(ii) How may you segment, position and target your market?

(iii) Which of Kotler's four levels of sustainability (pollution control/prevention; product stewardship; new environmental technologies; sustainability vision) are you using?

(iv) How through the marketing mix will you implement a sustainable strategy for your product?

REFERENCES

Banerjee, B. (2007), 'Managing sustainability', in S. Linstead, L. Fulop and S. Lilley (eds), *Management and Organization A Critical Text*. Houndmills: Palgrave Macmillan, pp. 155–181.

Bartelmus, P. (1994), *Environment, Growth and Development the Concepts and Strategies of Sustainability*. London: Routledge.

Bridge, R. (2008), 'Green means go for new firms', *Sunday Times*, March 9, p. 17.

Brown, G. (2004). 'Corporate Social Responsibility. A Government Update', DTI. www.csr.gov.uk

Carrigan, M., Svetla, M. and Szmigin, I. (2005), 'Ethics and international marketing', *International Marketing Review*, 22 (5), 481–493.

Carson, R. (1962), *Silent Spring*. Boston: Houghton Mifflin.

Clegg, S., Kornberger, M. and Pitsis, T. (2008), 'Managing sustainability: ethics and corporate social responsibility', in *Managing Organizations: An Introduction to Theory and Practice*. London: Sage Publications.

Crane, A. (2000), 'Facing the backlash: green marketing and strategic reorientation in the 1990's', *Journal of Strategic Management*, 8 (3), 277–296.

Daly, H. and Townsend, K. (1993), *Valuing the Earth: Economics, Ecology, Ethics*. Cambridge MA: MIT Press.

Dobscha, S. and Ozanne, J.L. (2001), 'An ecofeminist analysis of environmentally sensitive women using qualitative methodology: the emancipatory potential of an ecological life', *Journal of Public Policy and Marketing*, 20 (2), 201–214.

Fuller, D. (1999), *Sustainable Marketing Managerial–Ecological Issues*. London: Sage.

Georgescu-Roegen, N. (1993), 'The entropy law and the economic problem', in H. Daly and K. Townsend (eds), *Valuing the Earth: Economics, Ecology, Ethics*. Cambridge, MA: MIT Press.

Grande, C. (2007), 'Consumption with a conscience', *Financial Times*, June 19, p. 16.

Grant, J. (2007), *The Green Marketing Manifesto*. Chichester: John Wiley.

Grove, S.J. and Kilbourne, W.E. (1994), 'A Mertonian Framework for the analysis of the debate: advertising's role in society', *Journal of Current Issues and Research on Advertising*, 16 (2), 16–28.

Harrison, R., Newholm, T. and Shaw, D. (2007), *The Ethical Consumer*. London: Sage Publications.

Hart, S.L. (1997), 'Beyond greening: Strategies for a sustainable world', *Harvard Business Review*, January/February, 66–76.

Harvey, F. (2007), 'More than printers and cycle racks', *Financial Times*, June 7, p. 1.

Hutchins, D. and Young, W. (2005), 'Its not easy being green', *Financial Times*, October 28, p. 6.

Kangun, N. (1974), 'Environmental problems and marketing: saint or sinner?', in J.N. Sheth and P.L. Wright (eds), *Marketing Analysis for Societal Problems*. Urbana: University of Illinois Press, pp. 250–270.

Kilbourne, W.E. (2004), 'Sustainable communication and the dominant social paradigm: Can they be integrated', *Marketing Theory*, 4 (3), 187–208.

Kotler, P., Armstrong, G., Wong, V. and Saunders, J. (2008), *Principles of Marketing*, 5th European edition. Harlow: Pearson/Prentice Hall.

Kotler, P., Wong, V., Saunders, J. and Armstrong, G. (2005), *Principles of Marketing*, 4th European edition. Harlow: Pearson/Prentice Hall.

Laczniak, G. (1993), 'Marketing ethics: onward toward greater expectations', *Journal of Public Policy and Marketing*, 12, 91–96.

McDonagh, P. and Prothero, A. (1997), *Green Management A Reader*. London: The Dryden Press.

Meadows, D.H. (1972), *The Limits to Growth*. New York: Universe Books.

Parker, G. (2008), 'Cameron tells business to accept social responsibilities', *Financial Times*, March 17, p. 2.

Peattie, K. (2006), 'Sustainable marketing: marketing re-thought, re-mixed and re-tooled', in M. Saren, P. Maclaran, C. Goulding, R. Elliot, A. Shankar and M. Catteral (eds), *Critical Marketing Defining The Field*. Berkshire: Butterworth Heinemann, pp. 192–210.

Peattie, K. (2009), 'Rethinking marketing', in T. Cooper, (ed.), *Longer Lasting Solutions: Advancing Sustainable Development Through Increased Product Durability* Surrey: Ashgate.

Peattie, K. and Crane, A. (2005), 'Green marketing: legend, myth, farce or prophesy?', *Qualitative Market Research An International Journal*, 8 (4), 357–370.

Pezzey, J. (1992), *Sustainability: An Interdisciplinary Guide' from Environmental Values in American Culture*. I. Cambridge: The Whitehorse Press pp. 321–362.

Raffael, M. (2004), 'Tales of the sea: Catch 22', *The Observer*, September 26, p. 2.

Roper Starch Worldwide (1996), *The Green Gauge Reports*. New York: RSW Inc.

Shell (2008), 'Clearing the Air', DVD.

Thompson, J. (1995), 'Sustainability, justice and market relations', in R. Eckersley (ed.), *Marketing the State and the Environment*. London: Macmillan.

Turner, R.K. (1993), *Sustainable Environmental Economics and Management*. London: Belhaven Press.

United Nations Development Programme (1992), Agenda 21. www.un.org

Van Dam, Y.K. and Apeldoorn, P.A.C. (2008), 'Sustainable marketing', in M. Tadajewski and D. Brownlie (eds), *Critical Marketing*. Chichester: John Wiley.

Veblen, T. (1899), *The Theory of the Leisure Class*. New York: Macmillan.

WCED (1987), *Our Common Future*. Oxford: Oxford University Press.

Wokutch, R.E. and Spencer, B.A. (1987), 'Corporate saints and sinners: the effects of philanthropic and illegal activity on organizational performance', *California Management Review*, XXIX (2), 62–77.

Woodhouse, P. (1992), 'Environmental degradation and sustainability', in T. Allen and A. Thomas (eds), *Poverty and Development in the 1990's*. Oxford: Oxford University Press.

www.autotrader.co.uk.

www.business-ethics.com.

www.greenpeace.org.uk.

www.iema.net.

www.sca.com.

CHAPTER 10

Social Marketing and Consumer Citizenship

Effi Raftopoulou

INTRODUCTION

This chapter examines social marketing, a relatively recent development in marketing thought, broadly concerned with social change. Social marketing relates to the use of marketing concepts and technologies to promote particular ideas or behaviours, with the aim to assist in the solution of social problems. Some of the most prominent social marketing applications include anti-smoking, safe driving and other health-related campaigns. Such campaigns have been arguably very successful in raising awareness and promoting behaviour change. As a result, an increasing number of organizations and government departments are adopting marketing for the promotion of social causes. For example, the UK government has been, over the past few years, consistently amongst the top spenders in advertising expenses, demonstrating the increasing importance of marketing tools for contemporary governments (Hastings, 2007).

Through social marketing, marketing use has extended beyond the commercial sphere and has radically changed the nature of our participation as citizens in the solution of social problems. For example, we are frequently reminded through advertisements and promotions of the benefits of recycling for the environment, and we are greatly assisted and encouraged in our efforts through easy access to recycling facilities and monetary or other incentives. This makes social marketing a particularly interesting and important field as it concerns very significant aspects of social life.

This chapter explores the field of social marketing. Perhaps it would be too ambitious to offer a universally accepted definition of social marketing, so, in order to better understand the field, we first examine the history of its development and then we discuss the scope and nature of the field alongside some of the relevant academic debates. We then outline the main concepts as described in the literature and examine the potential as well as the difficulties and criticisms of social marketing. The following section initiates the discussion by describing the birth of the social marketing concept.

LITERATURE REVIEW

The Birth and Evolution of Social Marketing

The idea that marketing tools and methods can be used outside the domain of commodities was first expressed by Wiebe (1951–52), who suggested that social causes can be promoted more successfully if tools and principles similar to those in commercial marketing are used. Taking this point forward, a seminal article by Kotler and Levy (1969) proposed that marketing use should also be explored in the context of non-physical 'products', such as services, organizations and people. They maintained that a wide range of not-for-profit organizations, groups or individuals, for example museums, universities or politicians, were already undertaking marketing activities, in one form or another. Their proposal for a broadened concept of marketing received mixed reactions, with some marketing academics expressing enthusiasm, and others being rather sceptical.

The initial reluctance to adopt marketing in the non-commercial arena focused upon the notion that the concept of marketing loses its meaning if extended outside the realm of market transactions or economic exchange (Laczniak and Michie, 1979). Thus, it was felt that the traditional boundaries of the discipline should be maintained, as it is difficult to define a field that involves transactions for which the nature of 'exchange' cannot be accurately determined. Further to this, it was argued that marketing is not merely a framework or tool that can be applied in any field of study (Luck, 1969). In consequence, a broader view of marketing was seen as imperialistic and problematic, particularly as it resulted in unclear boundaries and responsibilities for marketers. Nevertheless, the proponents of the extension of the marketing concept argued that even in commercial marketing, the notion of 'exchange' is not restricted to monetary exchange, but may also include symbolic aspects. The debates on the broadened concept of marketing went on in academic circles, with several advocates and opponents.

Following a period of introspection and debate around the limits and scope of the field of marketing, a range of different subfields emerged, including educational, arts, place, relationship, political and social marketing. These subfields are seen as part of the natural evolution of the marketing field, brought about by the increased needs of non-business organizations for marketing services. Social marketing in particular is seen as a positive response by marketers to the intensified criticism of marketing for its negative impact on society.

The term 'social marketing' was first introduced by Kotler and Zaltman in 1971 as: '... the design, implementation, and control of programmes calculated to influence the acceptability of social ideas and involving considerations of product planning, pricing, communications and marketing research' (p. 5). Thus, this first definition linked particular marketing tools and methods with the promotion of social ideas. During those early years of development of the field, its tools were increasingly adopted by practitioners, but most campaigns consisted primarily of advertising elements. Thus, social marketing was often identified with social advertising. It was, however, argued that practitioners should adopt a wider-than-advertising approach, which would also include other marketing elements, such as marketing research, product development, segmentation and a more conscious marketing orientation. At that stage, the field lacked a sound theoretical basis and most social marketing projects were short of proper design and implementation. Despite these deficiencies, social marketing became quite popular particularly in the field of health promotion, a development which further advanced its establishment as a substantial field of marketing and boosted efforts for the formation of a more solid theoretical basis. Social marketing continued to expand in terms of applications in later years, with a wide range of organizations and governments promoting various social causes. Some examples include campaigns against gun crime, homophobia and anti-social behaviour or campaigns promoting recycling.

Although there still seems to be some disarray in terms of the boundaries and the scope of the field, social marketing has evolved significantly and is currently a well-established part of the marketing discipline (Andreasen, 2003). The field is also developing in terms of its theoretical basis to a more independent (from commercial marketing) foundation. One indication of this evolution is the establishment of specialized research centres such as the Social Marketing Institute in Washington, the Institute for Social Marketing (Open University and University of Stirling), the Centre for Social Marketing Research (University of Wollogong), the publication of social marketing textbooks (e.g. Kotler et al., 2002; Donovan and Henley, 2003; Andreasen, 2005) and the launch of an academic journal on the subject (the *Social Marketing Quarterly*). Although these developments point to the fact that social marketing is developing in terms of theory and application, there is a widely recognized need for further theoretical development of the field, perhaps away from commercial marketing analogies and tools (Peattie and Peattie, 2003).

Understanding Social Marketing: Clarifying Some Ambiguities

The initial definition of social marketing did not succeed in providing clear boundaries of the field and, in fact, even nowadays, the term is understood in rather different ways by marketing scholars. We examine some renewed attempts to define the scope of the field and discuss social marketing in relation to other marketing fields.

A recent, popular definition describes social marketing as:

> *the adaptation of commercial marketing technologies to programmes designed to influence the voluntary behaviour of target audiences to improve their personal welfare and that of the society of which they are a part. (Andreasen, 1994, p. 110)*

This definition associates social marketing with behaviour change. However, it has been suggested that social marketing should focus on the advancement of social ideas, rather than persuasion for behaviour change (e.g. Fine, 1990). Although most writers in the field adopt a broader view (one that encompasses both ideas and behaviours), others argue that by limiting social marketing to behaviour change, the field can be better differentiated from other disciplines (e.g. education) (Andreasen, 1994). Arguably though, an attempt to change people's behaviour may inevitably involve modification in their attitudes, values and ideas (Brenkert, 2002). Therefore, social marketing essentially extends beyond behaviour change. Levy and Zaltman (1975) also propose that social marketing plans may seek to achieve different levels of social change, i.e. short or long-term change. When such programmes aim for short-term change and address the individual, the intended outcome is behaviour change. However, if these plans focus on particular groups, their aim is administrative change or change in norms, whereas if they address society as a whole, their aim is change in policy. Similarly, if social marketing plans are focusing on long-term change and they target the individual, then their aim is a change in lifestyle, whereas if they target particular groups or society as a whole, their aims are organizational change and socio-cultural evolution respectively. Therefore, social marketing programmes can extend far beyond behaviour change, depending on their scope and objective.

The ambiguity in terms of the defining characteristics and scope of the field is also reflected in much of the theoretical and practical work in the field, where, quite often, the boundaries between social marketing and other related fields are unclear. Some scholars, for instance, adopt a perspective of social marketing that includes aspects of marketing relevant to social responsibilities. Nowadays, the term 'societal marketing' is seen as more appropriate for this field. The difference between 'social' and 'societal' marketing is that the former has as its primary aim to change attitudes, beliefs and behaviours of individuals or organizations for a social benefit, whereas the latter is concerned with socially responsible marketing practices (Webster, 1975).

Still another ambiguity concerns whether social marketing refers to all marketing activities undertaken by not-for-profit organizations. Public and not-for-profit organizations frequently engage in the promotion of social change, but they may also undertake marketing activities for the promotion of services, (for example, museum or library services). The terms 'non-profit marketing' or 'public sector marketing' (Fox and Kotler, 1980) encompass the whole range of activities such organizations undertake, whereas social marketing refers only to these activities aimed at social change. Furthermore, social marketing is often identified with health promotions, mainly due to the wide application and development of social marketing theory in this field. However, social marketing also deals with social change outside the domain of health (e.g. anti-racism campaigns). In addition, health communication activities extend further than social marketing (e.g. education), although social marketing appears to be the most developed and broadly accepted approach in public health promotion (Maibach and Holtgrave, 1995).

Private-sector firms can also engage in the promotion of social change, but social change is seen as their secondary and not their primary aim (as profit is their primary aim). The term 'cause-related marketing' is deemed to be more appropriate (Brønn and Vrioni, 2001). To summarize, as Webster (1975) points out, much of the confusion surrounding the scope and limits of non-commercial marketing fields can be attributed to the fact that some of these fields are defined on the basis of their 'product', whilst others are defined on the basis of the organization adopting the tools.

Although some of the above ambiguities relevant to the definition and scope of social marketing remain unresolved. Both academics and practitioners are unanimous in that 'social good' (or individual social welfare) is central, as it is the motivating force behind social marketing campaigns (Murphy and Bloom, 1992). Thus, whilst commercial marketers address the consumer, social marketing efforts target the citizen and promote their wares on the premises of personal and social well-being.

SOCIAL MARKETING ELEMENTS

A large part of the theoretical underpinnings of social marketing have their roots in commercial marketing. Similarly to generic marketing, social marketing is not a theory on its own; rather, it draws on other disciplines, such as psychology, sociology, anthropology and communications theory. The following elements are generally seen as central to social marketing: (i) consumer orientation, (ii) the notion of exchange, (iii) competition, (iv) long-term planning and (v) the marketing mix (Grier and Bryant, 2005). As a result of the ambiguities surrounding the field, there are several debates surrounding these concepts which are reflected in the discussion below.

Consumer Orientation

The consumer is seen as the focal point of all forms of marketing. The principle of 'consumer orientation' is also central in social marketing despite the slight incongruity of the term 'consumer' with the sphere of social ideas and behaviours. The focus on the consumer has arguably moved social marketing from 'expert-led' approaches, to consumer-driven and thus more inclusive and relevant approaches (Hastings and Saren, 2003). It should be noted that instead of the term 'consumer', the term 'target adopter' is often seen as more appropriate for social marketing.

The perceptions, needs and wants of the target adopters are central throughout all stages of marketing planning. Thus, substantial information on the target audience is crucial. This information defines who is being asked to change ideas, behaviours or attitudes, what their current ideas are and how best to approach them. Research, segmentation and targeting are essential elements of social marketing plans and they inform to a great extent the strategies adopted. Some common segmentation variables in social marketing programmes include current behaviour, future intentions, readiness to change and psychographics.

One of the main difficulties in adopting a consumer-centred approach is that it often proves complicated and costly for organizations to conduct market research, because (i) it is difficult to obtain valid and reliable measures for ideas and behaviours, (ii) it is hard to define the relative influence of particular factors on behaviour and (iii) certain target groups are hard to identify and reach (Bloom and Novelli, 1981). Further to this, the choice of a target audience is rather difficult and challenging, as it is often hard to decide which social group is most in need of a particular programme. Notwithstanding these difficulties, it is essential for social marketing programmes to understand and focus on the target adopters.

Exchange Theory

Exchange theory has arguably been key to any understanding of marketing, and has facilitated the broadening of the marketing concept outside its traditional boundaries. The theory of exchange proposes that consumers act primarily out of self-interest with the aim of achieving the greatest benefit while incurring the minimum cost (Bagozzi, 1978). This means that marketers have to create an offer of value for their target audience.

In social marketing, exchange theory implies that the marketer has to understand and offer benefits that the target adopter values. This entails an understanding of the costs (monetary or otherwise) involved in the attitude or behaviour change and a subsequent offer of incentives. Therefore, the 'change agent' (i.e. the organization, group or individual that invites people to change their behaviour, ideas or attitudes), has to create an offer that will be attractive to target adopters.

Since the marketing concept has been understood so far in terms of satisfaction and profit, and these terms become irrelevant in the context of social marketing, it is more difficult to conceptualize exchange in this respect (Peattie and Peattie, 2003). Furthermore, it has proved rather difficult in practice to create an attractive offer, as the costs involved in social or individual change are not often tangible (e.g. the time, effort and physical discomfort involved), noticeable, individual or immediate (e.g. when taking up recycling) and thus they are difficult to define and reduce. Exchange is symbolic, as well as material, and it often involves psychological, social or other intangible elements. In addition, exchange in marketing should be governed by the freedom to accept the offer and the desire to engage in the transaction. However, as Hastings and Saren (2003) argue, it is rather problematic for social marketers to ensure that target adopters are capable of communicating their views and able at all times to accept or reject the offer. Oftentimes, social marketing programmes are interwoven with other governmental actions towards a social issue, restricting the ability of the individual to freely determine their behaviour (e.g. a programme against child obesity that regulates the availability of particular foods in schools).

Competition

Apart from creating an attractive offer, a social marketing programme has to make that offer more attractive than that of the competition. In this case, competition no longer refers to products and companies that try to satisfy similar needs and wants with the company's product or service, but refers to other behaviours that compete with the one promoted. One example of this is the convenient choice of fast food, instead of eating healthy, home-cooked meals. The aim of the marketer is to identify what benefits can distinguish their offering from competitive behaviours. It is, however, quite difficult to identify the driving forces behind people's behaviours and attitudes, and rather challenging to create an offering that will persuade people to change their long-term, established behaviours and deeply held attitudes or ideas. Peattie and Peattie (2003) also suggest that social marketing efforts may face competition from commercial marketing when promoting opposing causes but also from other social ideas, apathy or unwillingness.

Long-term Planning and Sustainable Change

One of the main advantages of social marketing is arguably the strategic, long-term planning approach it offers to organizations. This is essential for behaviour change that takes a long time and needs commitment and close co-operation between an organization and the target audience. However, often it is the long-term commitment required in achieving sustainable change, and the complexity of the social issues involved, that make it hard to convince organizations to undertake and finance such activities.

The Marketing Mix

The framework of the marketing mix has been the cornerstone of social marketing plans, but the four traditional elements of the mix are redefined. Although in its emergence social marketing was restricted to predominately promotional or communication activities, it is nowadays generally agreed that such efforts should be based on an integrated marketing mix, and a conscious marketing orientation on the part of organizations (Hill, 2001).

In the context of social marketing, the product is perceived as the behaviour or idea promoted and the associated set of benefits. The main objective of social marketing programmes is to make this product relevant and attractive to the target audience. Andreasen (1997) suggests that the product in social marketing can be perceived in relation to three dimensions: the core idea (i.e. the belief, attitude or idea promoted); the associated behaviour (sustainable or single act) and the relevant tangible object or service that can assist behaviour change.

The multiple dimensions of the social market create great complexity in the definition of what the product is and what the benefits are. The marketer no longer has to deal with tangible elements and attributes such as packaging, name, physical attributes, positioning but with ideas, behaviours and attitudes that often involve careful consideration by the target adopter. Another challenging feature of the social marketing product is that there is less flexibility to shape the offering and it is difficult to convey associated benefits as it relates to behaviours and ideas. It is also more challenging to persuade people to change long-term and fairly stable behaviours, especially in complex economic, social and political climates, with often very limited resources. Frequently, social marketers have to deal with negative demand and apathy or resistance, so, in situations where the product benefits are intangible and relevant to society, rather than individuals, benefits are difficult to personalize and quantify.

Price, on the other hand, refers to all types of costs to the individual that the change of behaviour involves. Instead of 'price' the term 'transaction costs' is seen as more appropriate for social marketing as it encompasses all forms of cost involved, including monetary or not, tangible and/or intangible (Peattie and Peattie, 2003). Some examples of costs include embarrassment, loss of time, effort required and psychological discomfort. For instance, quitting smoking may involve the cost of nicotine patches, as well as the physical discomfort caused from withdrawal symptoms, and the time and effort to go to an anti-smoking clinic. The objective of social marketing programmes in relation to price is to reduce the costs involved in changing the behaviour, for instance through subsidising the cost of nicotine patches or through reducing discomfort through nicotine supplements. However, there is often difficulty in measuring the costs involved in the behaviour promoted and subsequently finding ways to reduce them.

Place refers to the place for the distribution of physical goods or services that facilitate behaviour change, but also to the place where the target audience will perform the intended behaviour. A social marketing programme has to ensure easy and convenient access, for example through provision of anti-smoking clinics in a large number of places, wide availability of nicotine patches.

The final element of the marketing mix, promotions, is understood in the same way as in commercial marketing. It is one of the most challenging aspects of social marketing due to the sensitive nature of certain issues (e.g. sexual health) but also due to difficulties in identifying and reaching specific target audiences. Further to this, social marketing has been rather slow in taking on board recent developments in communication theory which acknowledge the interactive and social constructive nature of communication.

The next section discusses the potential of social marketing to contribute to social change. It also provides an overview of its main limitations and criticisms in the relevant literature.

THE POTENTIAL AND LIMITATIONS OF SOCIAL MARKETING

Social marketing is already seen as a field with significant potential to address social problems. Since its birth, social marketing was intended as a positive response to criticisms aimed at the field of marketing, and has played a significant role in weakening marketing's poor reputation for being manipulative and deceptive. Social marketing's potential is based on its ability to provide theoretical insights and technological advances acquired from behaviour studies in commercial marketing that can then be used for promotion of social issues and behaviours (Hastings, 2003). It is seen as a particularly appropriate approach in situations where new information and innovative practices relevant to social problems need to be disseminated, when counter-marketing is needed (e.g. smoking, drinking, etc.), or in relation to health problems (Grier and Bryant, 2005). It is a different approach to social change that focuses more on the audience and incorporates audience research and segmentation, leading to better targeted and more effective messages. Further to this, it introduces a more systematic planning process for behaviour change, thus enhancing effectiveness through planning and coordination.

Rothchild (1999) assesses social marketing in relation to other social change or 'public behaviour management' tools, namely education and law, and outlines their relative appropriateness and effectiveness. He suggests that education works through informing and persuading people to change their behaviours voluntarily. Individuals have free choice on how to respond to the proposed change and society adopts the costs of their behaviour. On the other hand, law or policy development work through coercion or threat of punishment. Coercion is seen as preferable when an individual cannot easily understand or relate to the benefits of behaviour change, and when the cost to society is considerable and difficult to ignore. Finally, a marketing approach works by offering alternative choices to people. The main principle is that the recommended choice is made more appealing or advantageous to the target group. Social marketing can overcome the short-comings of predominately educational approaches to influencing public behaviour, which are mainly expert-led and often rather traditional, paternalistic or culturally insensitive, thus often neglect the perspectives and needs of the target audience. Rothschild's paper demonstrates the relative benefits of social marketing in relation to education and law, and discusses the appropriateness of each tool. However, situations are not usually clear-cut situations and, quite frequently, policy intervention and education are also parts of a social marketing approach. It is also assumed that people are not willing to change their behaviour on their own for society's sake; and that they are only willing to change their behaviour if it benefits them as an individual in some way.

Despite the positive responses to social marketing, a number of difficulties have been identified in relation to the practical application, as well as important ethical issues (e.g. not targeting those most in need) (Andreasen, 2003). Some of these difficulties can possibly be traced to the direct transfer of commercial marketing ideas and tools into the social realm. This transfer does not give enough consideration to the different nature, scope and objectives, but also sensitivities and implications, of the two fields (Solomon, 1989). Social marketing programmes are often concerned with rather complex issues which cannot always be solved through single behaviour change. Further to this, in some areas the costs involved in behaviour change are too great, or the level of audience involvement is either too low or too high, thus necessitating a great facilitation effort.

A significant difficulty in adopting social marketing in some organizations (particularly not-for-profit ones) relates to the requirements for heavy investment of time, money and human resources. Managers of such organizations are also reluctant to adopt social marketing due to differences in culture and lack of training. In addition these organizations are characterized usually by limited resources, and accountability to public scrutiny, so there is unreceptiveness to marketing which is often associated with wasteful expenditures, manipulation and aggressive persuasion. The discomfort with the use of marketing arises from its image as a potentially unethical field, a tool that gives power to a group to influence public opinion in contested issues, and which is therefore not dissimilar to propaganda.

The use of marketing terminology (e.g. 'customers') has also been criticized for its inappropriateness, as it can dehumanize and devalue the people involved. Concerns have been expressed in relation to advertising, mainly due to its negative image and the general mistrust with which it is regarded, particularly in relation to glamorizing social issues and obscuring real political dialogue. The use of emotion appeals, such as fear and guilt, which are quite common in social marketing, are also seen as problematic and manipulative. Furthermore, there is a lack of clarity in terms of responsibilities for marketers, accentuated by a lack of regulation in the field of marketing.

The above concerns and criticisms relate essentially to the applicability of commercial approaches in the public domain. The issues arise from the significantly distinctive characters, conditions and tasks between the social and commercial domain. The nature of the relationship between the participants in the market is different from that in the social sphere, where exchange is often between unequal parties. Through the use of marketing, certain ethical, moral and political problems and conflicts are avoided and moral concerns are replaced with the logic of the market. Further to this, and despite the increasing adoption of marketing in not-for-profit organizations, the perception of citizens as consumers is still seen as unsuitable in that it distorts the nature of citizenship and pushes the boundaries between the state and the market. The idea of 'exchange' is also rather problematic in this context as it implies that the marketing organization may receive benefits from the transaction.

In addition to these concerns, social marketing has been criticized for focusing mainly on individual and short-term change. This can be rather ineffective for social problems that have both individual and social dimensions. In these cases societal factors (like public policy, social norms and the physical environment) sometimes pose a set of constraints on human behaviour and can play an important role in assisting or prohibiting behaviour change. Therefore an individual-level approach would be insufficient and has been accused of holding individuals responsible instead of looking at institutional or societal factors that determine their behaviour.

So far, social marketing is seen as a rather ineffective tool in influencing wider social groups (such as policy makers or law makers) and is seen to only address the information gap at an individual level. More importantly, the process by which one group of people seeks to cause change in other groups of people, in directions preferred by themselves, is essentially a political activity. This raises important questions in relation to who decides what behaviours need to change; on what basis; what means they use to achieve change; and who will be held accountable for these changes. Since common or individual well-being is not understood in the same way by all, any effort to improve it will inevitably involve power issues. Nevertheless, we cannot completely discount the potential of social marketing in contributing to positive social change, neither can we ignore the significant issues posed by the introduction of commercial practices into the public realm. The field is, to some extent, still trying to find its feet and delineate its purpose, scope and potential.

CONCLUSION

In this chapter we have discussed the field of social marketing, a relatively recent development in marketing thought but with widespread applications. We have then examined the historical development of the field, both as an

Case study: Changing public attitudes towards crime – marketing use by the police force

Following the success of long-running health and road safety campaigns in a number of countries (e.g. UK, Australia, Canada), a number of organizations in the public sector are keenly embracing the use of marketing tools and techniques. Realizing the importance of integrated, proactive and effective communications, a local police authority in the UK devised a Media and Communications Strategy. The strategy aimed to promote their work as well as raise awareness of and support for its role to provide an effective, efficient and fair police service for the local communities.

For this purpose, a dedicated Communications Unit has been established which works with a number of teams and key individuals in the police force, and maintains working relationships with various media partners. In an effort to be more 'customer focused', their strategy includes initiatives that encourage dialogue and feedback internally, but also with the communities and various stakeholders in order to support the police service.

Some of the objectives of the Communications Strategy include the strengthening of public confidence and trust, the positive promotion of the work of the police force, the change in public attitudes and behaviours towards crime and the improvement of the image of the organization both externally and internally. Further to this, the encouragement of community involvement has become a significant priority of the police force as it is believed that citizens' active participation can contribute to crime reduction. In consequence, a number of social marketing initiatives have stemmed as part of this strategy. Some examples include campaigns to encourage members of the public to hand over their firearms anonymously, anti-knife campaigns, campaigns for home and personal protection against theft as well as campaigns targeting young people,

academic discipline and as a technology applied to assist social change. As the field is relatively new, there is still lack of consensus about its definition. Instead of offering a definition, we tried to better understand what social marketing is about through an exploration of its main elements and through its relation to other marketing fields. Finally, we discussed the significant potential of this field of marketing in changing attitudes and helping solve social problems, also drawing attention to potential difficulties and areas of concern.

In view of the globalization of social issues (such as environmental issues, poverty or obesity), the field of social marketing offers an important additional tool that can assist social change, by reaching in a targeted manner a large number of people. As its applications are ever-increasing, marketers need to be aware both of its potential and its pitfalls and the need for better theoretical development of the field is also pressing.

INTERNET RESOURCES

Institute for Social Marketing, Open University and University of Stirling. http://www.ism.stir.ac.uk/

The National Social Marketing Centre, UK. http://www.nsms.org.uk/public/default.aspx

The Social Marketing Institute, Washington. http://www.social-marketing.org/

aiming to change their attitudes towards guns. In this manner, the police are addressing the relevant target groups and aim to change their behaviour or attitudes towards particular crimes.

One of their most recent campaigns aimed to combat terrorism. Following a year-long consultation with over a thousand local residents and workers about terrorism, it was concluded that public support is vital in the combat against terrorism. In particular, it was suggested that the police needs to build on public support and restore trust in public authorities in order to become more effective in deterring and preventing terrorism.

The advertising campaign lasted for five weeks and included local press advertisements, posters, postcards, window- and door-stickers, as well as a radio advert broadcasted by major commercial local radio stations. The objectives were twofold: (i) to create awareness of some items and activities that may be relevant to potential terrorists and raise public concerns and, (ii) to encourage the public to report suspicious behaviour in confidence. In support of the advertising campaign, a hotline has been launched in order to report suspicious behaviour and a form on the police website has been created for the same purposes. Their website further provides extensive information on the types of activities that can be suspicious, gives information on ways to report activities and provides assurance of confidentiality to members of the public.

Through this campaign, the police force offers a medium for public participation in their counter-terrorism activities. Apart from enabling citizens through the provision of relevant information that can help them better understand the ways in which they can help, the advertisements also offer reassurance that their officers will use their expertise in order to decide on how to use this information.

Social marketing network, Health Canada. http://www.hc-sc.gc.ca/english/socialmarketing/index.html

Weinreich communications. http://www.social-marketing.com/

KEY READINGS

Andreasen, A. (1994), 'Social marketing: its definition and domain', *Journal of Public Policy and Marketing*, 13, 108–114.

Bloom, P.N. and Novelli, W.D. (1981), 'Problems and challenges in social marketing', *Journal of Marketing*, 45, 79–88.

Donovan, R. and Henley, N. (2003), *Social Marketing: Principles and Practice*. Victoria: IP Communications.

Gordon, R., Hastings, G., McDermott, L. and Siquier, P. (2007), 'The critical role of social marketing', in M. Saren, P. Maclaran, C. Goulding, R. Elliott, A. Shankar and M. Caterall (eds), *Critical Marketing: Defining the Field*. Oxford, UK: Butterworth Heinemann, pp. 169–177.

Hastings, G. and Saren, M. (2003), 'The critical contribution of social marketing: theory and application', *Marketing Theory*, 3, 305–322.

SEMINAR EXERCISES

Discussion Topics

1. Outline the development of the concept of social marketing by identifying the 'turning points' that have shaped the field.

2. What are the main problems that social marketers may encounter? Which of these problems are common in commercial marketing as well? Are there ways to overcome these problems?

3. Argue for or against the use of social marketing by governments. Do you believe the use of public funds for these purposes is justified?

4. It is often argued that social marketing campaigns alone cannot bring about significant change so they have to be complemented by education initiatives or regulation. Consider the example of a seat belt campaign and critically discuss this view.

Group Exercises

1. Each student will provide an example of a social marketing campaign. The group will choose the most interesting campaign and answer the following questions:

    (i) Which organization is running this campaign? What type of organization is it?

    (ii) What is the social idea/attitude/behaviour promoted?

    (iii) What makes this campaign interesting?

    (iv) Do you believe it has the potential to achieve social change? Why/Why not?

2. Consider a campaign that aims to change people's eating habits.

    (i) What are the different influences on peoples' eating habits?

    (ii) What are the main difficulties an organization promoting healthy eating may encounter in terms of changing peoples' attitudes and behaviours?

    (iii) What types of incentives can such a campaign offer to target adopters to convince them to change habits?

3. Consider an anti-smoking campaign.

    (i) What do you believe are the objectives of the campaign? Which is the target audience?

    (ii) What is the social marketing product of the campaign?

    (iii) What costs are involved in changing the behaviour/idea/attitude promoted? How can the organization reduce these costs?

    (iv) How do you understand 'Place' in relation to the campaign?

REFERENCES

Andreasen, A. (1994), 'Social marketing: Its definition and domain', *Journal of Public Policy and Marketing*, 13, 108–114.

Andreasen, A.R. (1997), 'Challenges for the science and practice of social marketing', in M.E. Goldberg, M. Fishbein and S.E. Middlestadt (eds), *Social Marketing: Theoretical and Practical Perspectives*. Mahwah, NJ: Lawrence Erlbaum Associates, pp. 3–19.

Andreasen, A.R. (2003), 'The life trajectory of social marketing: some implications', *Marketing Theory*, 3 (3), 293–303.

Andreasen, A.R. (2005), *Social Marketing in the 21st Century*. Thousand Oaks, CA: Sage.

Bagozzi, R.P. (1978), 'Marketing as exchange: a theory of transactions in the marketplace', *American Behavioral Scientist*, 21 (4), 535–556.

Bloom, P.N. and Novelli, W.D. (1981), 'Problems and challenges in social marketing', *Journal of Marketing*, 45 (2), 79–88.

Brenkert, G.G. (2002), 'Ethical challenges of social marketing', *Journal of Public Policy and Marketing*, 21 (1), 14–25.

Brønn, P.S. and Vrioni, A.B. (2001), 'Corporate social responsibility and cause-related marketing: an overview', *International Journal of Advertising*, 20 (2), 207–222.

Donovan, R. and Henley, N. (2003), *Social Marketing: Principles and Practice*. Victoria: IP Communications.

Fine, S. (1990), *Social Marketing: Promoting the Causes of Public and Non-Profit Agencies*. Boston: Allyn and Bacon.

Fox, K.F. and Kotler, P. (1980), 'The marketing of social causes: the first 10 years', *Journal of Marketing*, 44, 24–33.

Gordon, R., Hastings, G., McDermott, L. and Siquier, P. (2007), 'The critical role of social marketing', in M. Saren, P. Maclaran, C. Goulding, R. Elliott, A. Shankar and M. Caterall (eds), *Critical Marketing: Defining the Field*. Oxford, UK: Butterworth Heinemann, pp. 169–177.

Grier, S. and Bryant, C.A. (2005), 'Social marketing in public health', *Annual Review of Public Health*, 26, 319–339.

Hastings, G. (2003), 'Social marketers of the world unite, you have nothing to lose but your shame', *Social Marketing Quarterly*, IX (4), 14–21.

Hastings, G. (2007), 'The diaspora has already begun', *Marketing Intelligence and Planning*, 25 (2), 117–122.

Hastings, G. and Saren, M. (2003), 'The critical contribution of social marketing: theory and application', *Marketing Theory*, 3, 305–322.

Hill, R. (2001), 'The marketing concept and health promotion: a survey and analysis of recent "Health Promotion" literature', *Social Marketing Quarterly*, 2, 29–53.

Kotler, P. and Levy, S.J. (1969), 'Broadening the concept of marketing', *Journal of Marketing*, 33 (January), 10–15.

Kotler, P., Roberto, N. and Lee, N. (2002), *Social Marketing: Improving the Quality of Life*. Thousand Oaks, CA: Sage.

Kotler, P. and Zaltman, G. (1971), 'Social marketing: an approach to planned social change', *Journal of Marketing*, 35, 3–12.

Laczniak, G.R. and Michie, A. (1979), 'The social disorder of the broadened concept of marketing', *Journal of Marketing Science*, 7, 214–231.

Levy, S.J. and Zaltman, G. (1975), *Marketing, Society and Conflict*. Englewood Cliffs, NJ: Prentice Hall.

Luck, D.J. (1969), 'Broadening the concept of marketing – too far', *Journal of Marketing*, 33 (July), 53–63.

Maibach, E. and Holtgrave, D.R. (1995), 'Advances in public health communication', *Annual Review of Public Health*, 16, 219–238.

Murphy, P.E. and Bloom, P.N. (1992), 'Ethical issues in social marketing', in S. Fine (ed.), *Marketing the Public Sector*. New Brunswick, NJ: Transaction Publishers, pp. 68–78.

Peattie, S. and Peattie, K. (2003), 'Ready to fly solo? Reducing social marketing's dependence on commercial marketing theory', *Marketing Theory*, 3 (3), 365–385.

Rothchild, M.L. (1999), 'Carrots, sticks and promises', *Journal of Marketing*, 63, 24–27.

Solomon, D. (1989), 'A social marketing perspective on communication campaigns', in R.E. Rice and C.K. Atkin (eds), *Public Communication Campaigns*. London: Sage, pp. 87–104.

Webster, F.E. (1975), 'Social marketing: what makes it different?', *Management Decision*, 13 (1), 70–77.

Wiebe, G.D. (1951–52), 'Merchandising commodities and citizenship on television', *The Public Opinion Quarterly*, 15, 679–691.

CHAPTER 11

New Technologies of Marketing Research

Elizabeth Parsons

INTRODUCTION

The concept and practice of marketing research has changed dramatically in recent years. The opening up of world markets through globalization, and the increased speed up of business transactions brought about by technological developments, have changed both our understandings of markets, and the tools we use to interpret them. While markets have changed, so too have consumers, who are now increasingly market literate and highly informed about the expanding choice of products, brands and services available to them. Marketing researchers, therefore, are operating in an increasingly complex environment. The emerging technological infrastructure of the internet has become indispensable for many consumers (Hoffman et al., 2004). This dialogical relationship between consumers and market researchers calls for new qualitative and quantitative approaches to understanding these new forms of data. Marketing researchers have also experienced a shift in their whole concept of the consumer. Researchers have moved away from demographic and psychologically informed views of consumers as information processors, having innate characteristics, wants and needs, towards a sociologically informed view of consumers whose identities emerge through their relations with others and the world around them. Where market research was previously focused on identifying pre-existing consumer attitudes and motivations in order to tap into these, research is now more squarely focused on understanding the social formation of consumer identity, in order to provide identities consumers will want to associate with. That is not to say that earlier traditions have been entirely replaced by a new wave of approaches, as Barker et al. (2001) suggest, instead we are seeing a new eclecticism in marketing research approaches:

> *there is a move towards a way of doing, using and thinking about market research which is quite different in character and application from what has gone before. This may represent both a shift towards the interpretivist pole of the continuum and more interestingly (and healthily) reflect a tangential shift towards a more eclectic industry – something we might call informed eclecticism. (Barker et al., 2001, p. 26)*

This chapter focuses on a range of emerging marketing research techniques that have augmented this eclecticism. The central focus in the chapter is on the way in which new technology has impacted on marketing research. The chapter explores the rise of ethnographic approaches to understanding consumers, particularly through the visual and the textual/linguistic. To this end the realms of videography, netnography, blogging and virtual life worlds are explored. The chapter then considers some of the advances in the use of data technologies for understanding consumers and markets. In closing the chapter includes a case study of Flamingo International, a qualitative market research organization which combines a range of the approaches discussed in the chapter.

VIDEOGRAPHY

Videography is a method which has recently emerged in consumer research. Its increasing popularity has been brought about by improvements in video technology and reductions in the price of equipment. It is now relatively easy to use video cameras and produce reasonable results. The technique of videography also offers considerable diversity, Belk and Kozinets (2005, p. 129) identify three main applications in consumer research:

1. *Videoing individual or group interviews* – This application adds a visual dimension to the more traditional voice recording of interviews. Being able to see the facial expressions and gestures of informants, as well as the proxemics and group dynamics, are helpful in interpreting meaning. Some of the difficulties associated with this technique, however, are that the video camera can be intrusive and make participants ill at ease and it may also prompt a degree of acting for the camera.

2. *Naturalistic observation* – This application has been widely used in tandem with an ethnographic approach to studying consumers. Here the emphasis lies in getting on the level with consumers to try and understand the world as they see it. In addition, the approach has

many advantages over traditional interview accounts of consumer behaviour because the way that people account for their activities and experiences is often very different from what they actually do in practice. It is usual in ethnography for the researcher to take detailed notes on their experiences in the field, this would typically be called a field diary, the benefit of using a video camera means that the researcher does not have to rely on their memory and ability to record the situation. Video also offers a richer source of information than observational notes. In addition, the recorded material can be a useful source of stimulation for discussion. The researcher and participant can watch the video together and reflect on their past comments and behaviours.

3. *Autovideography* – These videos are directed by the participant and therefore include material that they themselves feel is important. Giving the participant the camera to video themselves and their own experiences gives them control over the situation. The absence of the researcher means that the participant is more relaxed and may be more candid in what they choose to reveal.

The researcher, therefore, does not necessarily have to be in sole charge of the filming experience. Belk and Kozinets (2005) suggest that collaborative filming projects may be a further fruitful avenue for understanding consumers. They cite the example of a study of the new black elite in Zimbabwe which was conducted jointly by Belk and the MBA students of Africa University (2000). Because they were part of the community in question, the students could easily gain access for interviews and observation. However this familiarity between researchers and participants meant that issues relating to conspicuous and deliberate self presentation were perhaps more pronounced.

Webcam footage may also provide researchers with useful videographic data. Computers are often situated in the relatively private spaces of the home, such as bedrooms and studies, where researcher access may otherwise be difficult. As participants, (especially younger people), are becoming increasingly familiar with using this technology on a day-to-day basis, they may be willing to share footage of their home and office interiors, clothing and special possessions with researchers. Existing footage might also be used for analysis. This might consist of previous family videos of birthday parties and other holiday celebrations. Insights might also be drawn from home videos posted on websites such as You Tube. Video footage from webcams in parks, busy shopping streets and other public spaces may also provide insights into consumption behaviours and rituals. In addition to these new formats for data collection, Belk and Kozinets (2005, p. 137) highlight a range of possible genres for the resulting films. They observe that researchers should not be tied to the documentary format alone, but should extend their range of formats to include exposés, mockumentaries, heroic tales, journalistic tales, impressionist tales, realist tales and confessional tales.

Belk and Kozinets also usefully question the ways in which video data might be received by its audience. They observe that we are used to the uncritical acceptance of video footage as factual, and so warn against such a passive reading of this material. They suggest that researchers need to develop a 'critical visual literacy' (2005, p. 134) which is underpinned by an awareness that video is merely another story or version of reality.

> *While television journalism and documentary film making continue the positivist pretence that the visual cannot lie and presents the facts and the truth, documentary film makers, television editors, and video ethnographers all know that they are telling stories, creating (hopefully compelling) visual collages, and attempting to dramatically shape audience reactions. There is no such thing as a neutral image that is simply there as a fact, especially after the substantial creative winnowing that must take place in editing.*
> *(2005, p. 134)*

Videography can also be really beneficial in the corporate world. Recently the mobile phone company O_2 commissioned the video based market research company Voxpops International (see weblinks below) to use video to illustrate their main customer segments. The aim was to bring consumers to life for internal staff and sales purposes. The project involved twenty-four individual depth interviews with members of the O_2 consumer panel. Each interview was filmed in the respondent's home and additional time was spent filming the surroundings and lives of the individuals. The original intention of the videos was to illustrate each segment in an exciting and impactful manner. However, the depth interviews actually uncovered more information and insight than originally anticipated, and the reports have been used as part of O_2's annual research. Use of the final videos has also expanded to training courses to help O_2 marketers understand and refresh their knowledge of O_2 consumers (Voxpops International). Other examples of the use of video data by companies include: Heineken's video of interviews with potential consumers of their new product, which they use to persuade retailers to stock the product; VisitScotland's use of video interviews to understand the experiences of Scottish holiday makers; and Boots use of video interviews to find out what different consumer groups (particularly minority groups) thought about their range of products and services.

NETNOGRAPHY AND ONLINE COMMUNITIES

Netnography is a relatively recent research approach that has also been developed largely in the field of consumer research. Kozinets (1998, 1999,

2002, 2006) and Catterall and Maclaran (2001) have been key proponents of this approach. Kozinets describes netnography as follows:

> *"Netnography," or ethnography on the Internet, is a new qualitative research methodology that adapts ethnographic research techniques to study the cultures and communities that are emerging through computer-mediated communications. (2002, p. 62)*

Here the approach of ethnography has been adapted as a technique to study consumer behaviour in online worlds. In ethnography the emphasis is on immersion in the everyday life of the community in question in order to observe social life as it unfolds in situ (see Arnould and Wallendorf, 1994; Elliott and Jankel-Elliott, 2003).

Netnography has a number of distinct advantages over more traditional forms of marketing research. Discussion in online communities is entirely consumer directed, and thus offers insights into what really matters for consumers. As such, Kozinets observes that netnography offers the researcher 'a window into naturally occurring behaviours' (2002, p. 62). Also, when compared with the traditional interview format, there are much lower costs to collecting this data in terms of time, money and the emotional energy required. The researcher can merely download extracts of conversations for analysis. Due to its unobtrusive nature this approach is also useful for exploring sensitive research topics (see Langer and Beckman, 2005). Drawbacks of this approach are that the sample is limited to online users who are likely to possess specific characteristics, (such as reasonable levels of familiarity with technology and an existing interest in a particular subject). This means that they may not be representative of the larger population. In addition groups are often anonymous and therefore individuals cannot be identified along the lines of age, gender, profession, etc.

There are also significant ethical issues associated with the collection and use of this type of data. In netnographic research of a leading retailer, Maclaran and Catterall (2002) usefully identify the practicalities and ethical considerations involved. They observe the difficulties in gaining entry to a community structured by its own internal norms, hierarchies and vernacular. In particular they stress the importance of learning these rules and norms before trying to enter into discussion. Thus, they suggest a form of 'lurking' or observing exchanges for a period of time prior to participation. They also observe that the community members may have a number of different identities. In addition to the potential problems of deliberate fabrication, this means that the same participant could be interviewed more than once in a number of his/her different virtual identity guises. They also highlight the challenges raised by the lack of paralinguistic cues and, because of its asynchronous nature, the lack of spontaneity in participants' responses. In discussing interpretation and representation, Maclaran and Catterall (2002) highlight the enduring presence of the field which they see as an opportunity both to verify the researcher's interpretation with the community, and to engage in collaborative interpretation with community members. They also identify some of the ethical challenges of interpretation and dissemination. In particular they observe the 'publicly private' nature of online communications of this type, and suggest that 'researchers must distinguish between what is publicly accessible and what can be publicly disseminated' (2002, p. 324).

The communities under study in netnography are 'online communities'. Rheingold characterizes these communities as 'Social aggregations that emerge from the Internet when enough people carry on those public discussions long enough, with sufficient human feeling, to form webs of personal relationships in cyberspace' (1994, p. 5). Thus he marks online communities out from other more casual exchanges of news or information. Consumers are therefore developing 'relationships' in online environments (see for example Maclaran et al., 2006). However these relationships may often be quite fleeting. Consumers may dip in and out of these communities, using them as much as a source of information about a product or service, as for the experience of social bonding they may offer. Kozinets (1999) identifies four types of user: *tourists* who have only a casual attachment to the community; *minglers* who prioritize the social dimensions of the exchange and are not deeply involved in the topic of interest; *devotees* who have strong interests in the topic but lack social attachment to the group; and *insiders* who have both strong ties to the group and the topic in question, they are often longstanding founder members. Kozinets (2002) also identifies five different types of virtual communities:

1. Boards – These function as electronic bulletin boards (usenets/newsgroups).

2. Web rings – These bring together thematically linked web pages, these may be independent web pages.

3. Lists – These are email lists distributed to users united by a common interest.

4. Multiuser dungeons – These are themed virtual locations in which interactions are structured by role playing rules.

5. Chat rooms – These are un-themed virtual locations loosely organized around common interests.

A sixth type of online community not specifically mentioned by Kozinets, undoubtedly due to its relatively recent popular emergence, is the virtual life world. As with dungeons, these are themed virtual locations or islands where visual representations of users, called 'avatars', interact in three-dimensional space. They are distinct from dungeons in that interactions are not structured by role playing rules and social interaction proceeds in a manner similar to real life. Given the distinctly different nature of these virtual communities they are discussed in a separate section below.

Online communities allow consumers from a diverse range of cultures, social settings and geographical locations to connect through discussion of an array of products and services (see also Chapter 6). Topics include, for example, films, sports, music, eating out, travel and holidays, fast food, electronics, computers, cars, toys and so on. Discussion in these communities ranges from the general, such as where to obtain the best dining out experiences, to the very specialized: such as the technicalities of coffee making, which beans to use, how to best grind them, etc. Commentators observe that there is much to gain by expanding markets through these virtual communities (Hagel, 1997). Research has also identified a series of online 'brand communities'. For example there are newsgroups devoted to Harley-Davidson motorcycles (Schouten and McAlexander, 1995), Saab cars and Macintosh computers (Muniz and O'Guinn, 2001) and the Mini car (Beh, 2008). In consumption terms, these communities act to advocate, and give the seal of approval, to brands and products. They also act to create and disseminate (often quite detailed) information about brands and products and their use (Sandin, 2007). Kozinets (2002, p. 70) suggests that they may be usefully 'construed as individual market segments that are of interest in their own right'. However, while these communities can be useful to companies in providing feedback and information on consumer evaluations of the brand, they can also be a threat to the company. Consumer readings of these postings as an unbiased and 'truthful' source of information, combined with the large audiences some of these communities attract, can mean that negative postings can cause significant damage to a brand's reputation (see also Chapter 5). In marketing research terms however, it is very useful to know about negative feedback early on so that problems can be addressed.

BLOGS AND BLOGGING

Blogs are one of the more recent sites for marketing researchers' attention. Blogs have been described as follows:

> A blog (a contraction of the term "Web log") is a Web site, usually maintained by an individual, with regular entries of commentary, descriptions of events, or other material such as graphics or video (Wikipedia).

As Schroeder suggests in an online video interview (see internet resources in Chapter 5), blogs are another example of the increasing emphasis on visual methods of communication in today's society. They are largely about individual expression, and often involve a high degree of individual creativity. The activity of blogging is on the rise. A study by the marketing research firm Perseus Development found that over 4 million blogs have been created to date. However, blogs are often created and then left fallow as the novelty wears off. The same research found that 66 per cent of blogs had not been updated in the past two months. Blogs also seem to be the preserve of young people, with over 90 per cent being posted by the under thirties (Perseus Development, 2003).

At present blogs remain underused by marketing researchers. This is unfortunate as they are useful for consumer and market researchers for a range of reasons. Companies have used blogs to engage and interact with their consumer group, either with respect to individual products, or the brand itself. Here important insights can be gleaned around consumers' views of the brand or products, their experiences of using them, and perhaps, some of the problems they have encountered in using them. Blogs may be useful, therefore, not only to understand individual consumers, but also communities of consumers as they discuss and compare experiences. There are significant overlaps here with the online communities discussed above. The fact that blogs, by their very nature, are not subject to the control of companies, and are entirely the preserve of the consumer, means that the information they contain might be seen as very honest and candid. It must be remembered, however, that blogs exist as a form of very public self presentation for the consumer and, thus often focus on entertainment and the expression of creativity by individuals. In addition, they are often anonymous which means that their authors might typically 'talk up' their views and activities more so than they might in a one to one interview context.

Zhao and Belk's (2007) study of the blogs of young Chinese women found these women typically discussed shopping trips, dining experiences, holidays and clothing purchases. To this extent it seems that they are an edited reflection of what consumers deem as most interesting about their lives. Zhao and Belk observe that these blogs are: 'characterized by spontaneity and sudden bursts of creativity. Bloggers have worked blogs into their lifestyles, and thus what they record offers a unique opportunity to examine the personalized consumerist values of an emerging consumer society' (2007, p. 136). They also suggest that we may be able to learn a significant amount by talking to bloggers about the content of their blogs to discover their own interpretations.

While blogs have undoubtedly been underused in understanding consumers, they have been widely used by companies to monitor the activities of their competitors. To this end a range of blog tracking engines exist which search blog contents. These search engines provide information on both popular searches and the tags used to categorize blog postings. In addition, companies are using blogs to facilitate internal communication, and these blogs are a useful source of employee feedback. Companies using external blogs seem to have mixed success. The key to maintaining consumer interest is to make the blog interactive, interesting and useful. For example, Carling host a site called One All where users can create a web page and blog to discuss their own football team (see weblinks). Carling offer prizes to teams which have the most active blog pages. Individuals at Adobe have also set up successful blogs dealing with their various applications such as Flash and Dreamweaver. Here consumers can exchange expertise and Adobe can glean useful insights around consumer usage of their products.

VIRTUAL LIFE WORLDS

The marketing and consumer research potential of virtual life worlds, such as Second Life, Entropia Universe and There.com, has yet to be fully explored. Existing commentary suggests that they offer significant opportunity for understanding consumers. These life worlds take the self presentation found in blogs to another level. Here individuals are represented by their own digital 'avatars' which may or may not resemble their offline appearance. These three-dimensional virtual selves allow for significant play and creativity in identity formation. Recent research by the Global Market Institute (cited in Novak and Anderson, 2007) found two main motivations for people to use Second Life: 'because it is a creative outlet for me' and 'to escape real life, which I am not satisfied with'.

These virtual societies have an active commercial sphere where clothing, furniture and household goods can be purchased. The potentail for market insights is therefore significant. Avatars also run a range of businesses such as real estate brokering, event planning and advertising agencies. These goods and services can be purchased using virtual currency, which can then be converted by merchants into real world currency on a range of internet exchanges. A handful of avatar merchants (in particular fashion designers and land speculators) have been able to build up very significant incomes in this way, allowing them to give up their real world jobs and concentrate solely on their virtual career. At present marketing activity in virtual worlds is limited. However some companies have made a start. In the teen-oriented virtual world 'There', Levi Strauss promoted a new style of jeans by offering virtual pairs for sale at higher prices (in There.com currency) than the generic virtual jeans available. It is worth noting though that Levi's were disappointed with the outcome. Their head of internet marketing commented that they had hoped the experiment would tell them more about how much people were willing to pay for the new style, versus the generic jeans. They also hoped it would offer deeper insights into the sorts of activities for which people wore the jeans (Hemp, 2006).

Researchers have begun to explore the potential of these virtual worlds for offering insights into consumer behaviour (see for example a recent conference co-chaired by Solomon and Wood, 2008). There is certainly current untapped potential for marketers to understand consumers' priorities in a world where real world constraints are significantly loosened. Having said this, and as Bonsu and Darmody (2008) recently warn, the emancipatory potential for these new communities might easily be overstated. Marketing, after all, relies on seeking out and shaping people's dreams, and in virtual worlds these dreams are played out for all to see. Marketers could observe and collect data around how people both choose and interact with products and services, observing the features they prefer, and the ways in which they possess and adapt goods into their everyday virtual lives (Williams, 2007). Preliminary research by Kedzior (2007) observes that consumption in this context is centred on overcoming disembodiment and making existence in these virtual environments more real. To further explore consumer behaviour in this environment Tom Novak at the Sloan Center for Internet Retailing has created a Second Life island called eLab city (see weblinks). Users will live on the island and data will be collected on their shopping, working and leisure activities. One of the key issues yet to be fully explored is the relationship between individuals' online and offline experiences and personas, in particular, the extent to which individuals' online preferences might translate into real world behaviours. Little research exists pertaining directly to virtual consumer behaviour, although Cocciolo (2007a) conducted a study of blog discussions to explore Second Life users' opinions on the factors they thought influenced consumer behaviour in their virtual world. He found that users thought the tying of products and services into movies and virtual events were the most effective forms of influence.

Marketing researchers have also began to create avatars themselves, and either start up their own virtual marketing research business, and/or conduct research through virtual world participant observation, interviews, etc. To this end Menti (2007) has linked survey software to Second Life so that an automated, rather than human operated, 'avatar bot' can ask passers-by survey questions. This survey data has been analysed and collated in Global Marketing Insite research reports. Cocciolo (2007b) has also developed the survey tool 'Second Look', which uses touch screens within Second Life to administer surveys to avatars. In addition, the Social Research Foundation have recently launched an opinions panel in Second Life (see Internet resources). The 'First Opinions Panel' consists of 10,000 members of the Second Life community who participate in 'in world' research, and are paid in virtual currency (Linden dollars) for their participation.

More traditional marketing research techniques could also be applied to these worlds. For example, in creating an avatar on Yahoo, individuals are asked to make choices from a range of elements, including not only their physical appearance, but also pets and accessories, and the actual setting in which the avatar will appear. Some options include branded objects, such as Adidas shoes or Jeep Commander cars. Marketers could make links between product/brand choices and demographic and psycho-social factors as happens in traditional marketing research (see Hemp 2006, p. 54). As virtual worlds are likely to become more complex, online techniques of consumer profiling and segmentation will likely develop too.

While there is obviously much untapped potential for marketing research in the virtual world, the drawbacks are also significant. There are technology constraints in these virtual worlds, especially the processing power required to run them, but also the hardware capabilities of users to operate within them. In addition, for many, these worlds offer a form of escapism from real life, so there is resistance to the encroachment of real world commerce. Moreover, each world has its own specific culture and underlying norms and values which, as with cross-cultural research in the real world, require immersion to fully understand. These virtual worlds are becoming increasingly complex social environments, so understanding consumer behaviour in them is challenging. It must also be remembered that users are simultaneously negotiating their real world lives as they engage in virtual worlds. It is important for researchers to understand that the physical real world context of use has significant bearing on virtual consumer behaviour. Finally, as with all marketing research, the tracking of avatar data poses serious ethical problems, undoubtedly a code of ethics will need to be developed in this respect.

DATA CAPTURE AND DATA MINING

The impact that technological developments have had on marketers' ability to both understand and influence the consumer is perhaps most clear when looking at data driven marketing. Rather than trying to understand consumers' psychologically or sociologically based motivations for purchase, marketers rely here on mathematics to predict the probability of a consumer making a specific purchasing decision. In order to do this, companies collect vast amounts of data on consumers' spending histories. As consumers, we leave behind a trail of transaction data. For example, when ordering a book on the internet, information is logged on the books you look at prior to making your choice, the book you actually order, the amount you spend, the time and date of your order, and your personal financial, email and home address details. This information is then shared across a range of organizations including the website you visited, the supplier you purchased from (which may differ from the website owner) and the postal service. In addition, this information may be shared with other web providers, or sold to other companies as part of a data list. Companies typically assemble huge data bases of electronic point of sales transactions, online transactions and orders. Many organizations now have their own data warehouses which are purpose built and designed to collect and store data from the company's critical information systems as well as data from outside the company. These warehouses are built in advance to a 'data model', which is a very time consuming cross-functional effort. They can take from one to three years to build and cost in excess of £5 million (Peacock, 1998). To give an example, the US retailer Walmart, which logs every in-store transaction, has a data warehouse which is larger than that used by the US Internal Revenue Services for collecting taxes (Shaw et al., 2001). This warehoused data can then be matched with demographic data obtained for example via credit cards, store cards and loyalty cards. These collected data sets are then 'mined' for insights surrounding consumer purchasing patterns. Peacock defines data mining as follows:

> *Narrowly defined, data mining is the automated discovery of "interesting," non obvious patterns hidden in a database that have a high potential for contributing to the bottom line. "Interesting" relationships are those that could have an impact on strategy or tactics, and ultimately on an organization's objectives. (Peacock 1998, p. 10)*

Peacock's definition indicates that the central purpose of data mining is to support decision making within an organization. The whole mining process is automated, using various forms of 'machine learning' to extract information from data sets with little or no human involvement. These forms of machine learning are relatively recent and have their basis in artificial intelligence. The emphasis in these techniques is on discovery, in particular the discovery of relationships that were not apparent before. Two more recent examples of machine learning methods include neural networks (Vellido et al., 1999) and genetic or evoluntionary algorithms (Bhattacharyya, 2000). *Neural networks* involve both supervised machine learning – where the network is trained to recognize patterns – and unsupervised learning – where the network must learn to recognize patterns in the data. This pattern recognition is useful in applications such as perceptual mapping and segmentation. *Genetic or evolutionary algorithms* are used to construct decision rules similar to those obtained from decision-tree models. They are particularly useful in prediction and classification. These algorithms have parallels with evolutionary processes where two species members come together and share material to either regenerate or terminate the species line. As Malhotra and Peterson (2001, p. 222) observe, 'a genetic algorithm is particularly useful in solving poorly structured problems because it attempts to find many solutions simultaneously'. They also observe that because these algorithms are best used on a small data set with a relatively small number of relevant variables, they can be used in conjunction with other techniques such as decision tree modelling, which might be used initially to derive a smaller set from the whole data set.

While there is a vast array of applications for data mining, Peacock (1998) identifies four which have wide application:

1. *Customer acquisition* – Here data mining methods are used to discover attributes that predict customer responses to

communications such as special offers. Households from lists of non-customers are then identified using these attributes for mailings and other forms of communication.

2. *Customer retention* – Here data mining is used to identify customers who both contribute to the company's profits, but who are also likely to move to other companies. These households are then targeted with special offers not available to other customers.

3. *Customer abandonment* – Here data mining is applied to the purchase histories of customers to find which ones are costing the company more than they are contributing, i.e. in banking keeping small deposits but requiring a lot of servicing, or in online retailing, ordering goods but continually returning them. These customers are often discouraged from staying with the company. Though it should be noted that the ethics of some of these practices are questionable, as they often function to marginalize disadvantaged consumers such as those on low incomes.

4. *Market basket analysis* – Here product and brand purchase affinities are identified from purchase histories, and communications tailored and targeted accordingly.

In addition to the functions above, data mining might be used for developing new products, discovering cross-selling opportunities, managing customer churn, discovering patterns in customers' satisfaction, and tracking studies. These functions might typically be put into practice through direct marketing (Ling and Li, 1998; Bhattacharyya, 2000) and customer relationship management (Rygielski et al., 2002). To give some examples: American Express uses a neural network to examine the millions of card holder transactions in its database. This results in a series of 'purchase propensity scores' for each card holder. American Express uses these scores to match offers from affiliated companies to the purchase histories of individual card holders. These offers are then enclosed with their monthly statements (Peacock, 1998). The French retailer Casino uses data mining to support their just-in-time stock inventory strategy. A data mining system allows managers to mine real-time data, which offers an overall view of the business, this information is used to make critical decisions and ensure stock replenishment is managed more efficiently. Prudential Insurance recently combined demographic data on 10 million households with its life, securities, real estate and credit card operations systems. This data set was then mined to provide data on those households more likely to be interested in annuity products. A pilot using this new data set generated twice the responses of a random sample drawn from the whole data set (Peacock, 1998).

Shaw et al. (2001) argue that data mining techniques have been underused in areas such as consumer profiling and customer relationship management. Moreover Bucklin et al. (1998) argue for a more complete application of these techniques. They observe that marketers should move away from mere marketing decision support, towards the actual automation of marketing decisions. However, while data mining can identify patterns and relationships, it cannot as yet tell marketing managers what to do with that information. Data mining can help with strategic decisions, but not provide the answers.

> *We are not forecasting the demise of the marketing manager. What we are predicting is that marketing decisions made by managers may shift from the short-run, the tactical, and the maintenance of the established to the long-run, the strategic, and the launch of the innovative. Indeed, our outlook is quite positive. Tomorrow's marketing manager will enjoy more leverage, spend more time on "the hard important problems," including the rules for automation, and focus on decision domains where data are scarce and models do not yet work well.* (Bucklin et al., 1998, p. 236, emphasis in original)

CONCLUSIONS

The fragmentation and dynamics of postmodern markets means that traditional methods of researching consumers and markets are increasingly less likely to produce the kinds of insights that marketers need to guide future action. To this end, the approaches to consumer and marketing research discussed in this chapter are being used in increasingly eclectic ways within companies. As Ereaut (2004) observes:

> *The heroic qualitative researcher with diverse skills is giving way to the specialist. Expert teams are being put together by agencies for clients, of ethnographers, semioticians, futurologists, data miners, discourse analysts and others working together. They analyse their own and each other's data. Qualitative and quantitative sources get integrated, meta-analyses created, key implications drawn.* (2004, p. 146)

This eclecticism goes hand in hand with the rise of lifestyle marketing where members of a lifestyle group are identified by shared interests, activities or identities. This also involves a move away from the discovery of innate identities towards understanding and constructing identities consumers will want to identify with. Moreover the approaches discussed above are vital in understanding the new dialogical relationship with the consumer brought about by new technology. Market researchers are no longer conducting research 'on consumers' but 'with consumers'.

Case study: – Flamingo International (by Sharmila Subramanian, Flamingo International)

Flamingo International was founded by Kirsty Fuller and Maggie Collier in 1992 and is one of the most successful qualitative research agencies in the world. With offices in London, New York, San Francisco, Singapore and Tokyo, Flamingo International sees itself as a truly global qualitative research agency. The challenge for Flamingo International has always been to provide insights and thinking for brand building, informed by a future facing understanding of people and cultures across the world.

In order to deliver strong thinking and insight for its clients, Flamingo has had to adapt and evolve to negotiate a rapidly changing brand-consumer landscape. This landscape has moved from an advertising-led communications model, that relied on consumers responding to brands handing down meaning, to a world where consumers construct meaning for themselves, and are responding to more experiential forms of communication. Brands now have to engage with consumers who are increasingly:

- **Empowered**: proliferation of choice means consumers have more purchase power than they have ever had before.
- **Connected**: technology has facilitated new modes of connection and sharing for consumers.
- **Expressive**: consumers are not just spectators anymore, but often the creators within their world.
- **Modular**: consumer lives are increasingly compartmentalized, in terms of their lifestyles, identities and media use.
- **Committed**: there is an increasing desire to seek depth and texture through commitment to causes and interests.

It is clear to see the role that technology plays in consumer empowerment. Mobile telecommunications and the internet have changed the way people live their lives across much of the world. It is often the youngest people in society who are the most evolved, having grown up in a world where new technologies are the norm. The rise of the blogosphere and social networking sites indicate how comfortable young people are with broadcasting the details of their lives to a large network of people.

In this changing landscape, brands are required to change the way in which they interact with consumers. This also has a significant impact on the way in which qualitative research is conducted. In order to uncover consumer motivations and behaviours, it is imperative that the right methodologies are used. As new technologies have grown in importance, Flamingo International has adapted to this change, utilizing the internet as a medium of investigation.

Flamingo's online research methodologies

Online discussion groups

Online chat is a normal and routine mode of communication for many people. Moreover, it provides an opportunity for people to express themselves, free from the pressures that face-to-face communication can bring. This is one of the reasons why Flamingo International utilizes online discussion groups as part of its offering, having developed its own online chatroom. This works in the same way as a physical discussion group, with a moderator, participants and clients watching from behind a 'virtual' mirror, their presence being invisible. This medium works particularly well with a teenage target, especially when the subject matter is sensitive.

In this environment, there is great potential to gain access to deeper, more reflective and personal insights from consumers. Moreover, it is a particularly good medium to use for time-poor respondents who are unwilling to physically travel to participate in a discussion. The global reach of the internet also allows for people from around the world to take part in the same discussion in real time. On multi-market studies, this can prove an invaluable way of getting an immediate insight into a number of different cultures at the same time. This approach has also been successful when gaining access to experts on specific subjects. Online discussion groups allow experts from all over the globe to communicate in the same place at the same time.

Whilst online discussions are not appropriate for every subject matter, they provide an invaluable means of engaging with consumers on their own terms, in an environment in which they feel increasingly comfortable.

Blogs

Traditionally, participant diaries have been utilized in qualitative research as a means of consumers illustrating their lives and behaviours, through photographs, drawings and other visual material. Whilst this approach is still highly appropriate for certain consumer targets, blogs are an increasingly appropriate alternative. This is especially true for teenagers and young adults, who are familiar and at ease in the blogosphere. This trend has been harnessed by Flamingo International as a research tool, with blogs working as online diaries, enabling researchers to access people's lives over a period of time (Figure 11.1). Moreover, this medium provides an intimate, private and personal forum to express thoughts and opinions in an honest way. Importantly, blogs allow for participants to reflect, thinking over their answers in greater depth, which often leads to more considered and inspiring content. As audio and visual content are increasingly housed in digital rather than physical format, blogs often provide a more convenient medium for displaying audio-visual content.

Both of these examples of new research methodologies highlight how Flamingo has adapted to the new media landscape, and understood how consumers act within it. Beyond this, Flamingo are looking at new ways to utilize the internet further such as asking consumers to illustrate their social networks using existing online photo sharing sites. This has the potential to unlock a powerful and emotional consumer narrative for brands. As brands face new challenges from the empowered consumer a change in methodologies is

FIGURE 11.1 *An example of an individual blog by Flamingo International*

required. Harnessing and utilizing the power of new technologies such as the internet allows Flamingo to remain true to its mission of providing insights and thinking for brands of the future.

INTERNET RESOURCES

Carling One All, where users can set up blogs of their favourite team. http://www.carling.com/oneall/

eLab city, a virtual island set up for consumer research purposes. http://www.elabcity.com/

Flamingo International, qualitative marketing research company. http://www.flamingo-international.com/

Second Life Brief, a site where findings from consumer research in Second Life are reported. http://www.slbrief.com/

The Social Research Foundation which has set up the First Opinions Panel in Second Life. http://www.socialresearchfoundation.org/index.html

Voxpops International, a video based marketing research company. http://www.voxpops.co.uk/

KEY READINGS

Belk, R.W. and Kozinets, R.V. (2005), 'Videography in marketing and consumer research', *Qualitative Marketing Research: An International Journal*, 8 (2), 128–141.

Catterall, M. and Maclaran, P. (2001), 'Researching consumers in virtual worlds: A cyberspace odyssey', *Journal of Consumer Behaviour*, 1 (3), 228–237.

Malhotra, N.K. and Peterson, M. (2001), 'Marketing research in the new millennium: Emerging issues and trends', *Marketing Intelligence and Planning*, 19 (4), 216–235.

SEMINAR EXERCISES

Discussion Topics

1. Identify the potential ethical issues associated with each of the research approaches discussed in this chapter (i.e videography, netnography etc.). In each case discuss how these issues might be addressed.

2. A company that produces trainers for a target market of 18–25 year olds is interested in designing a new trainer. Discuss how the company might use each of the methods in this chapter to input into the design process.

3. Reflect on the observations of Barker et al. that 'there is a move towards a way of doing, using and thinking about market research which is quite different in character and application from what has gone before' (2001, p. 26). Discuss the key ways in which you think market research has changed.

4. How do you see marketing research evolving in the future? (think here about both the methods and technologies that might be developed).

Group Exercises

1. Conduct some blog research on a brand of your choice (use a blog search engine such as Technocrati http://www.technocrati.com).

    (i) Compile a summary of your key findings about the brand.

    (ii) Given your findings, what advice would you give to the brand manager of your chosen company?

    (iii) What are the positive and negative aspects of using blogs as a form of market research data?

2. Conduct a search of You Tube (http://www.youtube.com/) for videos which you feel offer insights into one element of consumer behaviour. Construct a presentation using the clips where you describe:

    (i) Why you chose these particular video clips.

    (ii) Which aspects of consumer behaviour they help us to understand.

    (iii) In what ways you think data of this type is helpful/unhelpful in understanding consumer behaviour.

3. Using Kozinets' (2002) mini netnography of online coffee culture for guidance conduct a mini netnography in an online community associated with a product/service of your choice.

    (i) Summarize your key findings.

    (ii) What insights into consumer behaviour does your study offer?

    (iii) What recommendations would you make to a company involved in selling the particular product/service?

    (iv) How might you extend the study further?

REFERENCES

Arnould, E. and Wallendorf, M. (1994), 'Market-orientated ethnography: Interpretation building and marketing strategy formulation', *Journal of Marketing Research*, XXXI (November), 484–504.

Barker, A., Nancarrow, C. and Stone, M. (2001), 'Informed eclecticism: A research paradigm for the twenty-first century', *International Journal of Market Research*, 43 (Quarter 1), 3–28.

Beh, K.H. (2008), *Unity in Diversity? Relationships in the Mini Brand Community*. Unpublished doctoral dissertation: De Montfort University.

Belk, R.W. and Kozinets, R.V. (2005), 'Videography in marketing and consumer research', *Qualitative Marketing Research: An International Journal*, 8 (2), 128–141.

Belk, R.W. and the MBA students of Africa University (2000), *Consumption Lifestyles of the New Elite in Zimbabwe*, 21 minute video. Salt Lake City, UT: Odyssey Films.

Bhattacharyya, S. (2000), 'Evolutionary algorithms in data-mining: Multi-objective performance modelling for direct marketing', *Proceedings of the 6th International Conference on Knowledge Discovery and Data-mining*, 465–473.

Bonsu, S.K. and Darmody, A. (2008), 'Co-creating Second Life: market – consumer cooperation in contemporary economy', *Journal of Macromarketing*, 28, 355–368.

Bucklin, R., Lehman, D.R. and Little, J.D.C. (1998), 'From decision support to decision automation: A 2020 vision', *Marketing Letters*, 9 (3), 235–246.

Catterall, M. and Maclaran, P. (2001), 'Researching consumers in virtual worlds: A cyberspace odyssey', *Journal of Consumer Behaviour*, 1 (3), 228–237.

Cocciolo, A. (2007a), 'Marketing in the virtual world: Understanding consumptive behaviour in Second Life', Unpublished essay. http://www.thinking projects.org/wp-content/cocciolo_sl_cr.pdf

Cocciolo, A. (2007b), 'Second Look: A research platform for Second Life', *Annual Meeting of the American Educational Research Association*, March 2007.

Elliott, R. and Jankel-Elliott, N. (2003), 'Using ethnography in strategic consumer research', *Qualitative Market Research: An International Journal*, 6 (4), 215–223.

Ereaut, G. (2004), 'Evolution and revolution in qualitative research', *Admap*, 454 (October), 146.

Hagel, J. (1997), 'Net gain: Expanding markets through virtual communities', *The McKinsey Quarterly*, 1, 141–153.

Hemp, P. (2006), 'Avatar-based marketing', *Harvard Business Review*, June, 48–57.

Hoffman, D.L., Novak, T.P. and Venkatesh, A. (2004), 'Has the internet become indispensable', *Communications of the ACM*, 7 (July), 37–42.

Kedzior, R (2007), 'Virtual consumption: Toward understanding consumer behaviour in a virtual world', *16th EDAMBA Summer Academy*, Soreze, France, July 2007.

Kozinets, R.V. (1998), 'On Netnography: initial reflections on consumer research investigations of cyberculture', *Advances in Consumer Research*, 25, 366–371.

Kozinets, R.V. (1999), 'E-Tribalized marketing: The strategic implications of virtual communities of consumption', *European Management Journal*, 17 (3), 252–264.

Kozinets, R.V. (2002), 'The Field Behind the Screen: using netnography for marketing research in online communities', *Journal of Marketing Research*, 39, 61–72.

Kozinets, R.V. (2006), 'Click to connect: Netnography and tribal advertising', *Journal of Advertising Research*, September, 279–288.

Langer, R. and Beckman, S.C. (2005), 'Sensitive research topics: Netnography revisited', *Qualitative Market Research: An International Journal*, 8, 189–203.

Ling, C.X. and Li, C. (1998), 'Data-mining for direct marketing: Problems and solutions', *Proceedings of the 4th International Conference on Knowledge Discovery and Data-mining*, 73–79.

Maclaran, P. and Catterall, M. (2002), 'Researching the Social Web: marketing information from virtual communities', *Marketing Intelligence and Planning*, 20 (6), 319–326.

Maclaran, P., Broderick, A., Stevens, L., Theadopoulis, A., Goulding, C. and Saren, M. (2006), 'The Commodification of romance? Developing relationships online', *Journal Finanza, Marketing e Produzione*, 39–45.

Malhotra, N.K. and Peterson, M. (2001), 'Marketing research in the new millennium: Emerging issues and trends', *Marketing Intelligence and Planning*, 19 (4), 216–235.

Menti, M. (2007), 'Market research technology in virtual worlds'. http://msurveys. com/secondlifehtml.

Muniz, A.M. and O'Guinn, T.C. (2001), 'Brand community', *Journal of Consumer Research*, 24 (4), 412–432.

Novak, T. and Anderson, G.A. (2007), 'Consumer behaviour research in Second Life: Issues and approaches', paper presented at *Association for Consumer Research Pre-conference, Consumers online: Ten years later*. Memphis, TN.

Peacock, P.R. (1998), 'Data mining in marketing: Part 1', *Marketing Management*, winter, 8–19.

Perseus Development (2003), 'The Blogging Iceberg: Of 4.12 million weblogs, most little seen and quickly abandoned'. http://perseus.com/survey/news/release_blogs.html

Rheingold, H. (1994), *The Virtual Community: Finding Connection in a Computerised World*. London: Secker & Warburg.

Rygielski, C., Wang, J. and Yen, D.C. (2002), 'Data-mining techniques for customer relationship management', *Technology in Society*, 24, 483–502.

Sandin, J.A. (2007), 'Netnography as a consumer education research tool', *International Journal of Consumer Studies*, 31, 288–294.

Schouten, J.W. and McAlexander, J.H. (1995), 'Subcultures of consumption: An ethnography of the new bikers', *Journal of Consumer Research*, 22 (June), 43–61.

Shaw, M.J., Subramaniam, C., Tan, G.W. and Welge, M.E. (2001), 'Knowledge management and data mining for marketing', *Decision Support Systems*, 31, 127–137.

Solomon, M.R. and Wood, N.T. (2008) Conference programme for 'Virtual Social Identity and Consumer Behaviour', *The 27th Annual Advertising and Consumer Psychology Conference*, May 2008, The Society for Consumer Psychology, Philadelphia. http://www.myscp.org/pdf/ACPprogram.pdf

Vellido, A., Lisboa, P.J.G. and Vaughan, J. (1999), 'Neural networks in business: A survey of applications', *Expert Systems With Applications*, 17, 51–70.

Williams, M. (2007), 'Avatar watching: participant observation in graphical online environments', *Qualitative Research*, 7 (1), 5–24.

Zhao, X. and Belk, R.W. (2007), 'Live from shopping malls: Blogs and Chinese consumer desire', *Advances in Consumer Research*, 34, 131–137.

CHAPTER 12

The Global Consumer

Emma Surman

INTRODUCTION

There was a time when travel to a foreign land meant an encounter with a foreign culture, a different language, foods, habits, customs and shopping experiences. There was the possibility of an encounter with the exotic, but we would almost certainly discover something very different to that which we would experience in our everyday lives at home. Today, whilst foreign travel may still provide us with the opportunity to see, do and consume something different, we will also see and experience much with which we are familiar. Global brands that are recognized throughout the world such as Coca-Cola, Nike, Benetton, Mercedes-Benz, Starbucks and Microsoft mean that many of the products on offer and the shops or restaurants we spend our money in are the same, whichever city or country we are in. Globalization is a process that describes the way the activities in which we engage on an everyday basis, in many cases without us realizing or stopping to reflect on them, increasingly link us to people and activities through-out the rest of the world. Most of the clothes, electrical goods, toys and other manufactured goods we purchase are produced or assembled in China before being dispatched to our local stores. Similarly, the food we eat in the UK is no longer dependent on what we grow here. The produce available at the local shops or supermarkets means that we can easily consume the tastes and delicacies of other cultures.

Services too are increasingly being delivered by people located in a different, often remote, geographical location to ourselves. Banks, insurance providers, mobile phone, and computer companies have engaged in a process of closing their local telephone call centres and back office operations, and relocating these to countries such as India, the Philippines and South Africa. This process of outsourcing means that when filing a claim after a car accident, or when calling the help desk for assistance with your problematic internet connection, you frequently find yourself speaking to someone from another country. From the food we eat to television programmes and films we watch, the car we drive to the music we listen to, it is clear that the presence of globalization can be detected.

These global links occur in all aspects of our lives: economic, political, technological, commercial and, most pertinently for this chapter, the cultural. In this chapter we will explore the impact that globalization has had on cultures around the world. Does the fact that people, regardless of where they live, have the opportunity to buy the same products, see the same advertisements, watch the same films and TV shows and recognize the same celebrities, mean that differences between nationalities and cultures are diminishing and we are all becoming more homogeneous? Is the increasing availability of global brands leading to a common global culture? Alternatively, does the proliferation of global brands mean that we increase the choice available to consumers, as the global adds to, rather than replaces, the local? By doing so, does it offer the possibility to consumers of liberation from the limitations imposed on them by their local experiences? As consumers or marketers, the impact of these global processes, and the type of cultures they are leading to, is of great significance.

This chapter will provide an overview of the process of globalization and the resulting debates. It will encourage you to question the power and influence of multinational companies and their relationship with consumers, the effects of globalization, the impact of branding, the relationship between global production, consumption and local cultures and the possibilities for fairer trade.

THE PROCESS OF GLOBALIZATION

Globalization, a term for which there is no agreed definition, was first used during the late 1960s and early 1970s (Held and McGrew, 2000). It has since become the 'buzzword' (Ellwood, 2001) or 'defining issue' (Legrain, 2007) of the modern era, frequently cited as either an answer to all of the world's problems or the explanation for all its ills. As these opposing perspectives suggest, it is also a term which is widely discussed and debated, and about which disagreements abound. These disagreements cover many aspects but include the following: (i) whether globalization is a separate and identifiable phenomenon, an important feature of contemporary society and a significant factor in current social change, or simply a continuation of previous trends that can be traced back to European colonialism, a modern label applied to an old process; (ii) the timescale over which it has taken place; and (iii) whether it is ultimately a positive or negative process for the world's population. It is far beyond the scope of this chapter to explore these debates in detail but it is pertinent to establish some key points of reference with respect to globalization in order to inform the subsequent discussion.

The introduction suggested that globalization was a process whereby we are increasingly linked to people and activities throughout the rest of the world. These links can be seen in the increased mobility (Robins, 2000) or flows (Beck, 2000) across national borders, of products, services, information, communication, people, images and ideas.One area in which this increased mobility is evident is that of cross-border commercial activity. Whilst trading internationally can be traced back at least two centuries (Keegan, 2002), changes have accelerated since World War II (Scholte, 2005). These include the de-monopolization of economic structures, the deregulation and globalization of markets, trade and labour (Featherstone, 1990), the global networking of financial markets and capital flows, the growing power of transnational corporations, the innovations in information and communications technology and the stream of images from the global culture industries (Beck, 2000). We thus find ourselves in a world in which any event is no longer simply 'local' (Beck, 2000), where we can instantly and easily make written, audio or visual contact with people located many thousands of miles away, and where an awareness of the world as one place is now widespread. Whilst this is a situation which many of us may take for granted, Scholte (2000, p. 85) identifies the extent and significance of this change:

> Whereas in earlier times only a narrow circle of intellectuals and
> businesspeople thought globally, and then only fleetingly, at the start
> of the twenty-first century globality is widely and deeply embedded
> in academic, commercial, official and popular thinking.

Although worldwide mobility and linkages have an impact on many aspects of modern life including the economic, political and commercial, of particular interest in this chapter is the extent to which globalization has impacted on cultural aspects of our lives. There was a time when it was the local (Held and McGrew, 2000) and/or national culture that was most influential. The increased mobility that characterizes the modern world has raised questions over the extent to which cultures are converging, and the way in which culture is being influenced and developed at the transnational level (Featherstone, 1990). This has led to concerns that globalization will result in the erosion of indigenous cultures in the face of the widespread adoption of the dominant, namely Western or US, culture. Global corporations, through the provision of standardized goods and services and through clever use of branding, have become one of the key players in this process of cultural globalization.

GLOBAL CORPORATIONS AND THE ROLE OF MARKETING

Henry Ford's offer to customers to 'have any colour you want so long as it is black', is often referred to as a way of explaining the role of marketing and the way it has transformed our lives. Labelled as embodying 'the production-ist mentality' (Morgan, 2007) whereby the market offering was standardized as a means of simplifying and thus reducing the cost of production, this approach was criticized for ignoring the customer. Alternatively, the market-ing approach suggested that firms could improve by developing a customer orientation and delivering what the customer wanted, rather than what it was most convenient for the company to supply (Morgan, ibid.).

This view of marketing as the consumer champion is reinforced in the marketing literature, where it is argued that marketing plays a social role, identifying customer needs and ensuring that they are fulfilled, satisfied or even delighted (see for example Jobber, 2007; Kotler and Armstrong, 2001). In subsequent years, marketing activities were developed and extended and the discourse of consumerism flourished, legitimizing a focus on customer service, not just in the private sector but increasingly across the public sector too (Morgan, 2007). Marketing thus became seen as the vehicle by which the customer would be provided with choice and freedom.

The increase in the prominence and influence of marketing occurred at a time when international markets were opening up to foreign competition. Whilst we may take the global marketplace for granted (Keegan, 2002), prior to the 1960s although a number of products were sold worldwide, they were very limited and were not subject to the tightly controlled branding strategies witnessed in today's corporate environment (Scholte, 2000). A number of fac-tors have been identified as drivers towards international trade in the mid and latter parts of the twentieth century. These include: developments in transport and communications links, the worldwide movement towards privatization and deregulation of markets (Keegan, 2002). In addition, common customer needs and requirements, pressure from overseas competitors in the domes-tic market, developments in technology (Johansson, 2006) and the desire to reduce costs and the opportunities for economies of scale (Levitt, 1983). In an international (and increasingly global) marketplace, companies were urged to seize the opportunity to develop highly standardized, high quality prod-ucts to be marketed around the globe (Levitt, 1983). An attempt to create a global product can be seen in the Ford Motor Company's endeavours to create a model of car that is attractive across the world. This included the develop-ment of the Fiesta, Mondeo and the Focus (Johansson, 2006). In recent times, attention has moved from selling standard products worldwide, to developing brands that can be marketed globally. Global brands are, according to Holt et al. (2004), judged differently by consumers, assumed to be of a higher quality and seen as providing membership to a wider cosmopolitan community.

Thus, in today's global marketplace companies, attention is not focused on the things it produces, but the images (Klien, 2000), with the focus on the creation, development and maintenance of brands becoming a core activity 'Machines wear out. Cars rust, people die. But what lives on are the brands' (Sir Hector Laing, 1998 in Klien, 2000). The brand has also become the point at which most value and profit can be generated for the business (Kaplinsky, 2000) and thus the point to which the majority of resources are directed (Klien, 2000).

The increasing importance of marketing, and specifically branding, to corporate activity, along with the globalization of markets, has had a significant impact on the organization of production (Scholte, 2005). The pressure to reduce costs, reap the benefits from economies of scale, and the move from full scale manufacturing to assembly, has meant that production facilities have been contracted out, outsourced or offshored to countries with lower labour costs and more favourable tax terms. The process of outsourcing is not confined to manufacturing activities, but more recently can be seen in service industries too as call centres and back office activities have also been transferred overseas. In a review of the evidence, Taylor and Bain (2005) concluded that 40–60% savings could be achieved when such processes are migrated to India.

The power of the brand and the opportunities for trade around the world mean that globalization is no longer just a marketing fantasy (Keegan, 2002) and global brands can now be consumed in many countries throughout the world. The issue for debate in this chapter is the extent to which these standardized products and the images, marketing communications and branding with which they are associated, are leading to a standard culture around the globe.

HOMOGENEOUS CONSUMERS

Ritzer (2007) is one author who argues that the increasing availability of, and demand for, global products, is linked to a spread of uniform culture, which is threatening the diverse and distinctive cultures that have traditionally existed across the world. This cultural convergence or 'sameness' is, it is argued, a direct result of the rise in power of the modern multinational corporation. Thus the increasing powerful, dominant and resource rich Western corporations, utilizing the latest in information and communication technologies, are able to influence cultures which have traditionally been far beyond their geographical reach.

Essential to their (transnational corporations) success is the ability to deliver suitably packaged imagery and symbolism which will convey their definitions of the services they provide. (Smith, 1990, p. 174)

The images and symbols that are conveyed as part of the branding process come predominantly from the developed Western economies; hence the values, images and lifestyle that they disseminate are also mostly Western. The result is a convergence in culture that occurs in the direction of the West (Ritzer, 2007). This convergence in culture is resulting in the homogenization of the consumer and the consumption process, leading to a high degree in similarity in, amongst other things, clothing, appearance, eating habits and choice of entertainment. But this homogenization is not limited to the provision of global goods and services, for in order to sell goods, companies also need to export the mechanisms which create and support the desire and opportunity to consume these products. Citing the example of credit cards, Ritzer (2007) argues that this US invention which occurred during the 1950s has now become an accepted and usual method of transaction across the world. However, the convergence in cultures is not limited to the use of this method of payment, but extends to the attitudes commensurate with its use. For the increasing use of the credit card brings with it an acceptance of debt and a neglect of savings in order to fund an ever increasing level of consumption. Not only has the USA exported a means to fund increased levels of consumption, but also the places in which consumption can take place. Described by Ritzer (ibid.) as 'cathedrals of consumption' he provides examples now evident across the world, in which we are encouraged to consume. These include: fast-food restaurants, shopping malls, casino-hotels, theme parks, cruise ships, superstores, home shopping television and internet shopping. Thus, in the homogeneous world of the global consumer, we all consume similar products in similar environments, as well as fund our purchases in a similar manner.

This move towards cultural convergence which is led by global corporations is labelled by Ritzer as 'grobalization' (ibid.). This term is used to encapsulate what he describes as the imperialistic ambitions of corporations to continually expand their power, influence and profit by operating throughout the world. As they do this, they overwhelm competing processes, which leads to the demise of local cultures.

> *What is needed is a world in which people continue to have the option of choosing the local – a world in which the local has not been destroyed as a viable alternative by grobalization (Ritzer, 2007, p. 210).*

THE HYBRID CONSUMER

An alternative perspective to Ritzer's is provided by those who argue that globalization leads to a greater diversity in cultures rather than greater convergence. It is argued that rather than replacing the diverse local resources and market offerings, global brands extend the range of cultural resources available by adding to the local and the national (Robins, 2000, p. 197). Thus, the process of globalization provides consumers with a greater number of products, services and symbols than were previously available.

In addition to extending the resources available, it is argued that rather than consuming commodities in a uniform manner, each consumer does so in a way which is individually meaningful to them, again leading to greater diversity. The postmodern perspective (see Chapter 3) is that consumption has become a means for the individual to express their identity, a means of both creating and presenting our 'selves' and forming connections with others (Firat and Venkatesh, 1995) and of becoming 'cosmopolitan' (Thompson and Tambyah, 1999) without having to visit or live in another country. As such, rather than being constrained by the global offerings of corporations, the consumer is seen as a creative agent (Elliott and Wattanasuwan, 1998) working to create something which may be unique with the cultural resources available to them. The combination of the increased availability of resources and the creative consumer leads to increased diversity:

> *Although the consumer learns and develops consumption symbols through socialisation processes and exposures to mass media, it does not mean that everybody who possesses the same product bought it for the same symbolic meaning. (Elliott and Wattanasuwan, 1998, p. 134)*

As consumers draw on the range of cultural resources available to them to piece together their identity, they may well draw on the cultural resources of other groups and 'culture swap' (Oswald, 1999) incorporating these into their personal identity leading to a 'creolization and fusion' of cultures, hybrid forms of consumption and a proliferation of pluralism and difference (Sandikci and Ger, 2002). In constructing their identities in this way, rather than fitting into categories that might be neatly defined by academics or marketers, the consumer can be seen to create their own (Schouten and McAlexander, 1995). These 'selves' may be constantly changing, or contradictory, indeed 'fragmentation' is seen as prime feature of the post modern experience' (Elliott and Wattanasuwan, 1998). According to this perspective, the consumer is no longer the victim of corporate branding and the activities of the marketer, instead consumption becomes a source of liberation (Firat and Venkatesh, 1995) and globalization and the increased number of products this leads to provides people with an increased degree of control over the forces that shape their lives (Oswald, 1999). However, studies have shown that the cultural diversity that does result from this process is a variation on certain common (global) themes, whereby activities at the local level are judged in relation to a global standard or norm. For example, although it is possible to identify local differences in the way that it is expressed, the concept of youth culture has been found to be becoming a universal or global phenomenon (Kjeldgaard and Askegaard, 2006).

Similarly, opportunities for local consumption are judged against established global standards or brands:

> ... a coffee shop is more or less like Starbucks in much the same way that a fast-food restaurant is more or less like McDonald's or a theme park is more or less like Disney World. (Thompson and Arsel, 2004, p. 633)

TOWARDS THE GLOBAL CONSUMER?

The term globalization may lack a common definition and be the subject of wide and differing opinions, but there is little doubt that the linkages between people and flows between nations have increased in recent decades. For corporations the process of globalization has provided opportunities to enter new markets and to expand their activities geographically. Marketing, and particularly branding, have become a powerful activity within this process. To build and maintain a successful global brand has become the dominant corporate aspiration, and as the number of global brands increases this process can be seen to pose significant issues for cultures and consumption across the globe. The issue which we have sought to explore in this chapter is whether the availability of global brands, and the symbols and images with which these are intricately bound, represent a constraint on consumer activity, leading to greater homogenization, or are a source of liberation and increased diversity.

It is important therefore, to explore this issue of liberation further. To do so three points are examined. The first is whether globalization can be seen as a source of liberation for everyone.

> Since a significant segment of the world's population is either untouched directly by globalization or remains largely excluded from its benefits, it is a deeply divisive and, consequently, vigorously contested process. The unevenness of globalization ensures it is far from a universal process experienced uniformly across the planet. (Held and McGrew, 2000, p. 4)

As Kaplinsky (2000) notes, whether you benefit from globalization depends on the terms in which you participate in it. Globalization can be seen to have provided an opportunity for the development of the super rich, a group of footballers (David Beckham), musicians (Vanessa Mae), businessmen (Bill Gates), artists (Damien Hirst), for example, for whom the opportunity to market globally has been highly lucrative. However, for those working long days in the factories of China and India to manufacture goods for Western markets in return for a tiny wage, without hope of ever being able to afford the global brands on which they work, or the farmers in India whose water supply has been depleted, leading to crop failure since the building of a Coca-Cola bottling plant (Dispatches, 2007), the process of globalization might not be seen as quite as liberating. As the process of globalization gallops on, all indicators of inequality are increasing, as is the number of people living on a dollar a day or less (Kaplinsky, 2000). According to Robins 'Globalization is an uneven and an unequal process' (2000, p. 198).

The second issue for consideration is the idea that the availability of global brands adds to, rather than depletes, local offerings. Data indicates that by 1990, the largest 350 global companies conducted 40 per cent of cross-border trade (Rugman and Verbeke, 1990). Furthermore, a handful of large corporations can now be seen to dominate a number of sectors. In 1998, the ten biggest firms controlled 70 per cent of computer sales, 85 per cent of pesticides and 86 per cent of the telecommunications market. Global chains owned a third of the world's hotel rooms, and Visa, MasterCard and American Express had 95 per cent of the world's credit card business (Scholte, 2000). We have thus seen a concentration of market share amongst the largest players, as large companies account for significant proportions of the total marketplace.

The third issue that it is pertinent to consider in respect of liberation is the relationship between consumers and the corporations. Firat and Venkatesh (1995) argue that liberation is achieved as consumers always have the possibility to subvert the market (switching brands or being brand disloyal) rather then being seduced by it. The market for beauty creams, now worth half a billion pounds in the UK (Dispatches, 2008), taps into our concerns about ageing and our desire to remain forever youthful. These creams are frequently marketed on the basis of their scientific sounding ingredients and their revolutionary anti-ageing processes, yet are not required to undertake or publish the results of clinical trials which test their claims (see case study in Chapter 8). In such a case, to what extent can the millions of women (and men) who buy these products be said to be liberated from the influence of the market, rather than seduced by the young looking models and impressive claims which target their inner fears?

Marketing likes to present itself as the champion of the consumer (Morgan, 2007), but others have questioned the extent to which marketing actually creates needs rather than fulfils them (Lasch, 1979 cited in Morgan, 2007). If this is the case, it is argued that consumers become 'governable' (Miller and Rose, 1997) and ultimately controllable by those corporations who stand to benefit from our spending.

While some authors argue that rather than making them a victim of the corporate marketers, consumption provides a means for people to influence their lives, to break free from the elements which constrain their activities and to exert some control on their world, the extent of this liberation appears to depend upon who you are, where you live and the terms in which you are engaging the process. It is also affected by the extent to

Case study: Bottled water – a pure or guilty pleasure?

Claridges is one of London's most famous hotels. In its own words it is the 'epitome of English style, the last word in luxury'. Visiting statesmen often stay there and whilst doing so use the hotel to entertain members of the British royal family. Building on this exclusive reputation the hotel has teamed up with one of the UK's top chefs naming one of its restaurants 'Gordon Ramsay at Claridges', thus positioning itself in the world of fine dining as well as that of luxury accommodation. Whilst enjoying the delights of Claridges' celebrity created food you can choose to accompany your meal with not just an impressive selection of wine but also with a choice of waters. Claridges' water list provides a collection of 30 of the worlds 'finest' bottled waters, with the most expensive costing the equivalent of £50 a litre. These waters are selected from around the world, from sources as exotic sounding as the icebergs of Canada, the volcanoes of New Zealand and the Nilgris mountains in India.

Described in terms more familiar to those reading a wine menu, the various waters make claims about their taste, health benefits and the foods to which they are best suited. Renaud Grégoire, the director of food and wine at Claridges, is quoted as saying 'Water is becoming like wine. Every guest has an opinion and asks for a particular brand.'

The last item on the water list is London tap water, which is available in a glass or a jug free of charge. Costing less than 1 pence a litre, in a blind taste test this tap water was actually rated higher than many of the more exclusive brands on Claridges' list.

The consumption of bottled water is increasing rapidly and is, in fact, the fastest growing sector of the soft drinks industry. In the UK, two billion bottles a year were consumed in 2003, an increase of 18% on the previous year. Yet in the UK and other developed countries we have a ready supply of water, available at a much more reasonable cost in our taps. This growing preference for bottled water is not because the water in our taps is contaminated or otherwise unsafe to drink, or according to the blind taste test quoted above, because it does not taste good. So, whilst tap water is safe, functional and palatable, people are prepared to pay a premium for water brought to them in a bottle from Canada, New Zealand or India. How can this be explained?

Drinking bottled water has become a lifestyle choice. Consumers might choose to drink it because they like the bottle, the convenience, or the values with which they perceive a particular brand to be associated. In short, the increase in consumption of bottled water can be explained by our concern with brands and the way in which they are used to make statements about the people we are, and the lifestyles we aspire to.

Whilst Claridges' menu features some of the more 'select' suppliers, such is the attractiveness of the bottled water market that the large drinks companies have been

which global corporations are able to dominate the marketplace, and the extent to which consumers as a collective or on an individual basis, are seen as able to avoid seduction by the powerful branding messages of the global corporations.

This chapter has taken globalization to be a process that increasingly links us to people and activities throughout the world. It has also discussed two opposing views as to whether this is resulting in a common global culture. Whilst some argue that, led by large global corporations and the focus on branding, we are seeing cultural convergence and homogenization, others have argued that local adaptation of global brands and practices has led to increased diversity and greater pluralism. The extent that globalization from either of these perspectives can be seen to be beneficial varies depending on the terms on which you are able to engage with it.

eager to get a slice too. Dasani, a bottled water product marketed by the drinks giant Coca-Cola was launched in North America in 1999 and became a huge success, becoming the second most popular bottled water. Eager to repeat this success in the European market, Coca-Cola sought to launch Dasani in the UK with a campaign costing £7m. After a series of public relations disasters and a health scare Coca-Cola subsequently decided to remove Dasani from the UK market just five weeks after launching it.

Dasani's first stumbling block came when it was discovered that the water they were selling was actually tap water distributed by the Thames Water Company. Unlike some of the waters on the market, which is bottled at (its natural) source and known as mineral water, Dasani is purified tap water. Coca-Cola claims that this purification process is highly sophisticated, based on NASA spacecraft technology and is termed reverse osmosis. Whatever it involves, it enables Cola-Cola to take a product costing 0.03 pence, process it, and charge 95 pence a bottle. The second, and subsequently fatal, blow in the UK came when it was discovered that Dasani had been contaminated with potentially carcinogenic bromate. Thus, far from purifying the water, Coca-Cola's highly sophisticated process appeared to be adding potentially harmful chemicals.

Whilst the purchasing of bottled water is an interesting example of the strength of the branding phenomena, its consumption to enable us to make statements about our lifestyle is not without consequences. Much more expensive, yet no healthier or safer than tap water, bottled water has been criticized as being very environmentally unfriendly and ethically questionable. Research for the BBC showed that drinking a one litre bottle of water can have the same impact on the environment as driving a car for a kilometre, in terms of CO_2 emissions. Our taste for globally sourced water also has consequences on local populations. Fiji water is one of the waters featured on Claridges' menu. Abstracted by an American company, from a water source discovered by the government with the help of British aid money, this source is used exclusively for bottled water and is not used by the local population. The water is then bottled and shipped tens of thousands of miles to exclusive outlets in the UK and USA. Meanwhile, a third of Fijians do not have access to safe drinking water and instead drink from local ponds and creeks, a factor which may in part explain the high number of cases of typhoid (a water borne disease) in Fiji each year.

Such findings have led Professor Tim Lang, the UK government's natural resources commissioner, to state that drinking bottled water should be made as unfashionable as smoking, and that when a large percentage of the world's population do not have access to safe drinking water. It is an example of one the gross inequalities in the world that we can buy water in bottles and see this as progress.

CASE STUDY SOURCES

BBC (2004), 'Soft drink is purified tap water', *BBC News*, March 1, 2004. http://news.bbc.co.uk/1/hi/uk/3523303.stm

BBC (2008), 'Bottled water: who needs it?', *Panorama*, February 18, 2008.

Boden, N. (2007), 'Tap water beats rival costing £50 a bottle, say experts', *The Scotsman*, December 19, 2007. http://news.scotsman.com/latestnews/Tap-water-beats-rival-costing.3602546.jp

Daily Telegraph (2008), 'Bottled water 'is immoral', February 17, 2008. http://www.telegraph.co.uk/earth/main.jhtml?xml=/earth/2008/02/17/eawater117.xml

Datson, T. (2004), 'Coca-Cola admits That Dasani is nothing but tap water', March 4, 2004. http://www.commondreams.org/headlines04/0304–04.htm

Doole, C. (2001), 'Bottled water 'a waste of money', *BBC News*, May 3, 2008. http://news.bbc.co.uk/1/hi/world/europe/1309841.stm

Garrett, B. (2004), 'Coke's water bomb', *BBC News*, June 16, 2004. http://news.bbc.co.uk/1/hi/business/3809539.stm

Wilson, B. (2007), 'Claridges to offer water from around the world', *Evening Standard*, October 12, 2007. http://www.thisislondon.co.uk/standard/article-23416339-details/Claridge's+to+offer+water+from+around+world/article.do

www.dasani.com

www.claridges.com

INTERNET RESOURCES

Australian Broadcasting Corporation, Globally Speaking. http://www.abc.net.au/global/culture/

Global Culture, a blog on global citizens and the quest for cosmopolitanism. http://global-culture.org/blog/index.php

The Global Policy Forum. http://www.globalpolicy.org/globaliz/index.htm

Killer Coke provides opposing views on Coca-Cola's behaviour as a global citizen. http://www.killercoke.org/ and the Coca-Cola website http://www.gettherealfacts.co.uk/

The Levin Institute, the State University of New York. http://www.globalization101.org/

The World Bank: http://www1.worldbank.org/economicpolicy/globalization/

KEY READINGS

Howes, D. (ed.) (1996), *Cross Cultural Consumption: Global Markets, Local Realities*. London: Routledge.

International Marketing Review (2005, issue 5), Special issue 'Ethics and International Marketing'.

Low, W. and Davenport, E. (2005), 'Has the medium (roast) become the message? The ethics of marketing fair trade in the main stream', *International Marketing Review*, 22 (5), 494–511.

Mirchandani, K. (2004), 'Practices of Global Capital: Gaps, cracks and ironies in transnational call centres in India', *Global Networks*, 4 (4), 355–373.

Schirato, T. and Webb, J. (2003), *Understanding Globalization*. London: Sage.

Steger, M. (2003), *Globalization: A very short introduction*. Oxford: Oxford University Press.

Witkowski, T. (2008), 'Antiglobal challenges to marketing in developing countries: exploring the ideological divide', in M. Tadajewski and D. Brownlie (eds), *Critical Marketing: Issues in Contemporary Marketing*. Chichester: Wiley.

SEMINAR EXERCISES

Discussion Topics

1. Identify the key factors that have led to/accelerated the process of globalization.

2. With reference to the case study 'Bottled water – A pure or guilty pleasure?' above, critically discuss the benefits and the pitfalls that have occurred as a result of globalization. Overall who are the winners and losers in this process?

3. Discuss the extent to which you think we are moving towards a global culture.

4. Identify the changes that have taken place in corporate activity with the development of globalization, and evaluate the role that marketing has played in this.

Group Exercises

1. Fair Trade: Read the article 'Has the medium (roast) become the message?' by Low and Davenport (listed in Key readings above) and discuss the following points:

   (i) Set out the main arguments for/against the involvement of big business in Fair Trade. Consider the perspective of: consumers, supermarkets and suppliers.

   (ii) What is more important, who sells Fair Trade or the volume of Fair Trade products which are sold?

   (iii) Whose responsibility is it to ensure that grower's interests are protected: the growers, product manufacturers, retailers or consumers?

2. Global Marketing Communications: Each group member should bring in a print advert of a brand that is advertised globally. They should discuss these in relation to the following questions:

   (i) In what ways can a global advertising campaign benefit a company?

   (ii) What issues should you take into account when developing advertising campaigns for world markets?

   (iii) What do you think the companies set out to achieve with the adverts? To what extent do you think they succeed?

3. Global tastes:

   (i) Each student should describe their favourite meal and identify where the influences have come from that have defined their taste. This could be done by getting each student to draw a mind map/spider diagram identifying these influences, i.e. influences could be friends, family, cultural feasts/celebrations travel, local geography, etc.

(ii) In groups, the class should identify what they see as a traditional English or (local) meal and explain their reasoning. Do any of the individual's favourite meals fit with this? If not why not?

(iii) From the discussion identify the main influences on food preferences, what does this indicate about the development of a global culture?

REFERENCES

Beck, U. (2000), 'What is Globalization?', in D. Held and A. McGrew (eds), *The Global Transformations Reader*. Cambridge: Polity Press, pp. 99–103.

Dispatches (2007), 'Mark Thomas on Coca-Cola', Channel 4, November 19, 2007.

Dispatches (2008), 'The truth about beauty creams', Channel 4, May 12, 2008.

Elliott, R. and Wattanasuwan, K. (1998), 'Brands as symbolic resources for the construction of identity', *International Journal of Advertising*, 17, 131–144.

Ellwood, W. (2001), *'The No-nonsense Guide to Globalization'*. Oxford: New International Publications Ltd.

Featherstone, M. (1990), 'Global culture: An introduction', in M. Featherstone (ed.), *Global Culture: Nationalism, Globalization and Modernity*. London: Sage, pp. 1–14.

Firat, A. and Venkatesh, A. (1995), 'Liberatory postmodernism and the reenchantment of consumption', *Journal of Consumer Research*, 22 (Dec), 239–267.

Held, D. and McGrew, A. (2000), 'The great globalization debate: an introduction', in D. Held and A. McGrew (eds), *The Global Transformations Reader*. Cambridge: Polity Press, pp. 1–45.

Holt, D., Quelch, J. and Taylor, E. (2004), 'How global brands compete', *Harvard Business Review*, September, 1–8.

Howes, D. (ed.) (1996), *Cross Cultural Consumption: Global Markets, Local Realities*. London: Routledge.

International Marketing Review (2005, issue 5), Special issue 'Ethics and International Marketing'.

Jobber, D. (2007), *'Principles and Practices of Marketing'*, 5th edition. Maidenhead: McGraw-Hill.

Johansson, J. (2006), *Global Marketing: Foreign entry, local marketing and global management, international edition*. New York: McGraw-Hill.

Kaplinsky, R. (2000), 'Spreading the gains from Globalisation: What Can be Learned from Value Chain Analysis?', *Journal of Development Studies*, 37 (2), 117–146.

Keegan, W. (2002), *'Global Marketing Management'*, 7th edition. Upper Saddle River, NJ: Prentice Hall.

Kjeldgaard, D. and Askegaard, S. (2006), 'The glocalization of youth culture: The global youth segment as structures of common difference', *Journal of Consumer Research*, 33 (September), 231–247.

Klien, N. (2000), *No Logo*. London: Harper Perennial.

Kotler, P. and Armstrong, G. (2001), *Principles of Marketing*, 9th edition. Upper Saddle River, NJ: Prentice Hall.

Legrain, P. (2007), *'Open World: The truth about globalisation'*. London: Abacus.

Levitt, T. (1983), 'The globalization of markets', *Harvard Business Review*, May–June, 92–102.

Low, W. and Davenport, E. (2005), 'Has the medium (roast) become the message? The ethics of marketing fair trade in the main stream', *International Marketing Review*, 22 (5), 494–511.

Miller, P. and Rose, N. (1997), 'Mobilizing the consumer: assembling the subject of consumption', *Theory, Culture and Society*, 14 (1), 1–36.

Mirchandani, K. (2004), 'Practices of Global Capital: Gaps, cracks and ironies in transnational call centres in India', *Global Networks*, 4 (4), 355–373.

Morgan, G. (2007), 'Marketing and critique: Prospects and problems', in M. Alvesson and H. Willmott (eds), *Studying management critically*. London: Sage, pp. 109–131.

Oswald, L. (1999), 'Culture swapping: Consumption and the ethnogenesis of middle-class Haitian immigrants', *Journal of Consumer Research*, 25 (March), 303–318.

Ritzer, G. (2007), *The Globalization of Nothing 2*. London: Sage.

Robins, K. (2000), 'Encountering globalization', in D. Held and A. McGrew (eds), *The Global Transformations Reader*. Cambridge: Polity Press, pp. 195–201.

Rugman, A. and Verbeke, A. (1990), *Global Corporate Strategy and Trade Policy*. London: Routledge.

Sandikci, O. and Ger, G. (2002), 'In-between modernities and postmodernities: theorizing Turkish consumptionscape', *Advances in Consumer Research*, 29, 465–470.

Schirato, T. and Webb, J. (2003), *Understanding Globalization*. London: Sage.

Scholte, J. (2000), *Globalization a Critical Introduction*. Basingstoke: MacMillan Press.

Scholte, J. (2005), *Globalization a Critical Introduction*, 2nd edition. Basingstoke: MacMillan Press.

Schouten, J. and McAlexander, J. (1995), 'Subcultures of consumption: An ethnography of the new bikers', *Journal of Consumer Research*, 22 (June), 43–61.

Smith, A. (1990), 'Towards a global culture?', in M. Featherstone (ed.), *Global Culture: Nationalism, Globalization and Modernity*. London: Sage, pp. 171–191.

Steger, M. (2003), *Globalization: A very short introduction*. Oxford: Oxford University Press.

Taylor, P. and Bain, P. (2005), 'India calling to the far away towns: The call centre labour process and globalization', *Work, Employment and Society*, 19 (2), 261–282.

Thompson, C. and Arsel, Z. (2004), 'The Starbucks brandscape and consumers' (anticorporate) experiences of glocalization', *Journal of Consumer Research*, 31 (December), 631–642.

Thompson, C. and Tambyah, S. (1999), 'Trying to be cosmopolitan', *Journal of Consumer Research*, 26 (December), 214–241.

Witkowski, T. (2008), 'Antiglobal challenges to marketing in developing countries: exploring the ideological divide', in M. Tadajewski and D. Brownlie (eds), *Critical Marketing: Issues in Contemporary Marketing*. Chichester: Wiley.

Index